IMAGES
of America

JEFFERSON TOWNSHIP ON LAKE HOPATCONG

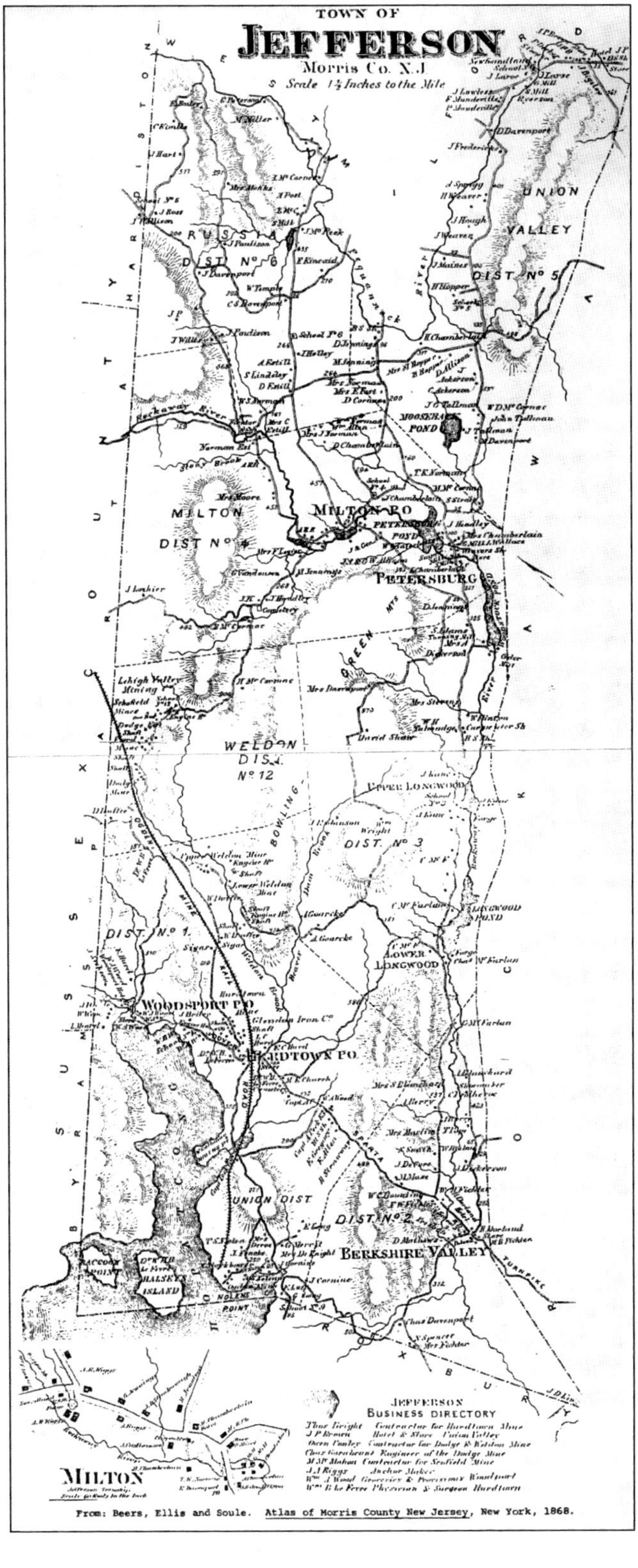

Jefferson Township is depicted on this map from the mid-1860s.

IMAGES
of America

JEFFERSON TOWNSHIP ON LAKE HOPATCONG

Lorraine C. Lees and R. Richard Willis

ARCADIA
PUBLISHING

ISBN 978-0-7385-0077-5

Published by Arcadia Publishing
Charleston, South Carolina

Printed in the United States of America

Library of Congress Catalog Card Number: 00-104082

For all general information contact Arcadia Publishing at:
Telephone 843-853-2070
Fax 843-853-0044
E-mail sales@arcadiapublishing.com
For customer service and orders:
Toll-Free 1-888-313-2665

Visit us on the Internet at www.arcadiapublishing.com

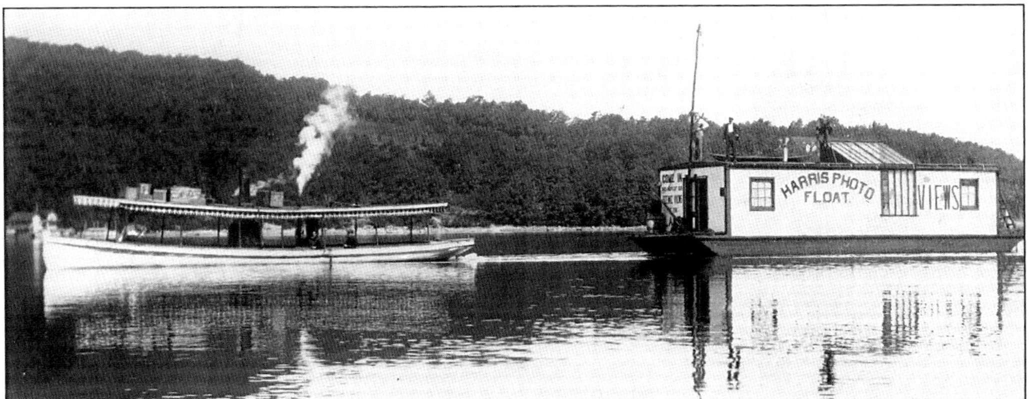

The Harris Photo Float was a large barge, or scow, measuring 16 feet wide by 50 feet long. The house that nearly covered the whole barge contained the Harris studio, sales area, darkroom, and kitchen. This photograph shows the barge being towed by the *Richard J*.

CONTENTS

Acknowledgments		6
Introduction		7
1.	All Aboard	9
2.	The Simple and Rustic Life	21
3.	Comfortable Places	37
4.	The Famous Lend a Hand	61
5.	Fun and Frolic	73
6.	Working Hard	87
7.	Helping Hands	109
8.	New Beginnings	119

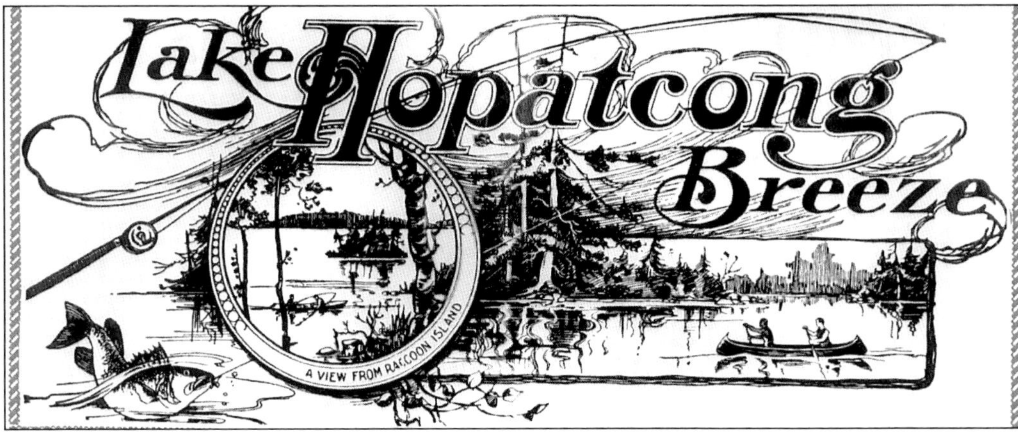

ACKNOWLEDGMENTS

Historically, parents often prove to be our best educators. It is from their guidance and knowledge that we often form our likes, dislikes, interests, and concerns. Both Richard and I are very fortunate to have had parents—Leona B. and Raymond R. Willis, and Florence and Michael Chabon—who took the time and effort to teach each of us to respect and care about our surrounding community.

It is our hope that this endeavor will help preserve the history of the area for past, present, and future residents and that our love, knowledge, and respect for Jefferson Township on Lake Hopatcong will encourage others to learn about, support, and take an interest in their community.

We wish to extend very special thanks to Martin Kane, Alma Moran, Alice Dow Muller, Evelyn Lauerman, Mrs. David Isherwood, Robert Goller, the Lake Hopatcong Historical Museum, Doris Crater Post, John DeBellis, Tim Clancy, Bert Engelkey, Fred Patak, Robert Drummond, Ed Crane, Alice Rutkoski, Ruth Ackerman, Robert Kays, and June Bright for sharing pictorial collections and stories. We greatly appreciate the generosity of all who have allowed us to borrow their treasures. Without their help, we would not have been able to complete our pictorial endeavors.

Without the Lake Hopatcong Anglers and Breezes, a large amount of our local history would have been lost forever. We are very fortunate that many people planned for the future by preserving the past.

Many thanks to my family (Chick, Michael, George, and Cynthia) for putting up with the constant confusion and for always extending their support and encouragement. Lastly, a word to coauthor Richard Willis: this would not have been possible without you. Thank you.

—Lorraine C. Lees

INTRODUCTION

Jefferson Township is a large municipality that is separated into two major sections, Lake Hopatcong and Oak Ridge/Milton, with the Mahlon Dickerson County Park in the middle.

Jefferson Township, once home to the Lenape Indians of the Delaware tribe, saw the influx of settlers in the late 1700s. On April 9, 1804, Jefferson separated from Roxbury and Pequannock and became incorporated. Jefferson originally occupied the shoreline of Little Pond and part of Great Pond.

During the latter part of the 1800s, Jefferson Township became a vital part of a summer resort on Lake Hopatcong. Nolan's Point was one of the major hubs in the area. The mining and ice industries flourished. Trains brought vacationers and new residents. Many left in the fall, but a large number chose to stay. War and the Great Depression brought many changes to Jefferson Township on Lake Hopatcong, but growth continued.

In 2004, Jefferson Township will celebrate its 200th anniversary. Residents will come and go, but history will continue to be made and our town will continue to progress.

"New Times, New People, New History, Built on Foundations out of the Past."

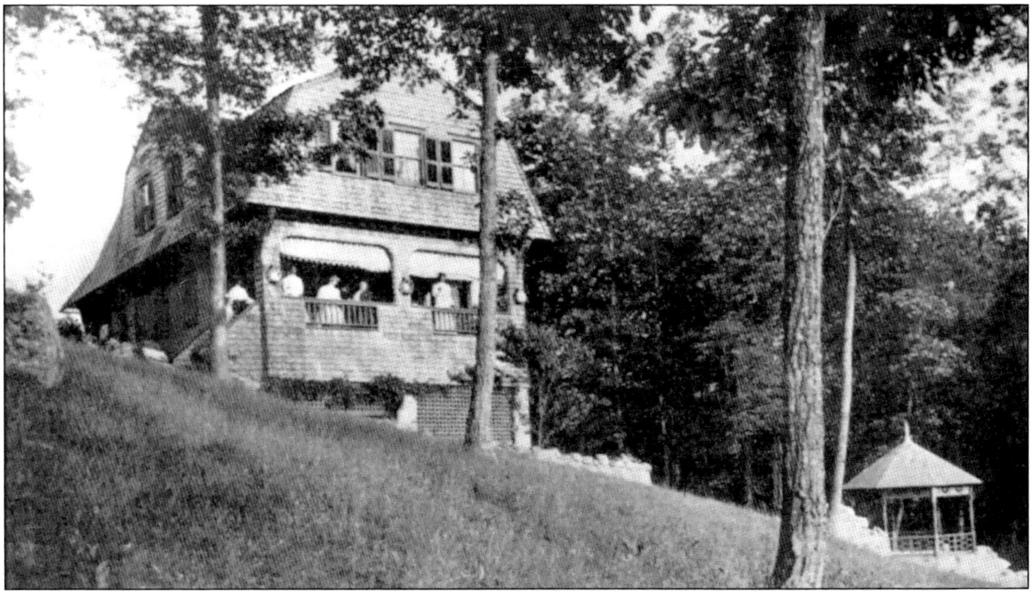

Rockledge Cottage, c. 1923, was the summer lake house of Senator Thompson of Somerville. It was located in the Castle Rock area of Jefferson Township, and it had a spectacular view of Lake Hopatcong. In addition to his political guests, Thompson often hosted theater personalities, such as George Burns.

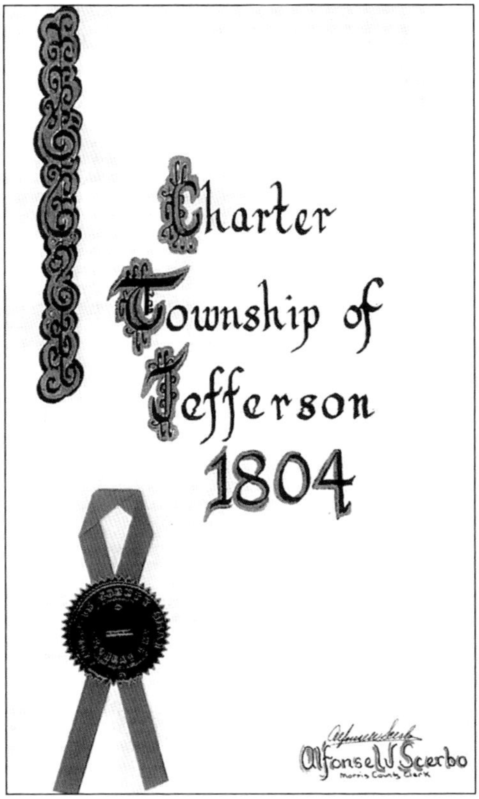

In April 1804, Jefferson Township became incorporated. A copy of the original charter is recorded in the Morristown Hall of Records. Alfonse Scerbo, a former county clerk, presented a copy of the charter to Jefferson Township.

One

All Aboard

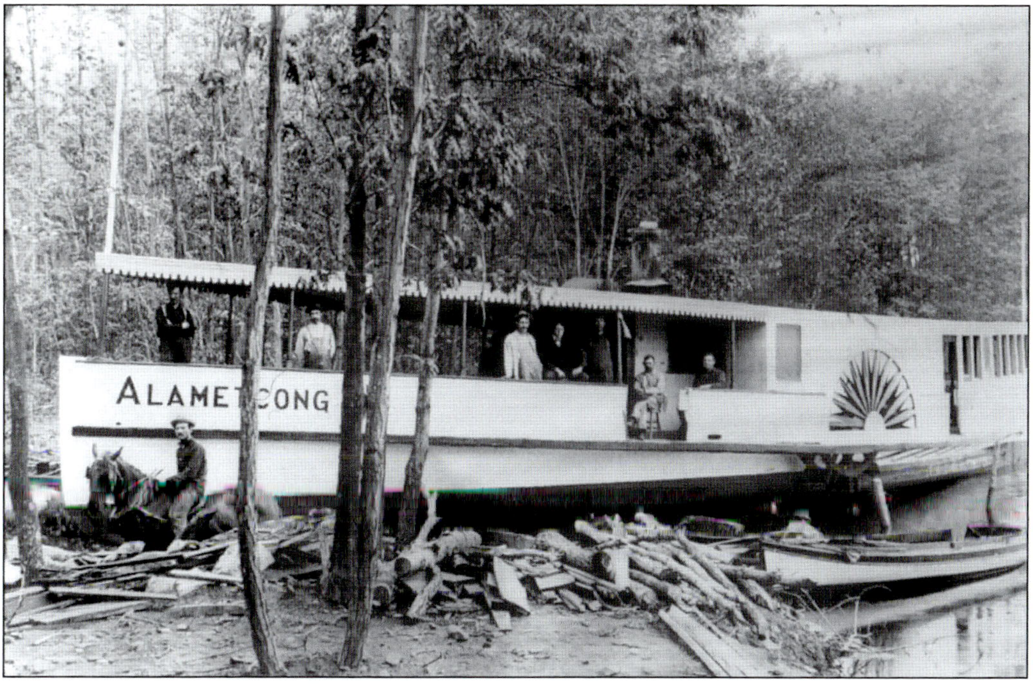

The original White Line consisted of four side-wheelers: the *Alametcong*, the *Nariticong*, the *Hopatcong*, and the *Musconetcong*. The *Hopatcong*, the largest, was referred to as the queen of the White Line. Theodore F. King was the president of this line.

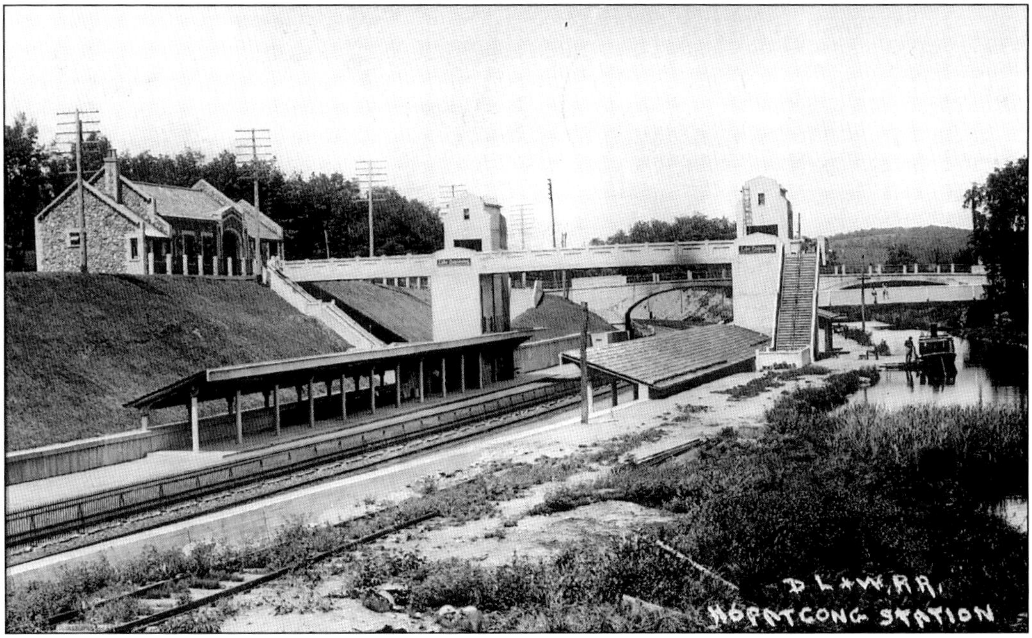

Many tourists arrived via the Delaware Lackawanna & Western train station in Landing and had to board awaiting passenger boats. In this *c.* 1910 image, the *Mystic Shrine* is docked in the Morris Canal and the walkway to Landing is over the canal. This walkway carried passengers to the Landing boat docks.

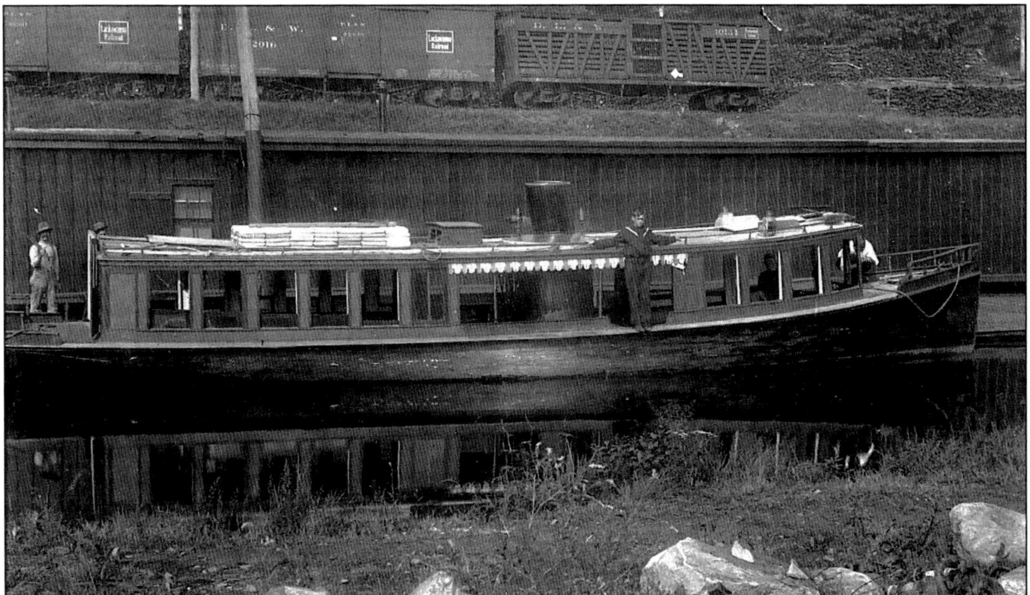

Unlike the White Line, operated by the Willis brothers, the Black Line traveled into the Morris Canal on a scheduled basis. The *Mystic Shrine*, the queen of the Black Line, picked up and delivered passengers at the Landing train station. Inclement weather was not a problem because the *Mystic Shrine* had windows that opened and closed. This photograph dates from *c.* 1915.

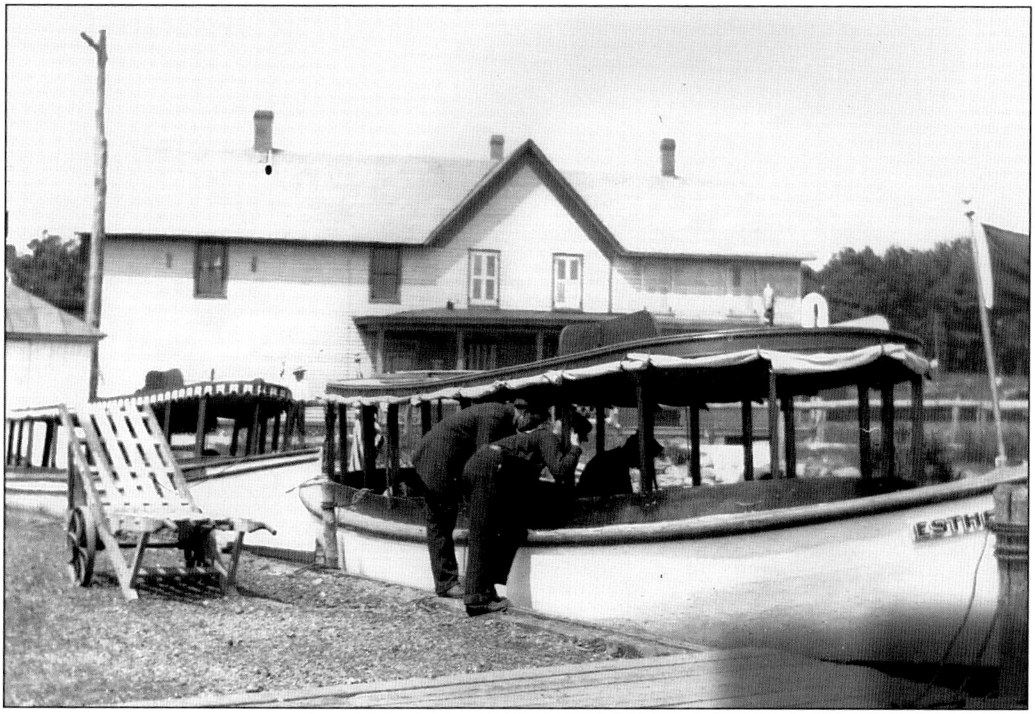

On the lake side of the Delaware Lackawanna & Western station in Landing, passenger boats await clients who need to be transported via water to their hotels, houses, and camps. Often passengers shopped at King's Store (background) before boarding their launches. This view dates from c. 1915.

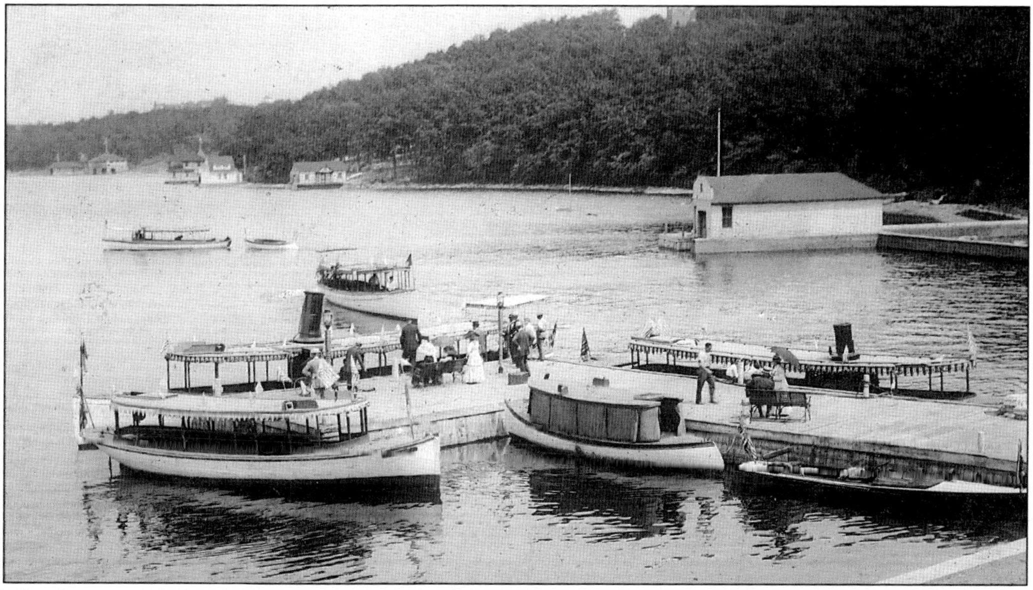

The Bertrand Island Transportation Company (BITCO) started out as the White Line. The second generation of boats, as seen in this c. 1910 picture, consisted of the *New Breslin*, the *Richard J*, the *Benedict CK*, the *Uncle Dan*, the *Esther R*, and the *LaFalot*. Their original port was Bertrand Island, the end of the trolley line.

Daily Report For

Date.., 1912.

I, William Willis, hereby report to the Bertrand Island Transportation Company, lessors, that the gross income for the use of said Company's boats, leased to me, and the income for dockage is as follows for the above date:

Uncle Dan, No. of passengers carried..................	Total Receipts, $..................
Benedict C. K., No. of passengers carried..................	Total Receipts, $..................
Esther R., No. of passengers carried..................	Total Receipts, $..................
New Breslin, No. of passengers carried..................	Total Receipts, $..................
Total Receipts, for use of Dock - - - -	$..................
Total,	$..................

From 1908 until 1916, William and John Willis of Nolan's Point leased the BITCO line. At the end of each day, the brothers completed a report and, each spring, they paid BITCO a yearly leasing fee, based on the previous year's receipts. They also kept additional records and paid for coal and dockage.

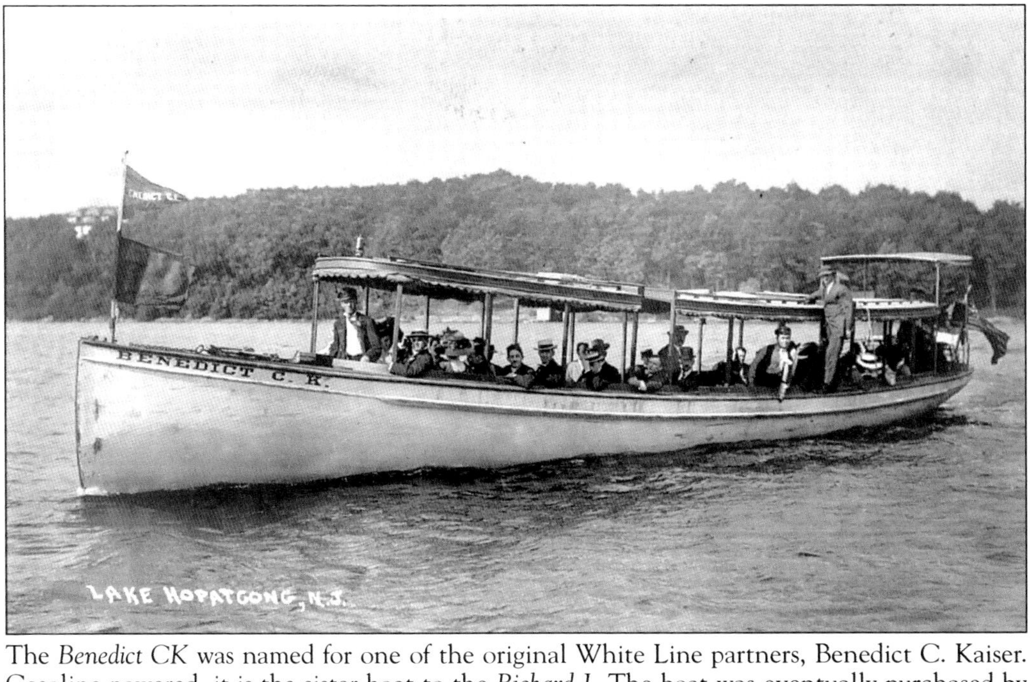

The *Benedict CK* was named for one of the original White Line partners, Benedict C. Kaiser. Gasoline powered, it is the sister boat to the *Richard J*. The boat was eventually purchased by George Hulmes, the Black Line owner, who renamed it the *Evelyn L.H.* for his daughter.

By the time Wilbur S. Willis reached his teens, he was already in charge of the *Uncle Dan* passenger boat. Willis is pictured *c.* 1908 in the traditional dress uniform of boat captain.

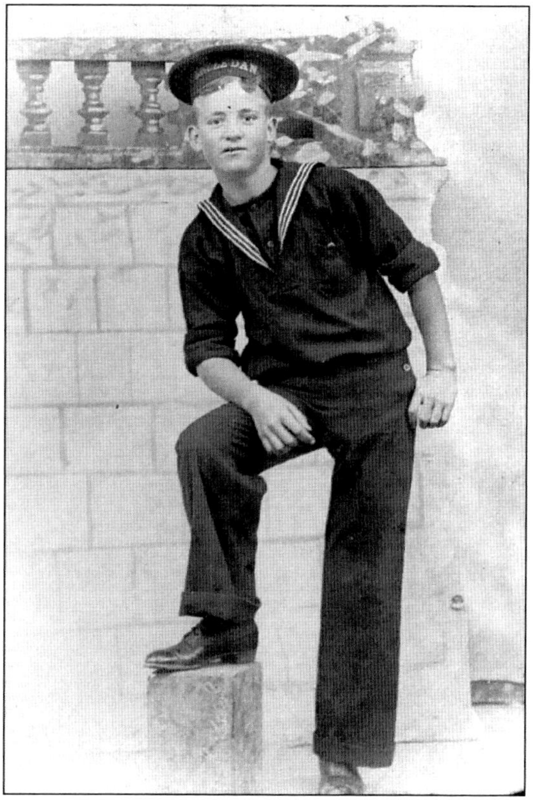

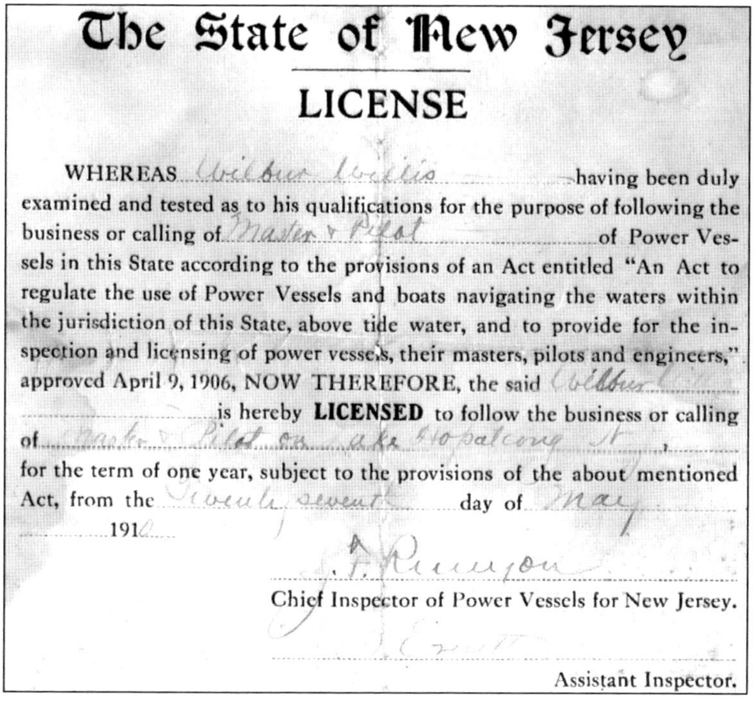

The State of New Jersey

LICENSE

WHEREAS Wilbur Willis having been duly examined and tested as to his qualifications for the purpose of following the business or calling of Master & Pilot of Power Vessels in this State according to the provisions of an Act entitled "An Act to regulate the use of Power Vessels and boats navigating the waters within the jurisdiction of this State, above tide water, and to provide for the inspection and licensing of power vessels, their masters, pilots and engineers," approved April 9, 1906, NOW THEREFORE, the said Wilbur W. is hereby **LICENSED** to follow the business or calling of Master & Pilot on Lake Hopatcong N. for the term of one year, subject to the provisions of the about mentioned Act, from the Twenty seventh day of May 1910

Chief Inspector of Power Vessels for New Jersey.

Assistant Inspector.

As early as 1906, the state of New Jersey required engineers, masters, and pilots to be licensed to operate power vessels and boats above tidewater. On May 27, 1910, Wilbur S. Willis of Jefferson received his license. In later years, he served as mayor of Jefferson Township.

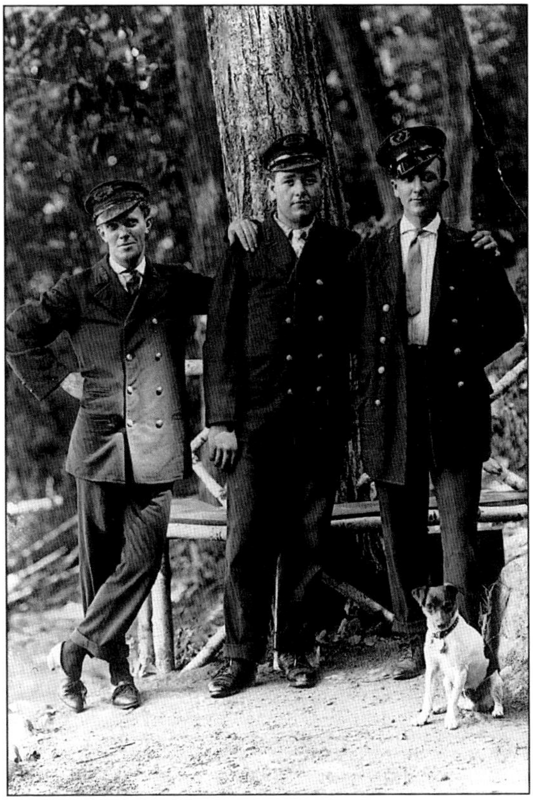

Most of the Willis Brothers employees were from the Nolan's Point area. Seen here, from left to right, are George Willis, captain; George Robinson Sr., engineer; and Tom Willis, purser. This Harris photograph, with Hypo (Harris's pet), was taken *c.* 1912. At the end of each day, the boats were stored at the Bryant Villa dock.

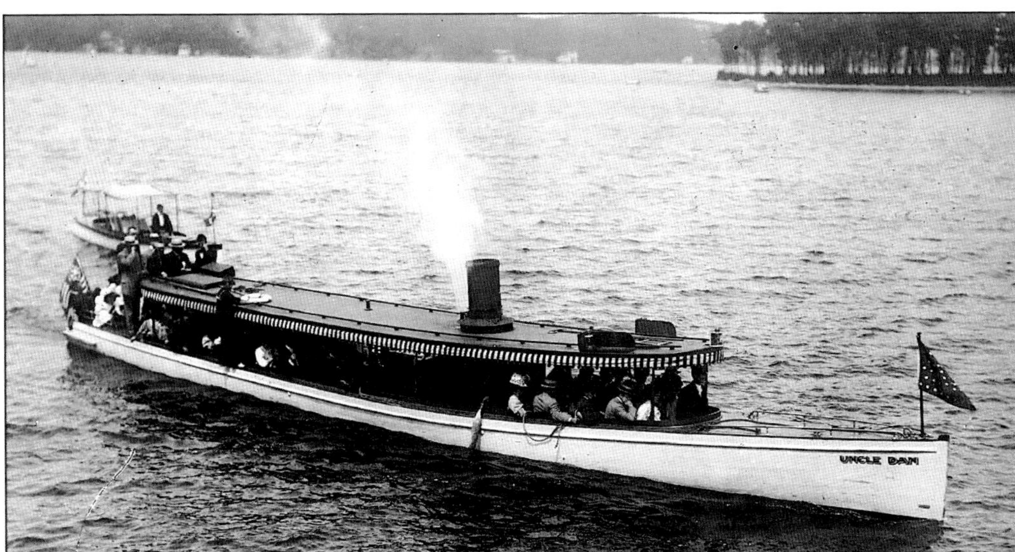

The *Uncle Dan*, pictured *c.* 1911, was the fastest passenger steamboat of the Willis Brothers delivery service. It was used primarily for express commuter service on Lake Hopatcong. It was built in Trenton and was delivered to the lake via the New Jersey canal systems.

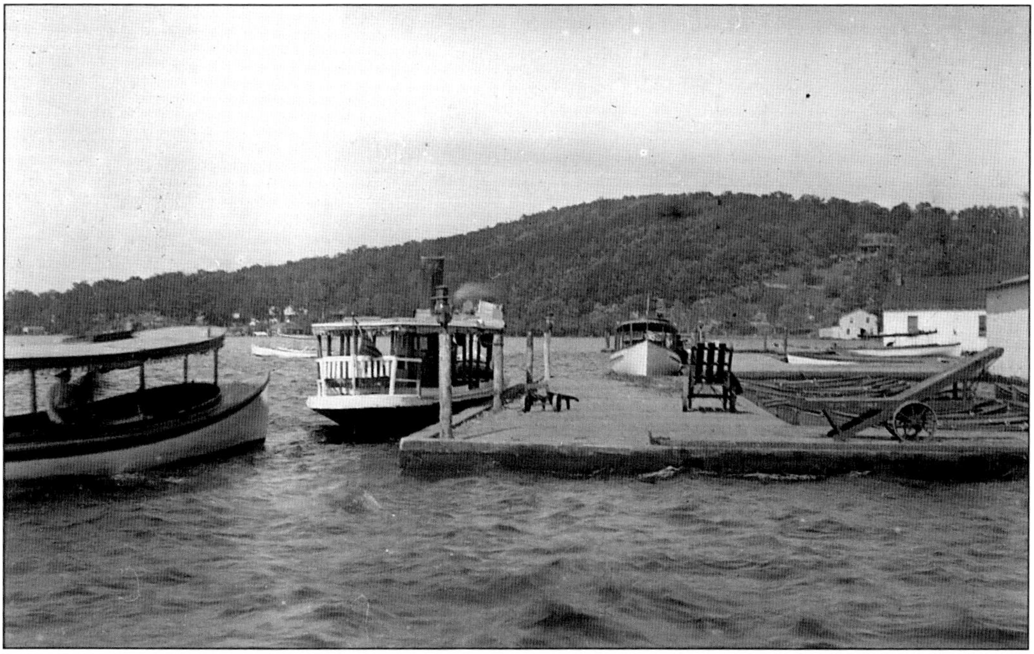

During the busy summer seasons, passenger boats would sometimes have to wait to unload or pick up passengers, as seen in this 1904 photograph. Baggage carts were available on the docks. However, these carts belonged to the Central Railroad and not the passenger boats.

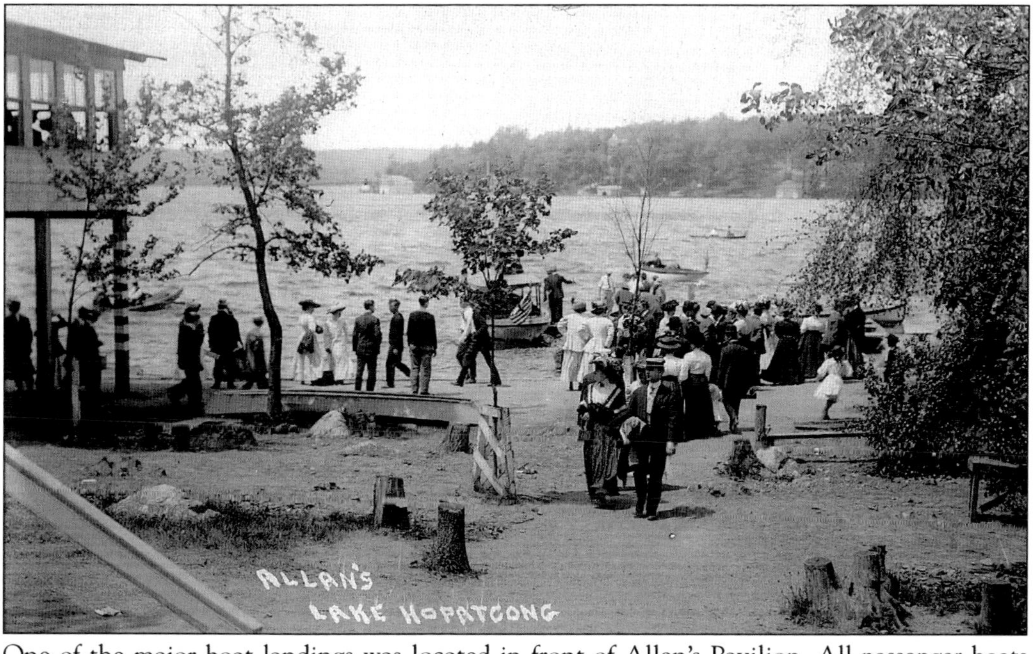

One of the major boat landings was located in front of Allen's Pavilion. All passenger boats used the same landings, and numerous patrons in long dresses or suits, as shown in this 1909 photograph, flocked to the point. An example of this landing is still visible in front of the Windlass Restaurant.

The Blue Line Boats

FOR LAKE HOPATCONG LOCAL TRAVEL

And for Short, Pleasant Excursions
for cottagers and hotel guests

On and after May 20, Daily and Sunday

EAST SIDE SERVICE

From Mt. Arlington Dock and Intermediate Landings,

Every Hour to and from Nolan's Point.
Every Second Hour to and from Raccoon Island.

WEST SIDE SERVICE

Five Trips Daily from all Landings on the West Side, from Mountain View Hotel to Davis Cove, ...

To and from Nolan's Point and Raccoon Island.

Fare, 15 cts. . . Round Trip, 25 cts.

THE BOATS ARE SMALL---NO BAGGAGE CARRIED.

See Time Tables, posted at Hotels, Docks, etc.

In addition to the White and Black Lines, there was a smaller boat line called the Blue Line, c. 1898. It had two boats called the *Daisy* and the *Dewey*. The boats did not have an express service to the trains, and they were not able to carry any luggage. This line was used for local travel from cottages and hotels.

Before arriving in Espanong Village or Nolan's Point, the Central Railroad train stopped at the Minnisink Station. Vacationers and local residents found this an easy commute.

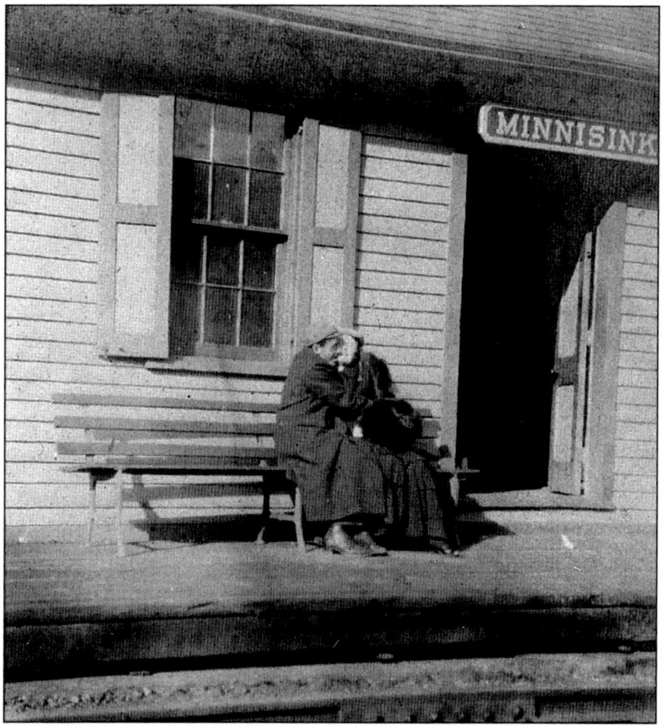

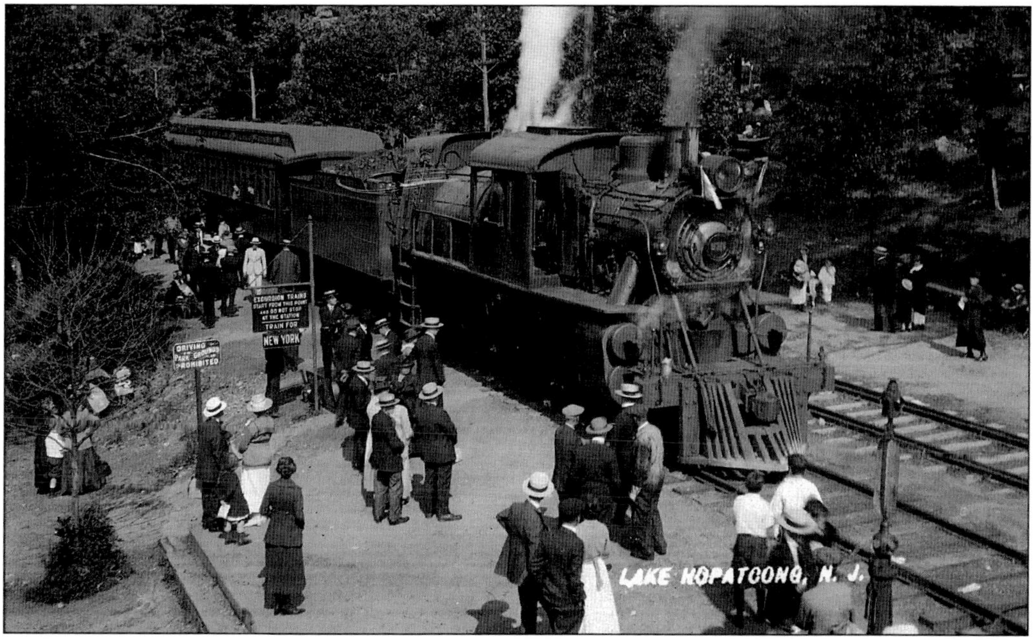

Unlike the Delaware Lackawanna & Western trains, the Central Railroad journeyed into Nolan's Point, starting in August 1882. However, passengers could not travel on this line until September 1882. As can be seen in this *c.* 1895 photograph, many people took advantage of this new service.

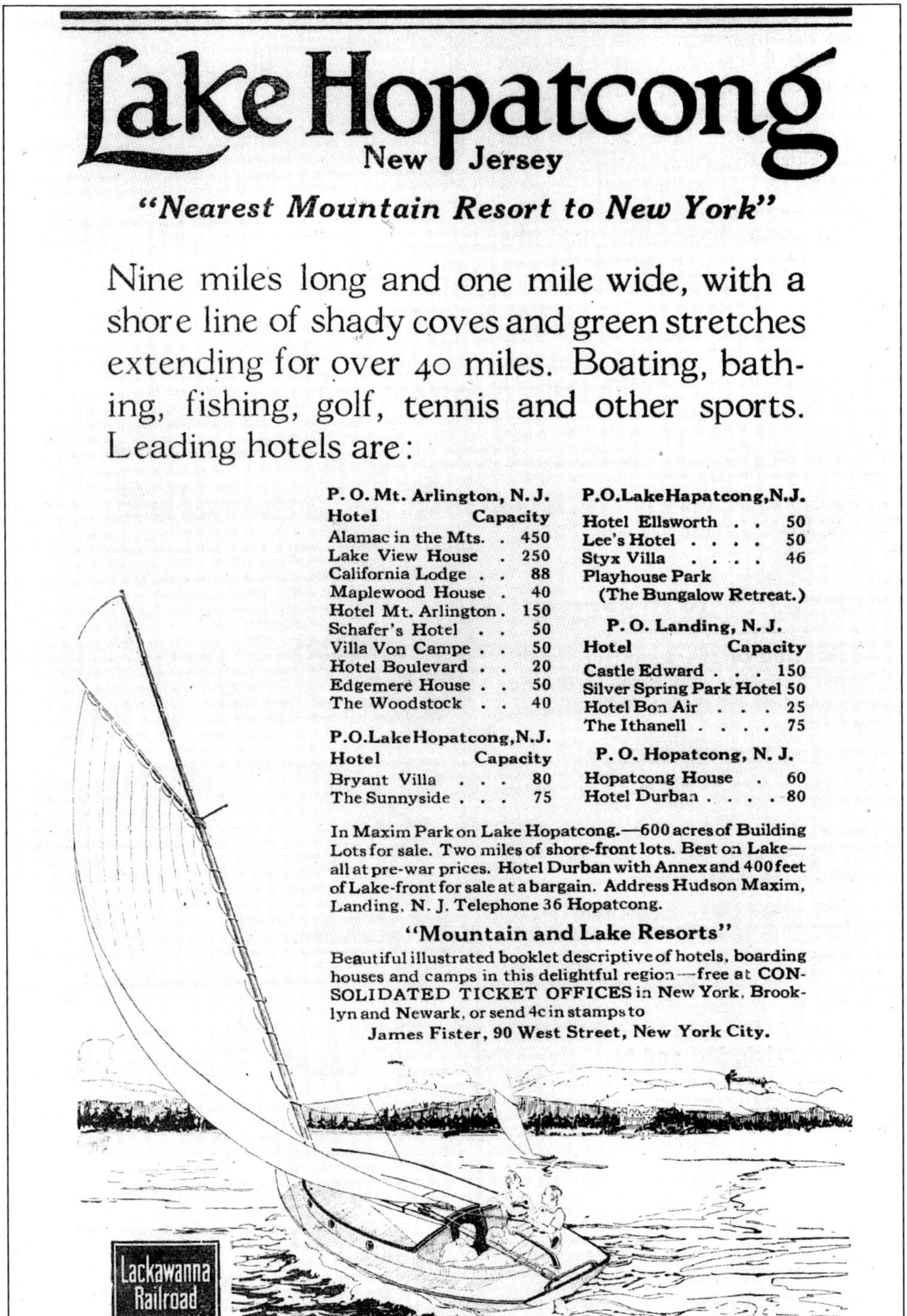

The Delaware Lackawanna & Western at Landing and the Central Railroad at Nolan's Point serviced Lake Hopatcong. Because of the lake's inaccessibility, advertisements were necessary to help promote tourism and to inform vacationers of how easy it was to get to the lake. These advertisements appeared in magazines and railroad literature. This one is from c. 1925.

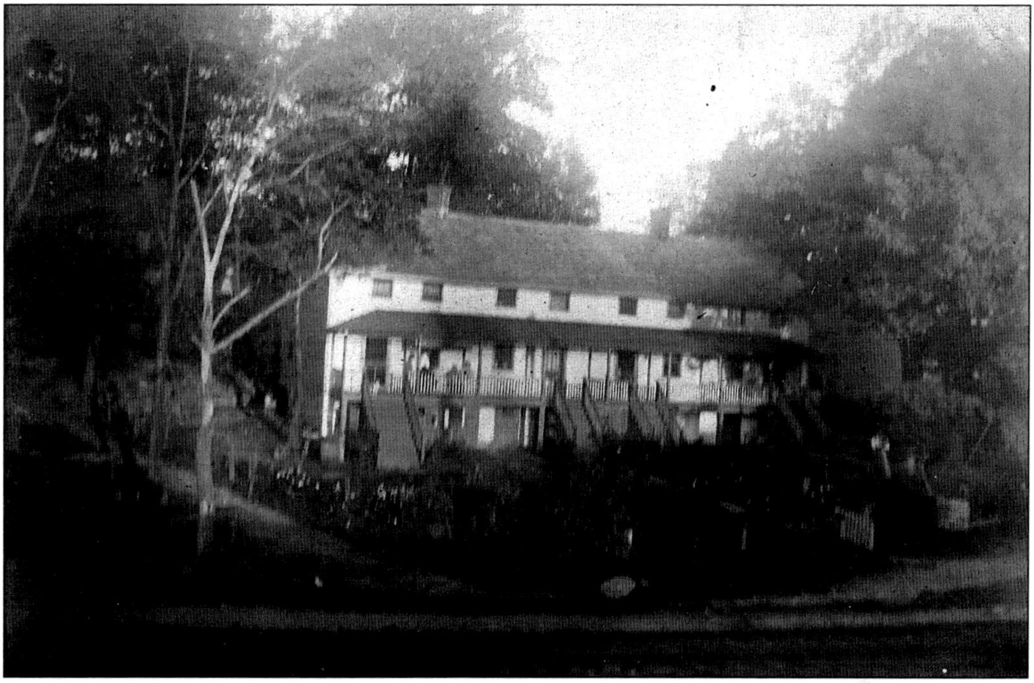

The Ogden Mine railroad workmen were supplied with living quarters on Nolan's Point near the railroad station. There were three row houses, each containing four apartments. These apartments were rented to the general public. However, when they were needed for the workers, the non-employees had to leave. One of the row houses still exists today.

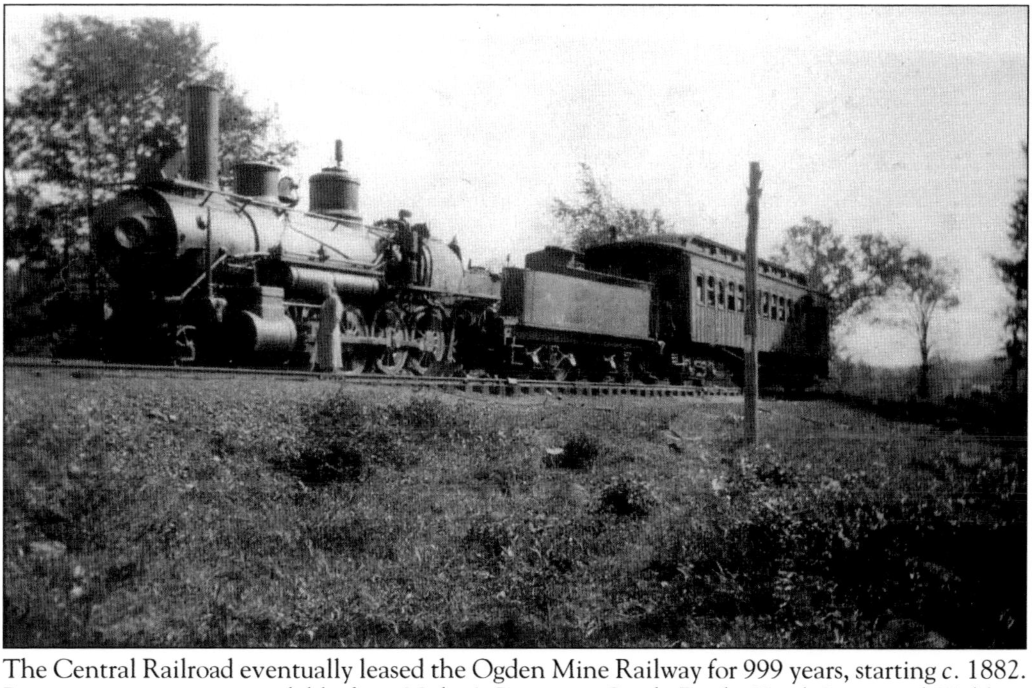

The Central Railroad eventually leased the Ogden Mine Railway for 999 years, starting *c.* 1882. Passenger service was available from Nolan's Point via Castle Rock, Hurd Cove, and Weldon, and it terminated at the Ogden Mine (Edison Mine).

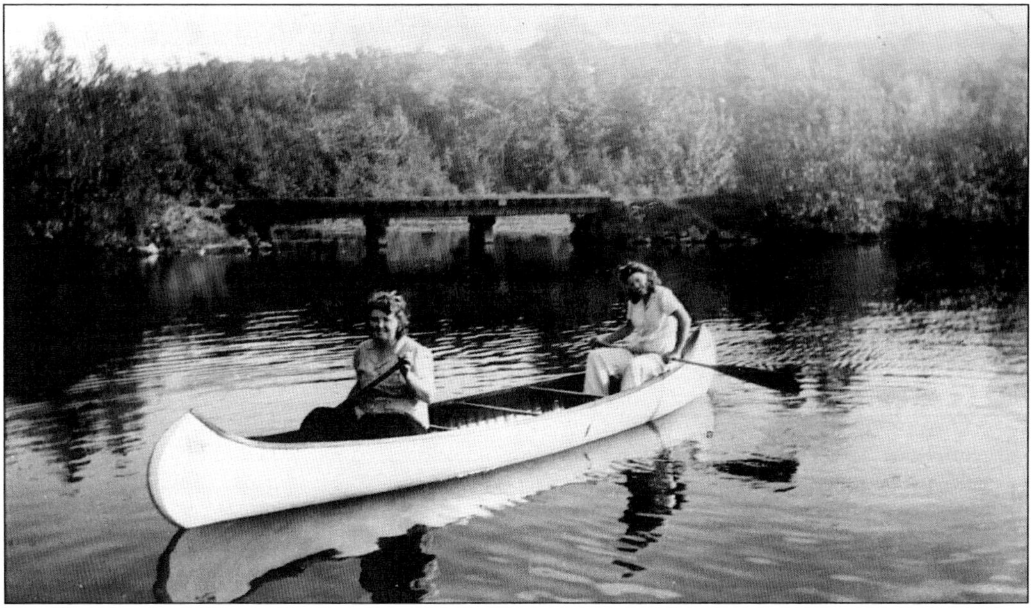

In order for a train to cross over Hurd Cove on its way to the Ogden Mines, it was necessary to construct a railroad bridge. This bridge was built *c.* 1865, and even though the top is gone, the pilings still exist in the waterways behind Chabon's Tavern.

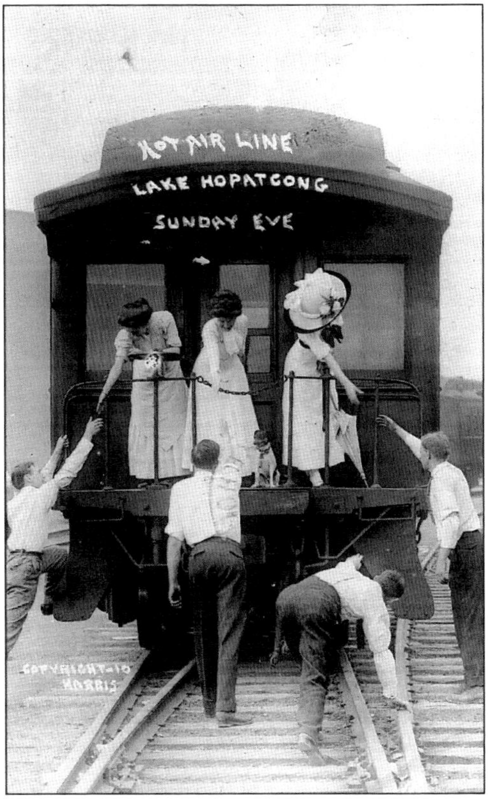

It is time to say goodbye to the lake and return home. Fond memories of our vacation will help us make it through the winter, and we will be back next year.

Two

THE SIMPLE AND RUSTIC LIFE

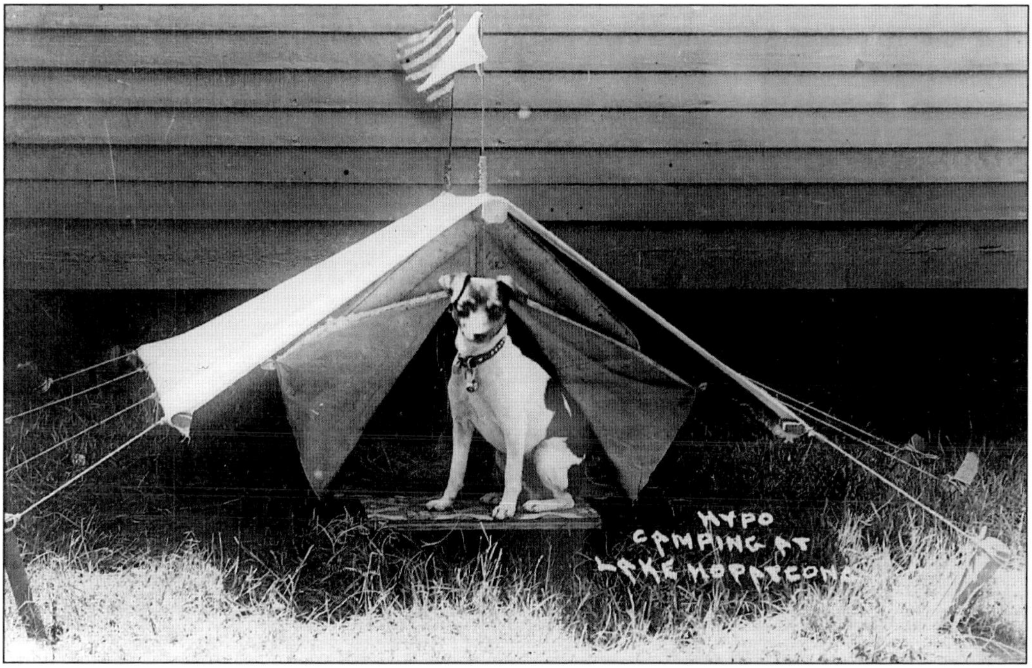

Camp Hypo was located behind the Harris studio on Nolan's Point. It was a very small dwelling that sheltered Harris's dog Hypo, whose name came from a photograph process. The dog appeared as Mr. Harris's logo in many photographs and postcards.

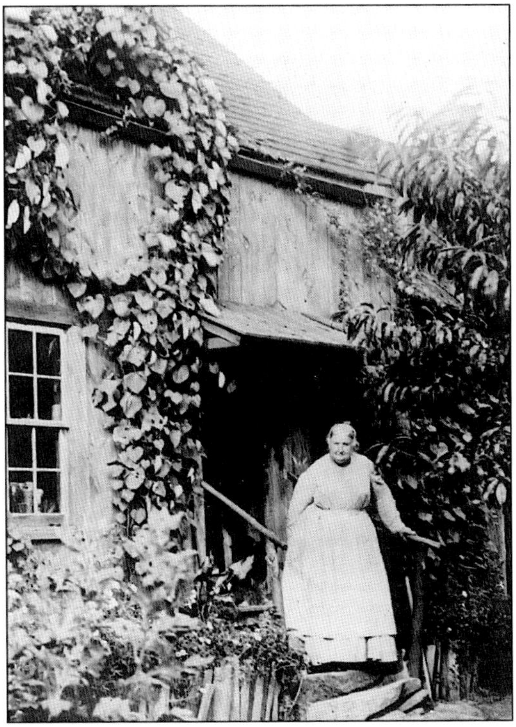

The Thomas S. Nolan House was erected in 1836 on what is today called Willow Street. It was one of the earliest houses on Nolan's Point and was called "Rustic Cottage." After the death of their parents, the Nolan boys were placed in an orphanage. However, their sister Jane remained. Nolan's Point is named after the Nolan family.

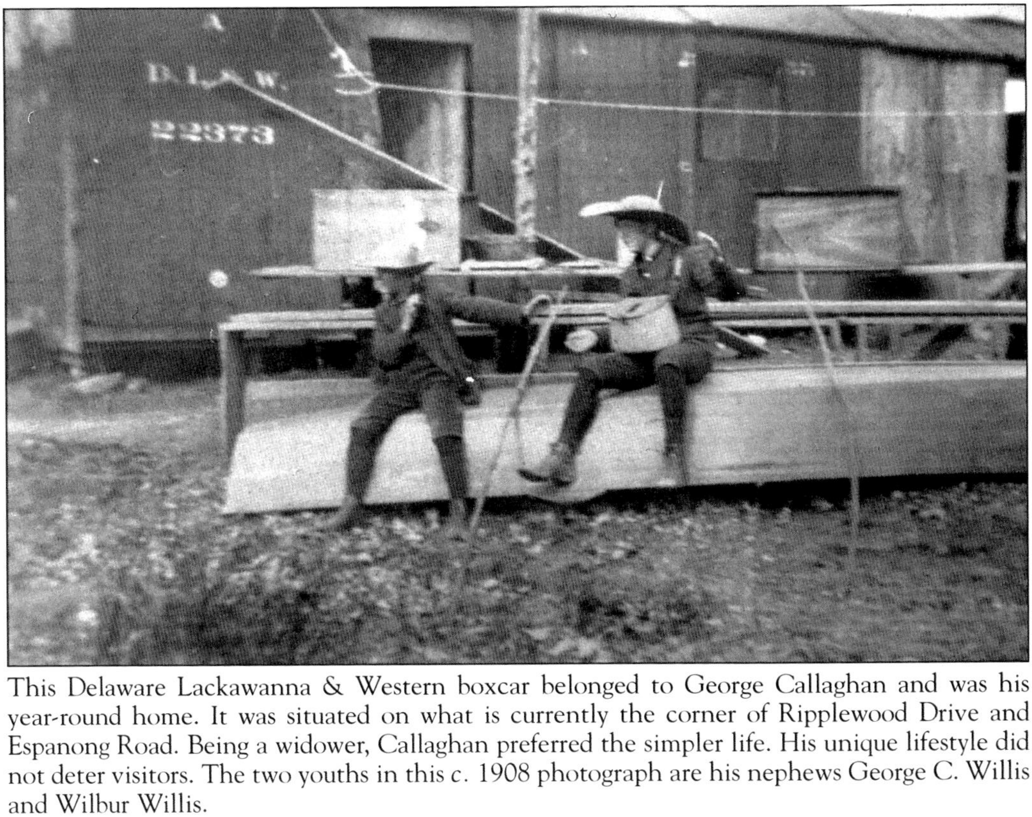

This Delaware Lackawanna & Western boxcar belonged to George Callaghan and was his year-round home. It was situated on what is currently the corner of Ripplewood Drive and Espanong Road. Being a widower, Callaghan preferred the simpler life. His unique lifestyle did not deter visitors. The two youths in this *c.* 1908 photograph are his nephews George C. Willis and Wilbur Willis.

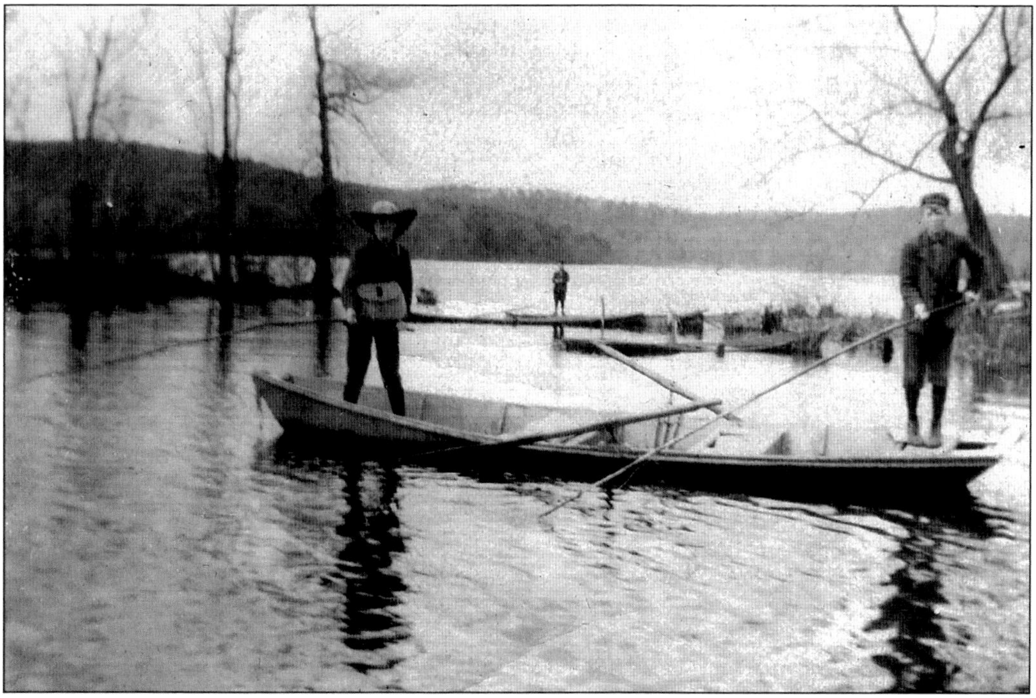

Fishing became not only a recreation but also a necessity. Directly behind George Callaghan's boxcar home, there was a small cove (today, the corner of Ripplewood Drive and Espanong Road). Callaghan was able to fish from shore or from boat and, during the winter, he also depended on ice fishing.

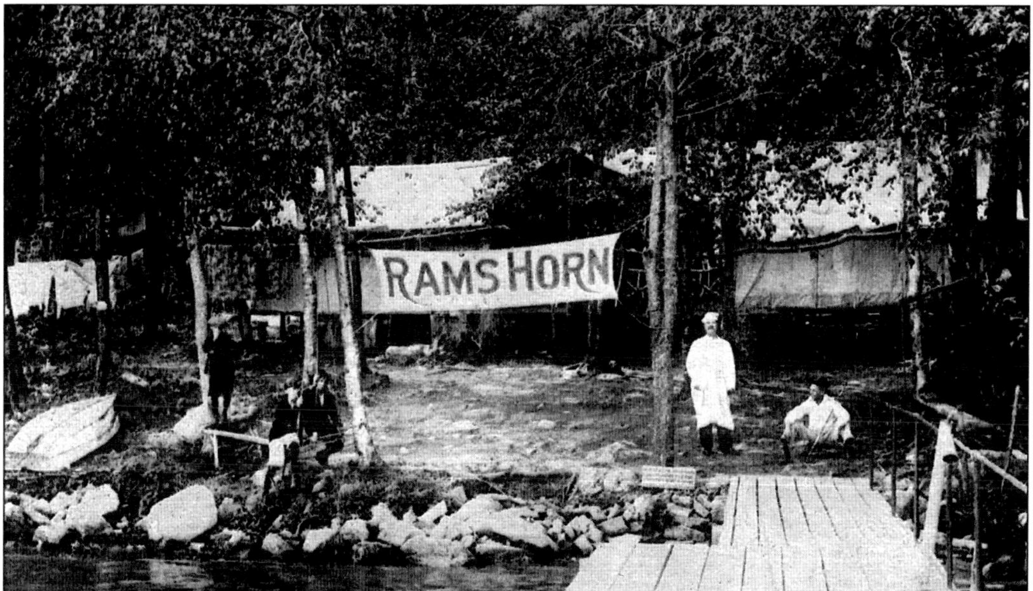

Halsey Island was the home of the Rams Horn Camp. During the summer of 1920, this camp became Camp Locora, with Mr. Jennings as the director. Thirty boys from Newark had the opportunity to partake in fishing, swimming, and boating, and competed with other camps around the lake in track and basketball.

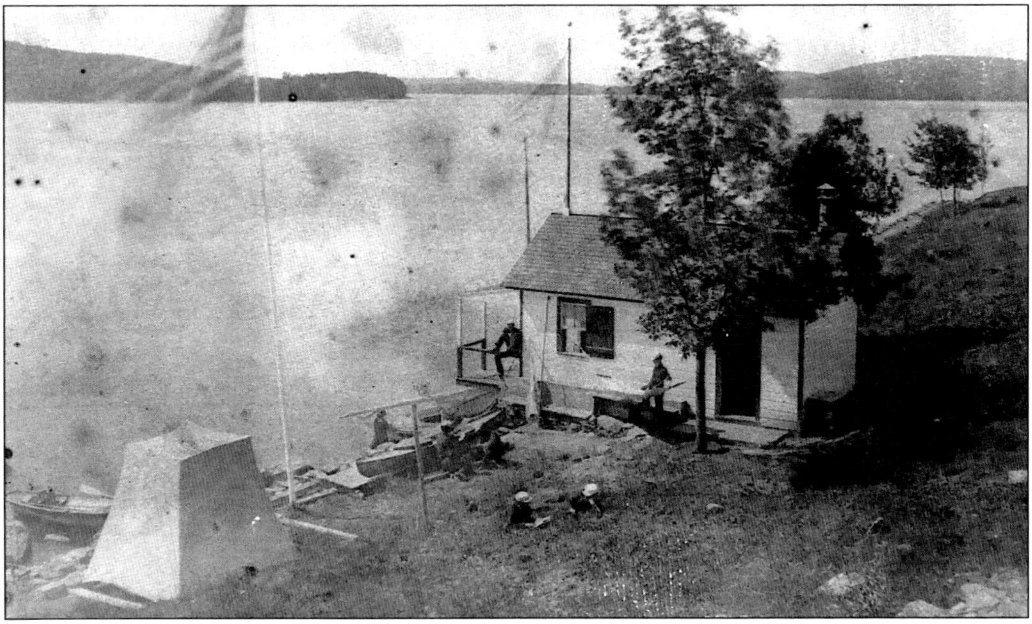

The Jolly Brothers Club was formed by four men from Brooklyn, New York. They came to Lake Hopatcong for fishing and sailing in 1884 and originally camped in Byram Cove. They then built a house near Nolan's Point. In 1888, they moved to the south shore of Great Cove and built a cottage there, where the club lasted for 50 years.

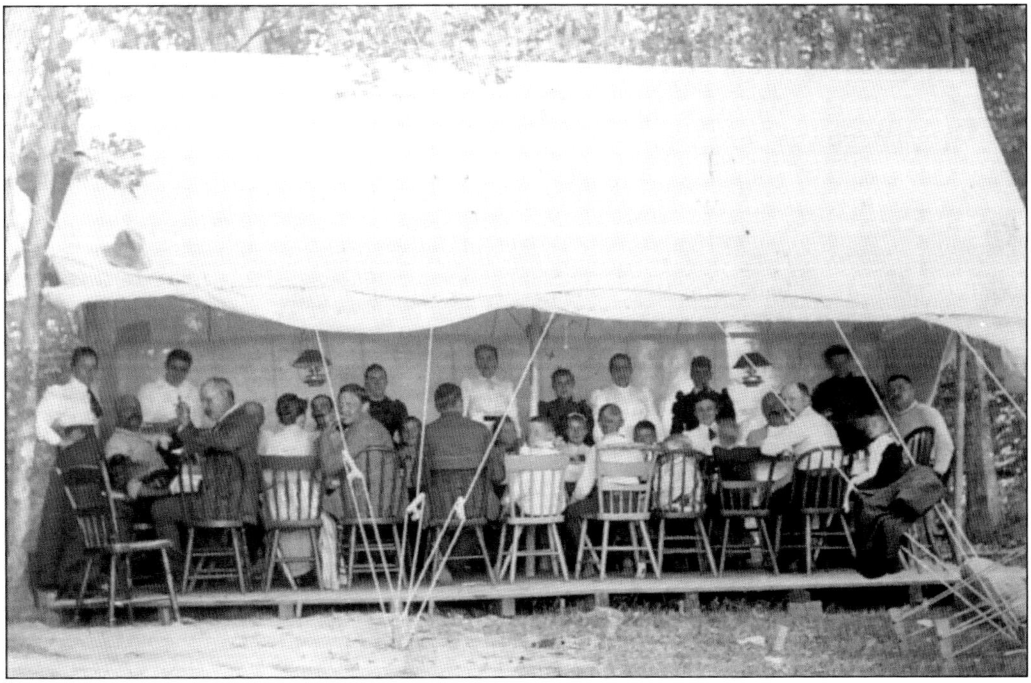

In 1874, a group of friends from Easton, Pennsylvania, formed the Ivanhoe Fishing Club. The members made their first trip to Lake Hopatcong in 1875, visiting Bishops Rock. By 1882, they had purchased land on Raccoon Island and erected a cottage on Point Breeze. The club remained at Lake Hopatcong for 50 years. "The object of this club is to fish and to enjoy life."

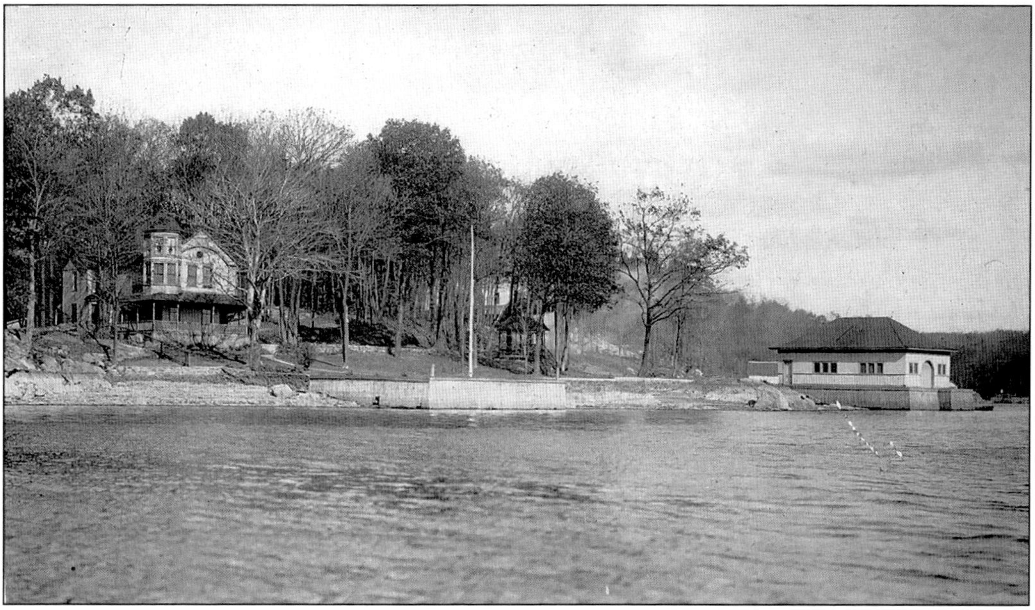

This summer cottage on Raccoon Island is believed to be the oldest, dating from *c.* 1850. It has a two-story turret and faces Halsey Island. The gazebo to the right of the flagpole, as seen in this *c.* 1910 photograph, is still standing today. The Hind family has owned the cottage since *c.* 1942.

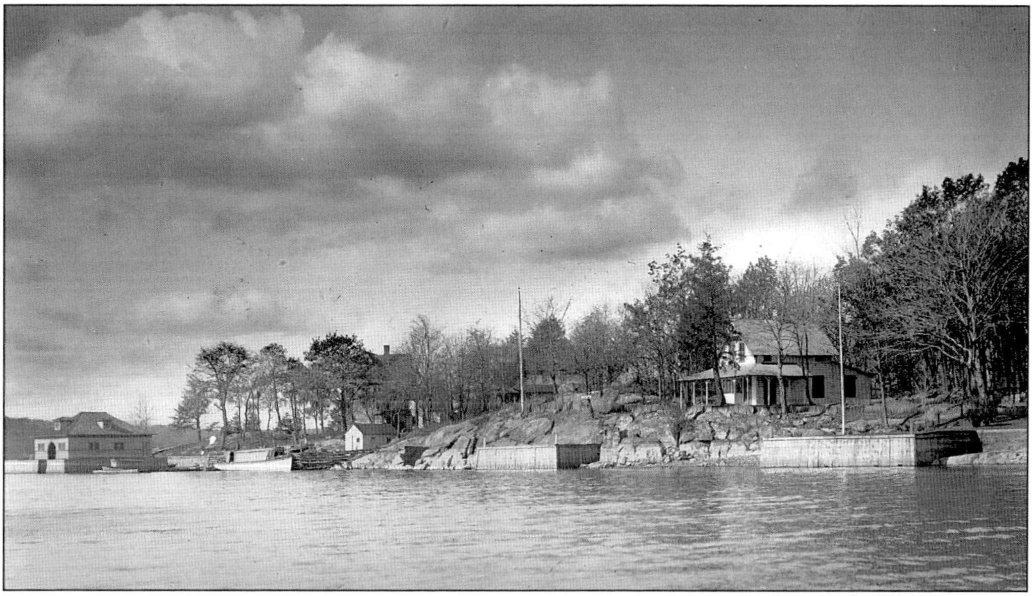

By the early 1890s, this cottage, owned by J.B. MacDuff, stood near the Hollywood Hotel and faced Prospect Point. Although the house appears to retain some of its original features, such as stained glass around the door, the seawalls on the edge of the property have been removed. John Carpenter is the current owner.

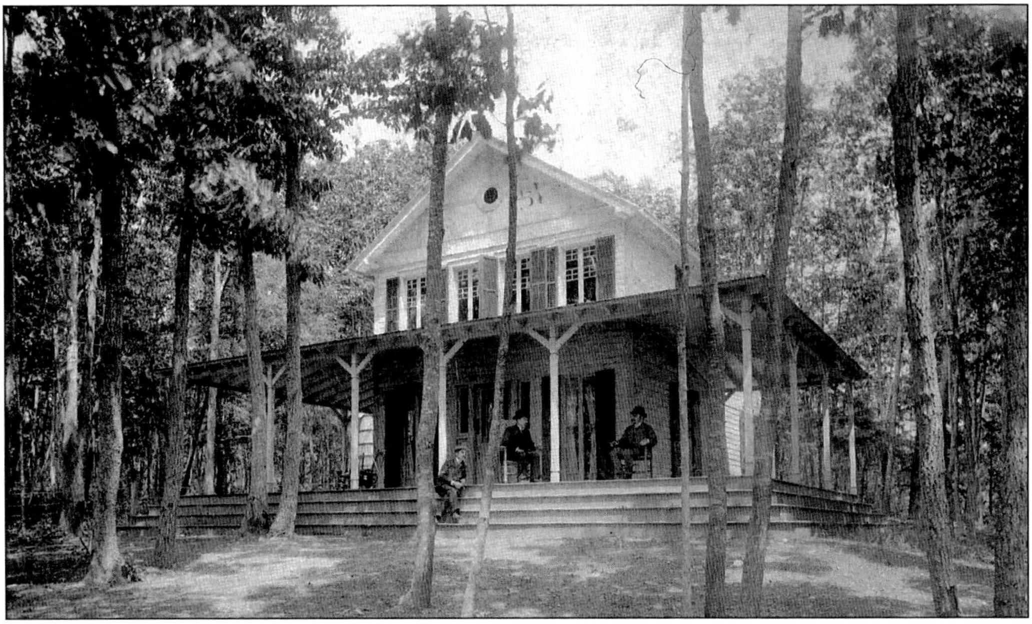

The Highwood Cottage was built in 1892 for Dr. David Engel and his wife, Amelia, of Brooklyn, New York. The property for this cottage was purchased from Oscar Megie and is located on the highest elevation of Raccoon Island. Five generations of the Engel and Lips families have occupied the summer residence since it was built.

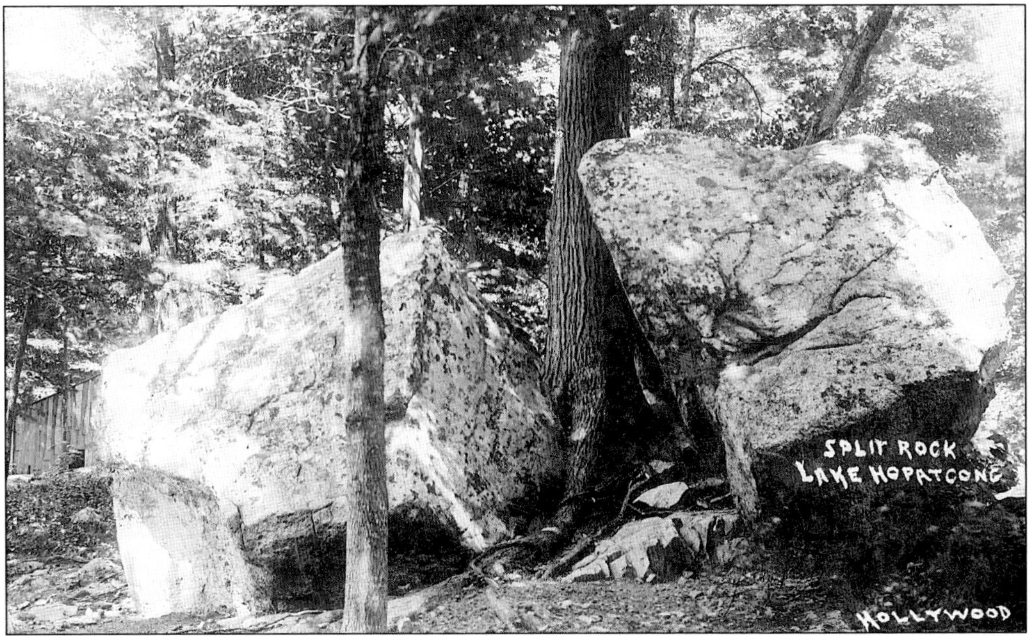

In this 1911 photograph, Split Rock, a natural wonder and fascination, is located behind what was the Hollywood Hotel. Although there is no longer a large tree between the rock sections, the rocks were and still are a curiosity.

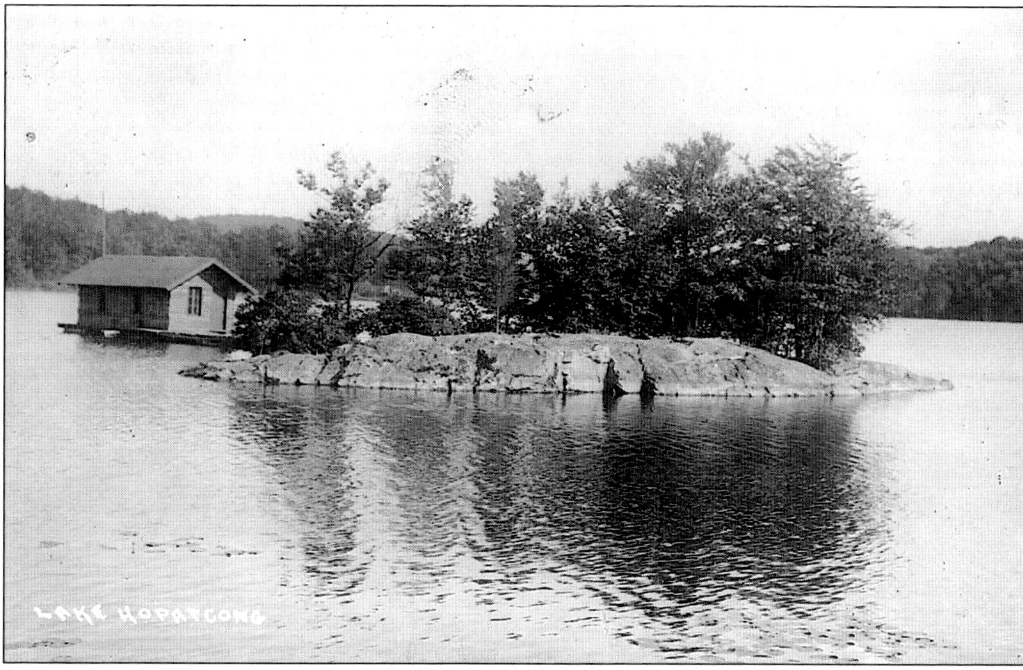

Just off the shores of Raccoon Island exists a small island that was the location for the boathouse, as seen in this 1909 postcard. In the winter of 1923, the boathouse was moved in sections across the ice onto Raccoon Island. Jay Picot Orben rebuilt the structure, which is still being used by the Orben family as a summer cottage.

Hemlock Craigs, a summer retreat on Raccoon Island, was built in 1908. It is believed that it was built by Mrs. Moore, the daughter of Oscar Megie. Sam McMillan, the current owner, is the fifth generation to vacation on Raccoon Island.

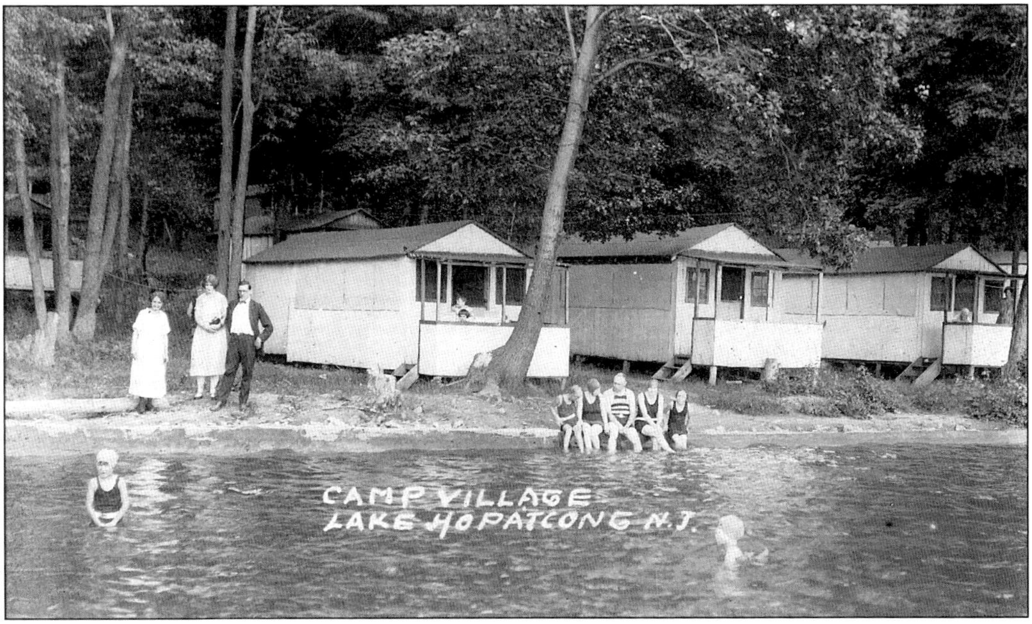

By c. 1909, Louis and Elsie Kraus had opened Camp Village on Prospect Point. Today CAPP Beach is located in this area. It was a colony of furnished semi-bungalows, half wood, half canvas, and was advertised as a highly respectable resort, which consisted of decent and honest people. Its season opened on Decoration Day (Memorial Day) and closed on September 30.

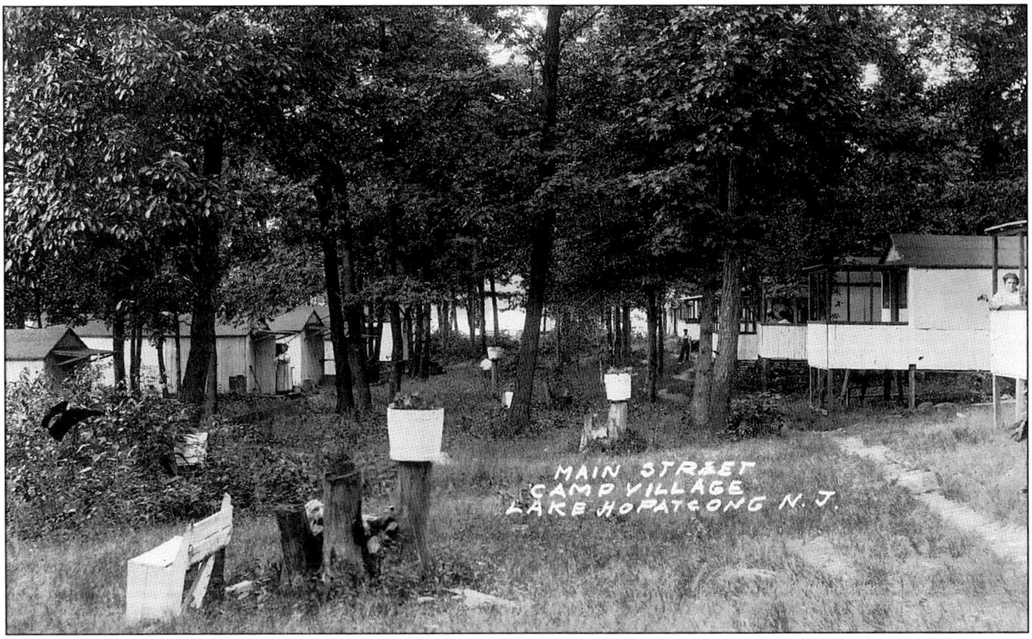

Camp Village had three classifications of bungalows: A, B, and C. Section A ($20 per week) was closest to the water; section B ($18 per week) was in the middle, and section C ($12 per week) was farthest from the water. Because they were situated on a slope, all bungalows had a view of the lake. Each bungalow had a front and back porch, one or two bedrooms, and a kitchen.

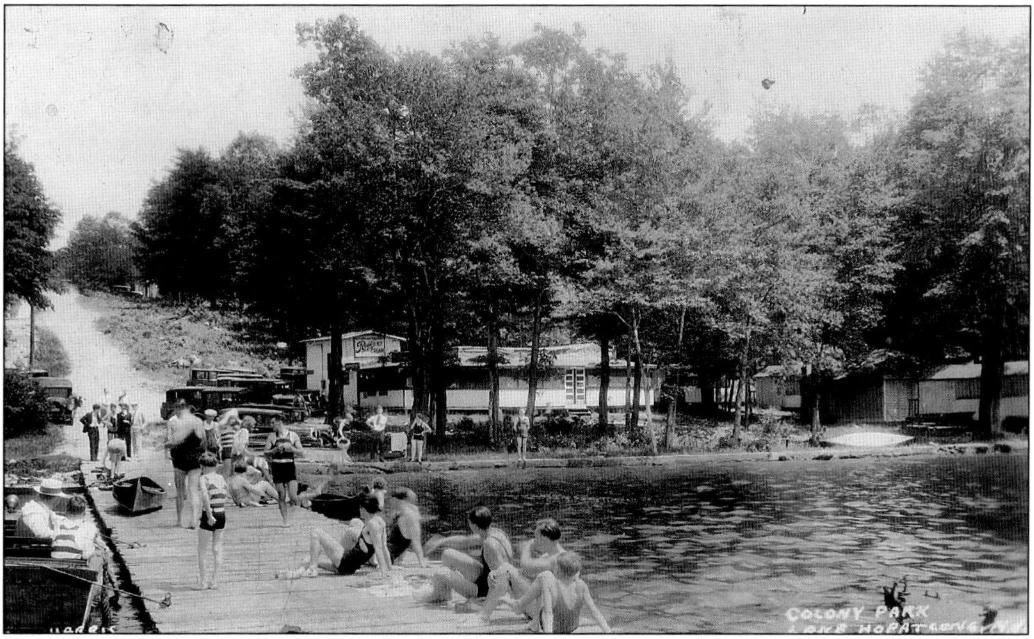

In addition to the bungalows, Camp Village had a general store and a small dance hall. Fresh breads, milk, and eggs were available every morning, and local produce and meats were also available. Campers were able to rent tables, lamps, chairs, and rowboats at very reasonable rates.

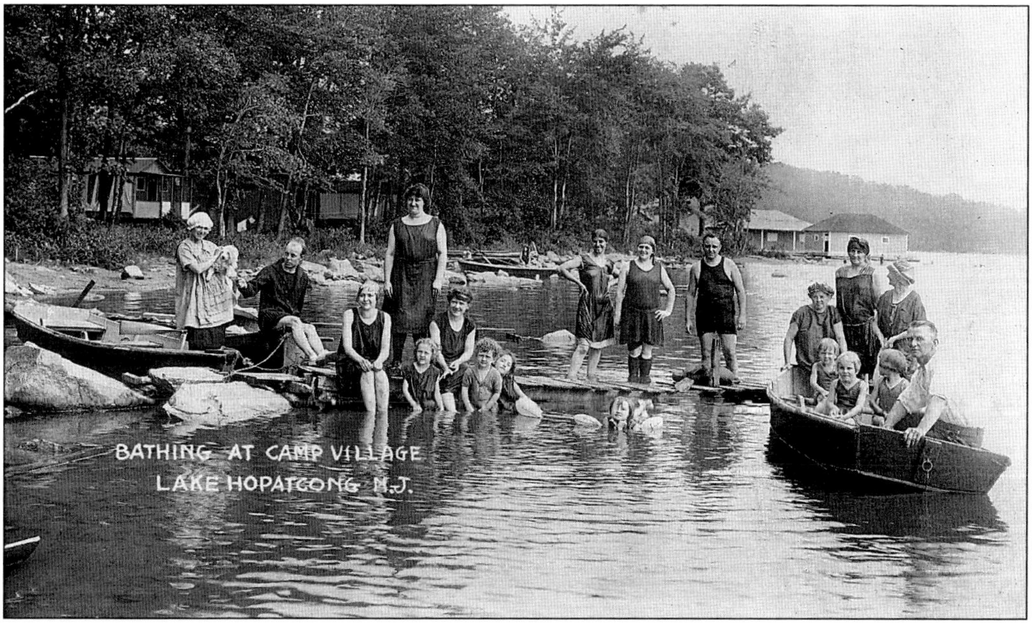

Camp Village's beach was 300 feet long and extended out into Lake Hopatcong approximately 200 feet. It had a gradual slope from six inches to five feet deep. A dock, which was built for diving, had a depth of about 10 feet of water at the end.

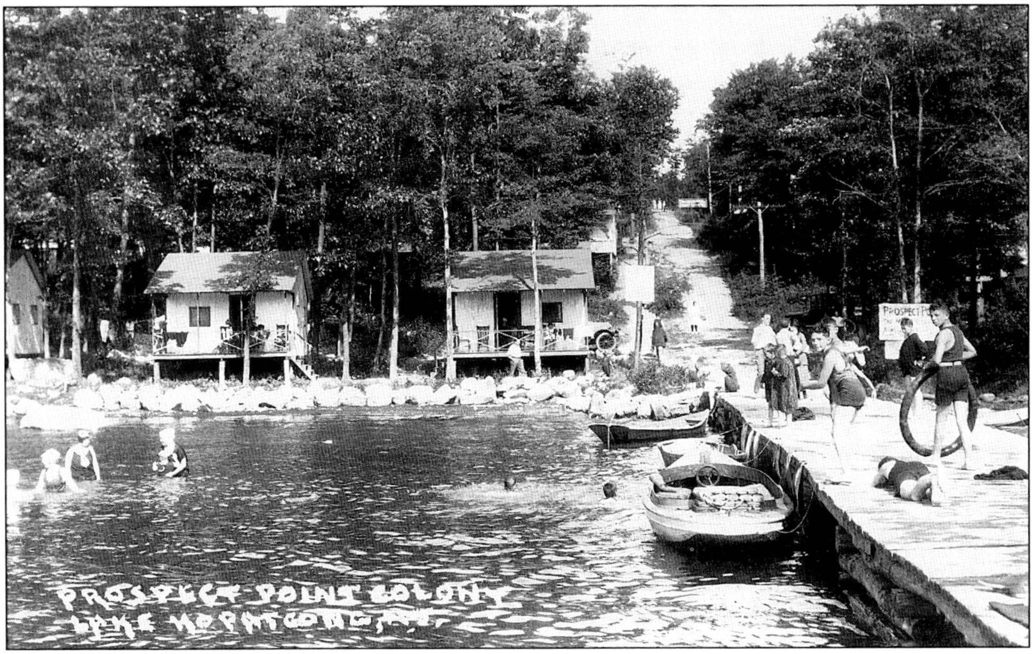

Unlike Camp Village, Prospect Point Colony was a group of wooden bungalows that were built c. 1918. These bungalows were located on the opposite side of the road from Camp Village. They were also furnished and were rented by the week, month, or season.

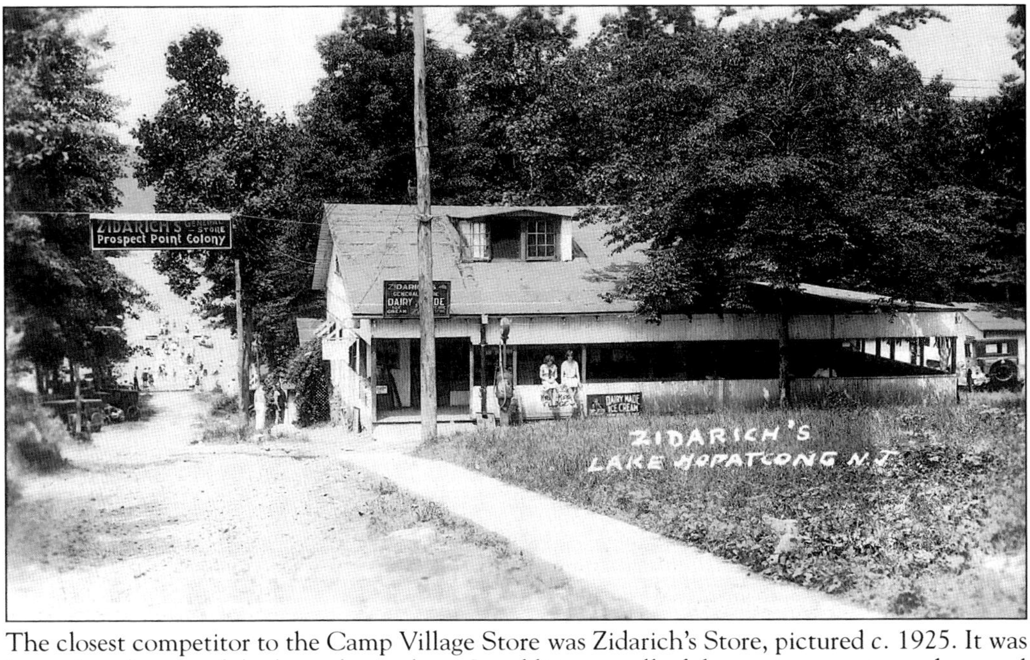

The closest competitor to the Camp Village Store was Zidarich's Store, pictured c. 1925. It was located at the top of the bungalow colony. In addition to all of the same groceries and general goods, Zidarich's had a gas pump. Unfortunately, according to Zidarich's grandson James Nunn, it exploded c. 1929.

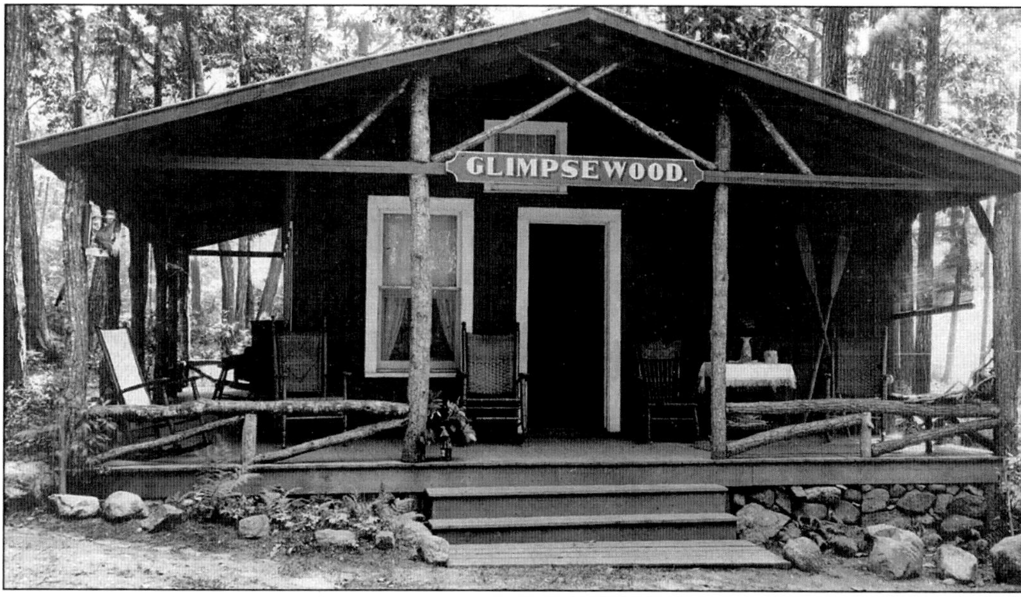

Glimpsewood Cottage was built in 1905 by Walter V. Messler Sr. of Morristown. Messler was employed by the Central Railroad as an engineer. The cottage took only two weeks to build. Messler did not like the lake, so the front porch was built facing Castle Rock. After Messler's death, his family moved the porch to face the lake. Glimpsewood has changed little over the years and is still owned by Messler's granddaughter Mrs. Robert Morgan.

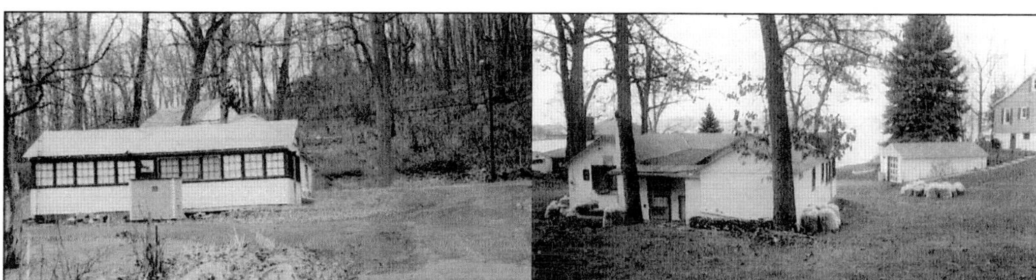

In 1888, the Phi Sigma Social Club obtained a formal charter from the state of New Jersey and became incorporated. The club consisted of doctors, lawyers, contractors, and other professionals from Phillipsburg. The club's goal was to promote friendship while enjoying sporting activities. On August 28, 1907, the club purchased property on Castle Rock Road and a tent camping area was laid out. A kitchen and dining area was erected first and eventually a second building was added to house community and sleeping areas. In the late 1930s, these two buildings were joined together by a glass-enclosed porch. The year 2001 marked the 112th birthday of the Phi Sigma Club. The club continues to own and use the property on Castle Rock Road. It is still a men's club, but a family group can occasionally enjoy the facilities.

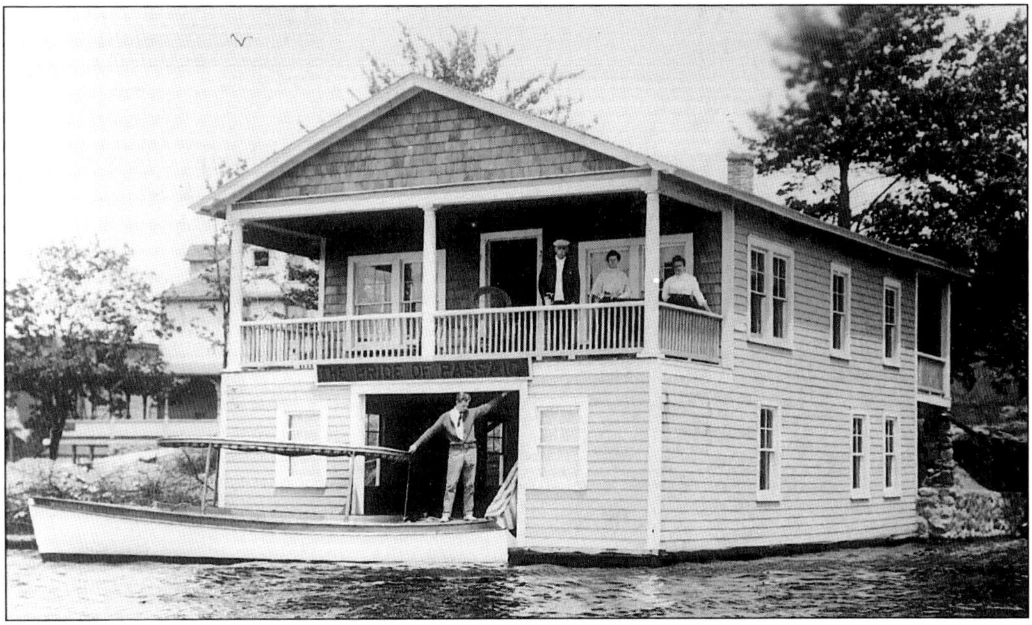

The Pride of Passaic was located next to Lee's Pavilion on Nolan's Point. This was a gathering place for the local youths. Unfortunately, it was destroyed during the 1924 fire that also destroyed Lee's Pavilion. The boat *C.D. Ely* was housed in this boathouse.

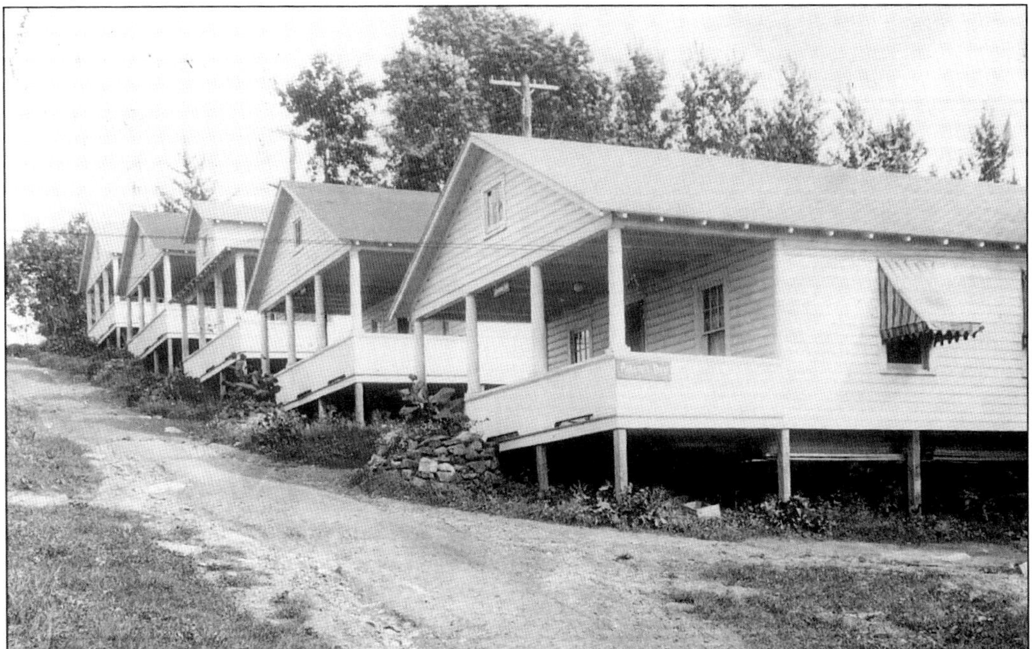

In addition to Lee's Pavilion, Andrew Lee also had a bungalow colony on what is currently called Lee Avenue on Nolan's Point. These bungalows, pictured *c.* 1920, were used by patrons that did not want a hotel environment. Domestic water came from Lake Hopatcong via a reservoir located above these bungalows. Many of these bungalows have been converted to year-round homes and still exist today.

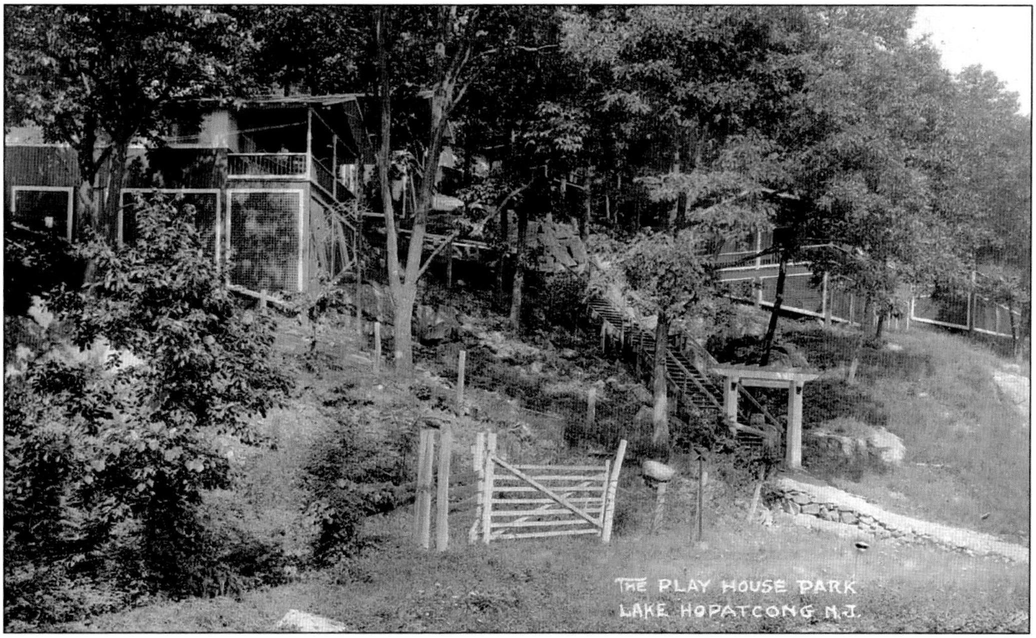

Around the 1930s, Playhouse Park was advertised as "the Bungalow retreat for people of refinement and discrimination." It was located on Great Cove and consisted of 30 cottages. Each cottage had three to five rooms, electricity, and a bathroom. The cottages also had access to a bathing beach, boating, fishing, and golf. Bungalows were available for a weekend, week, month, or season.

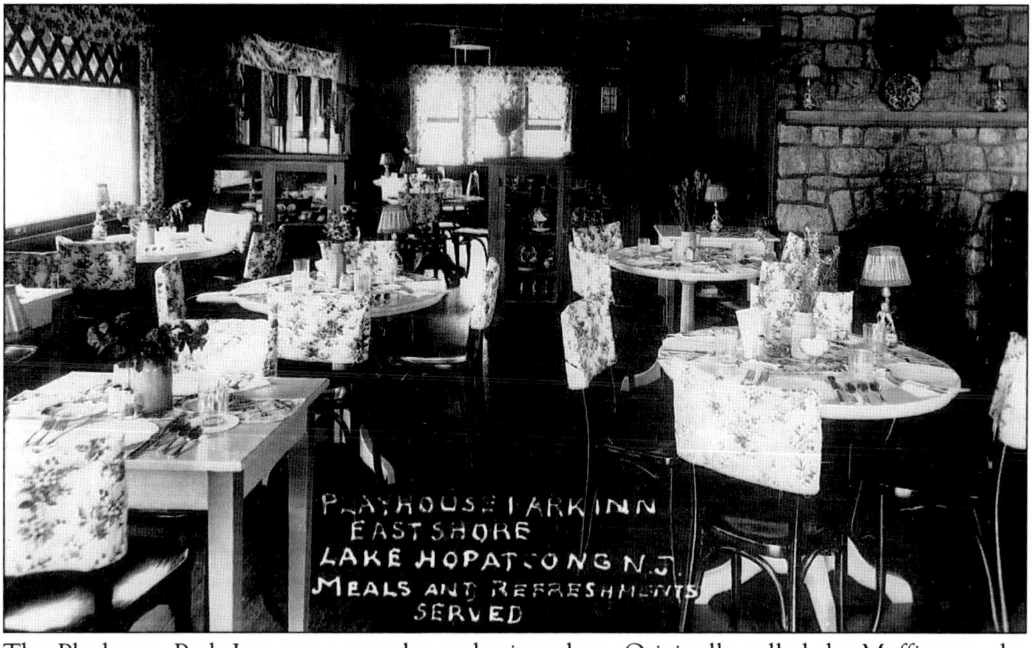

The Playhouse Park Inn was a popular gathering place. Originally called the Muffinette, the Playhouse Park Inn served excellent food to park residents and tourists.

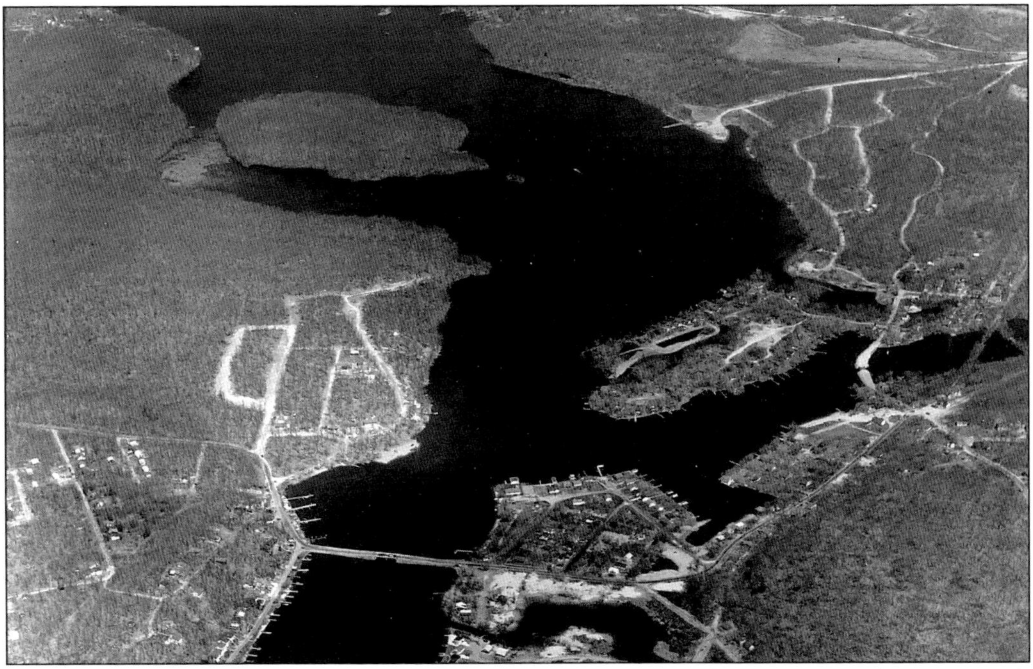

Lify Island, located at the northern end of Lake Hopatcong, is being preserved in a natural, pristine state. No development has or will occur on the island. Through the joint efforts of the township and Lake Hopatcong Regional Planning Board, Jefferson Township currently owns it. Between Lify Island and the mainland, there is a high-priority wetland that is home to a large wildlife population of ducks, geese, fish, and heron.

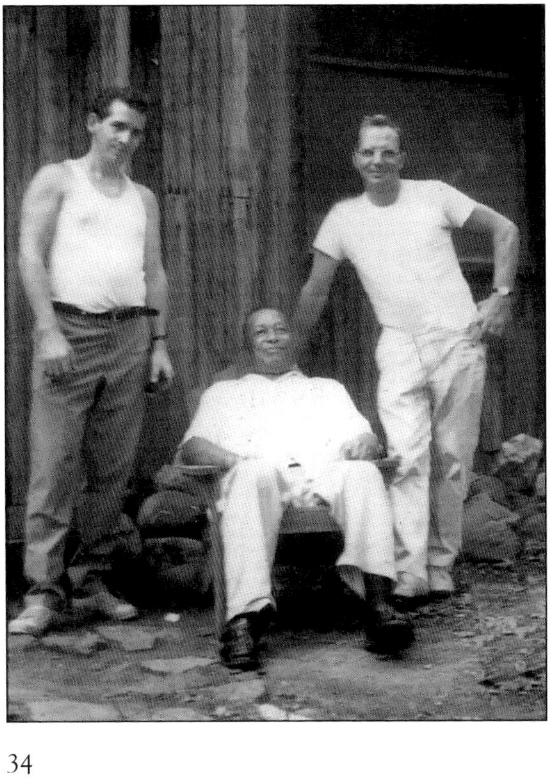

William Peterson, better known as "Pete," became a summer resident on Lify Island in the mid-1920s. He is seen here sitting in a chair *c.* 1970. He was born in Georgia but lived on Staten Island, where he was a cook for prominent families. Major Stewart and his partner, owners of the center of the Lify Island, gave Peterson lifetime rights to use the island. For many years, he brought Boy Scouts from Staten Island to Lify Island on the Smith family boats. In later years, many locals visited him.

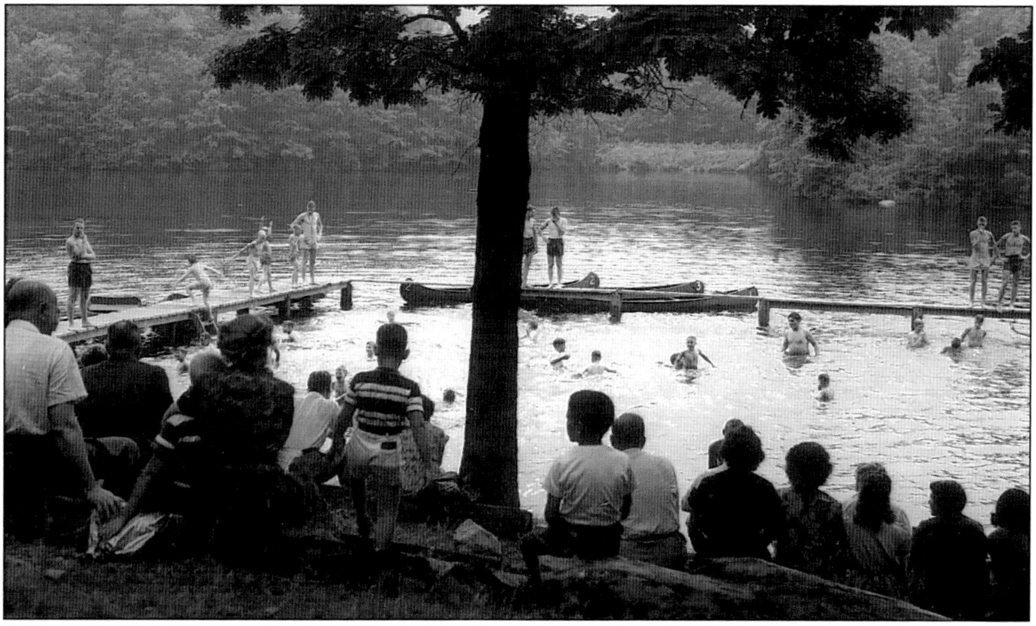

By 1937, Camp Ranger, located on Weldon Road, catered to boys from 8 to 13 years of age. The major goal of this camp was to help the boys strive for success and happiness. The ground and equipment were donated by a group of Montclair men. The programs were styled after many Maine camps and were often referred to as "Maine in New Jersey." Swimming, recreation, and competition were a major part of the program.

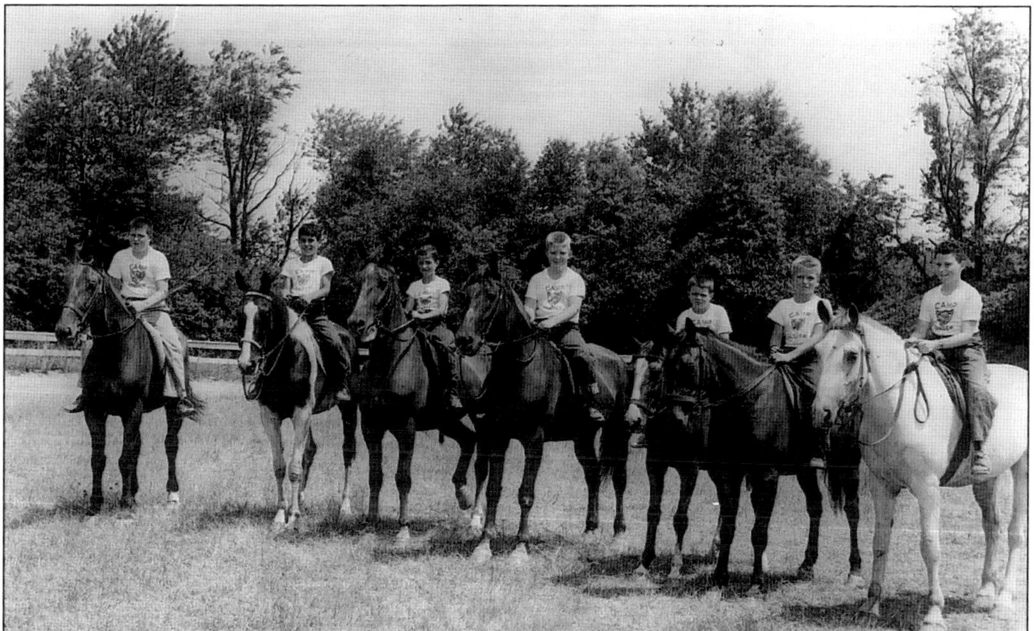

Camp Ranger was limited to 70 boys for a period of eight weeks. In addition to caring for themselves, the responsibility of caring for fellow campers and animals helped the boys develop self-esteem and respect. In 1962, the camp became Camp Clifton; in 1998, Jefferson Township bought the camp and renamed it Camp Jefferson.

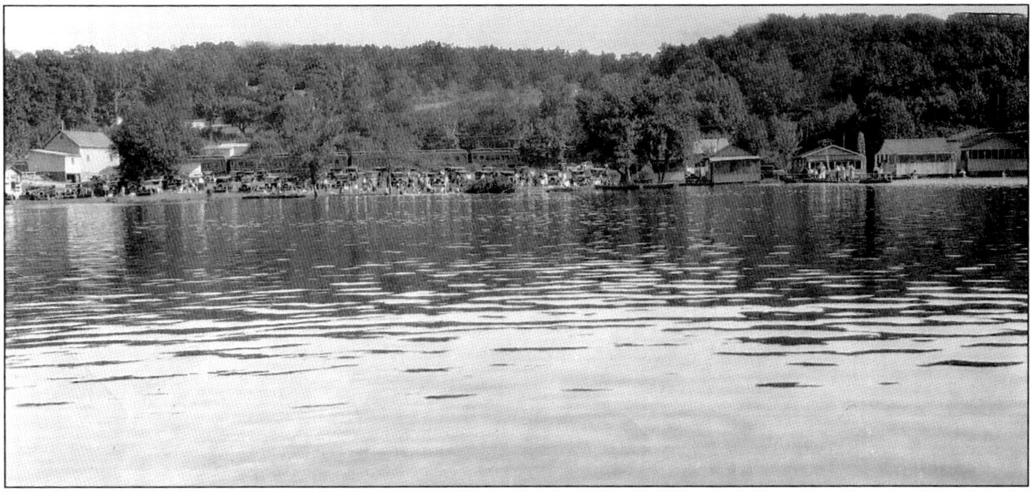

Callaghan's Cove had not only a tavern and a boardinghouse (Erin House) but also a swimming area and bungalow colony. Access to this area was easy because the Central Railroad had a stop at the hotel. This photograph was taken *c.* 1925.

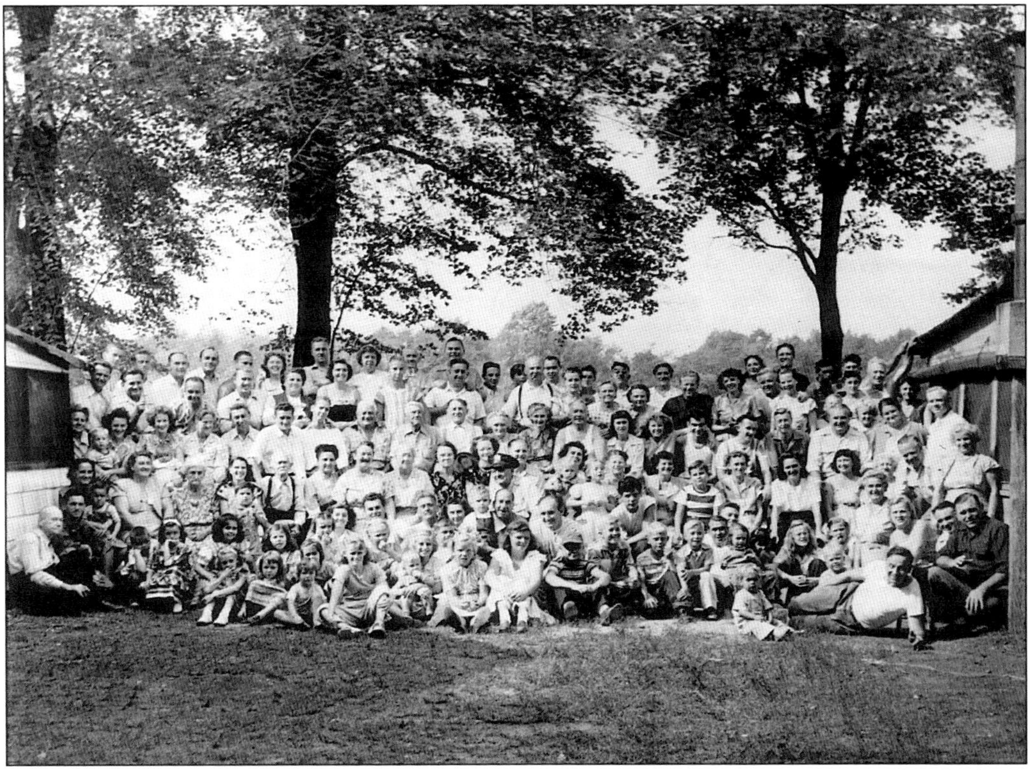

A bungalow colony existed on both sides of the cove: one on the Erin House (Callaghan) property, and the other at what is currently Sandy Point property. These bungalows were rented by vacationers for the week, month, or entire summer season. Picnics, fireworks, boating, swimming, and fishing were enjoyed by all. This *c.* 1947 photograph shows locals and vacationers enjoying each other's company.

Three

COMFORTABLE PLACES

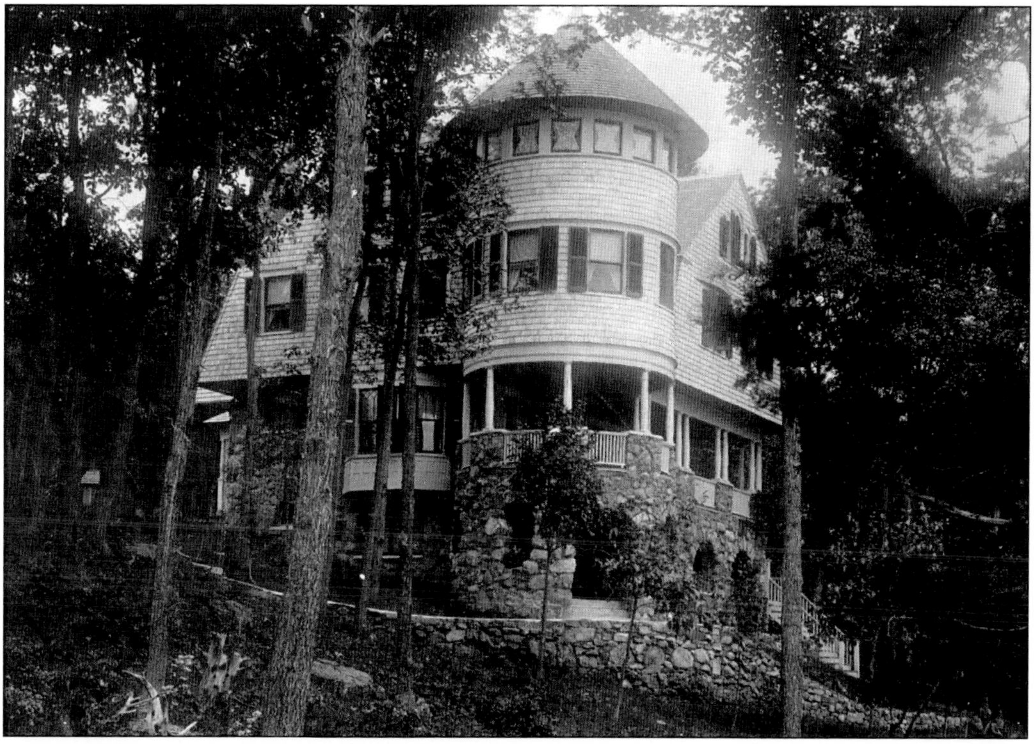

The Ardsley Hotel was located on Halsey Island, which was accessible only by boat. The Ardsley was built in the late 1800s by the Hoffman family of Somerville and was opened as a hotel in 1920. It was located on the side of the island facing Nolan's Point. Unfortunately, it was destroyed by fire in 1927 and was never rebuilt.

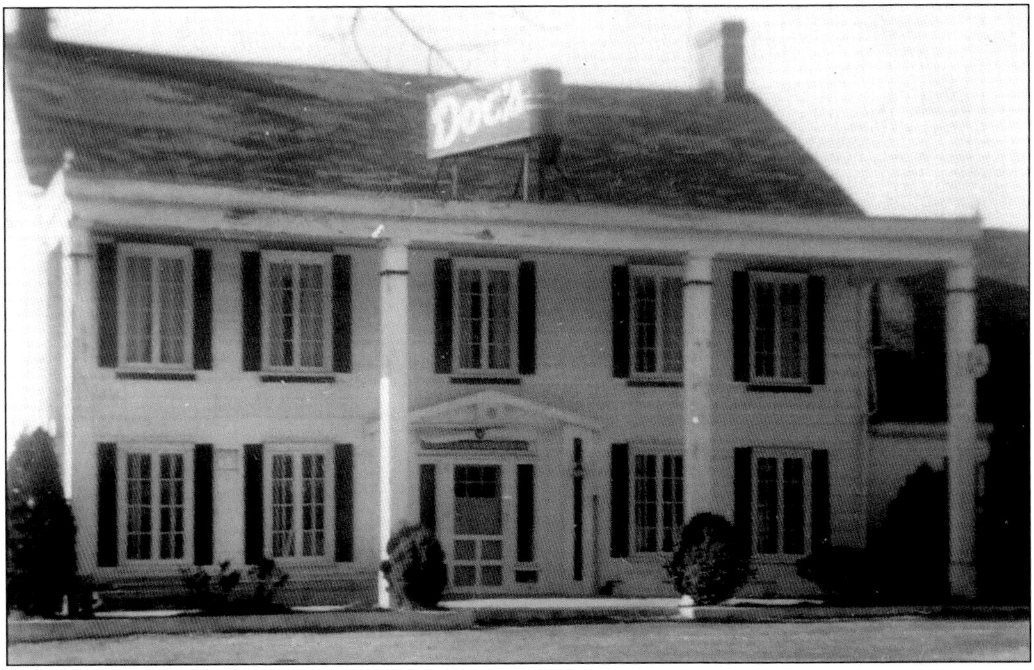

On April 9, 1804, incorporation meetings for Jefferson Township were held at Seward's Tavern. The tavern was located on Dover (Sparta) Road, also called Union Turnpike. John Seward was the proprietor. The name was eventually changed to the Mountain House, and it became a two-family house. In 1947, the name was changed again to the Airport Inn because of a small airport behind it. Its name was Doc's at the time of this photograph. In 1964, it was called the Vunderbar. In 1974, it became Squires Pub & Spirits, a local tavern and store. The building still exists and is currently unoccupied.

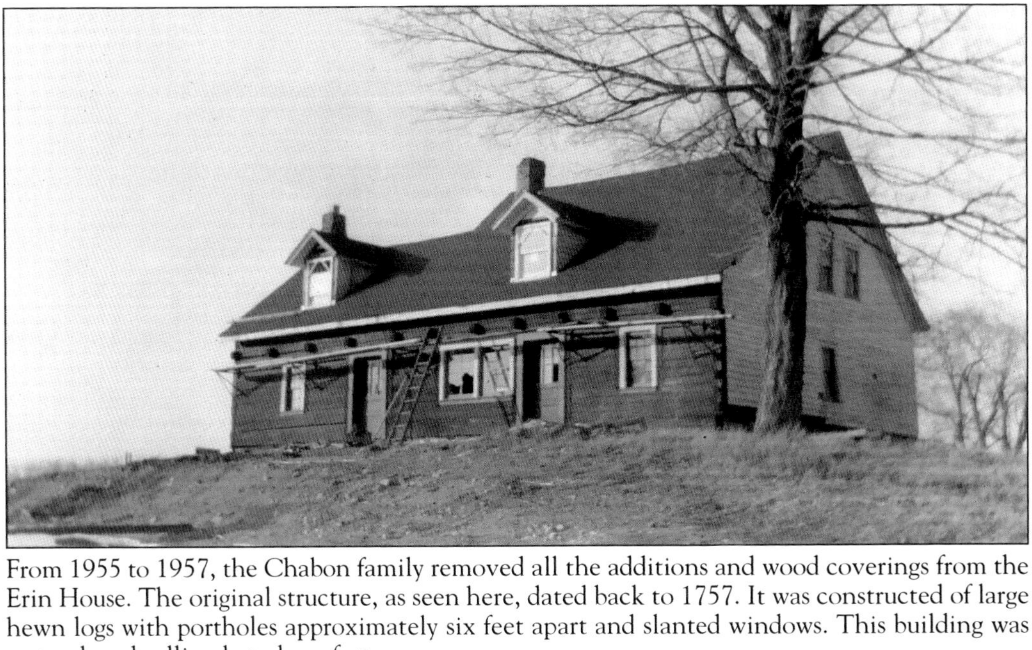

From 1955 to 1957, the Chabon family removed all the additions and wood coverings from the Erin House. The original structure, as seen here, dated back to 1757. It was constructed of large hewn logs with portholes approximately six feet apart and slanted windows. This building was not only a dwelling but also a fort.

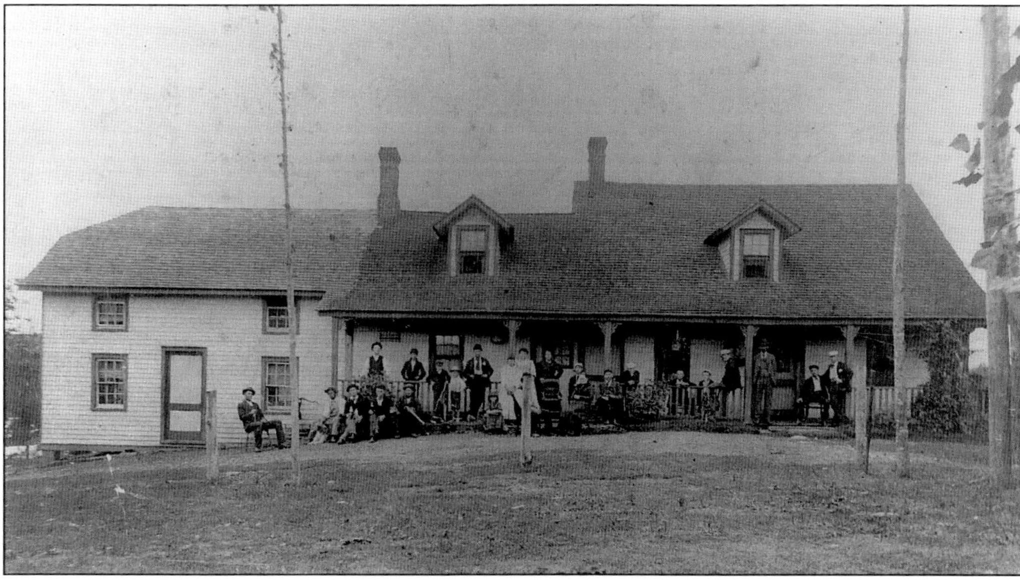

The Callaghan family poses in front of the Erin House, located on Hurd Cove. The family purchased the property from the estate of Aaron Peck. By the late 1890s, a large addition of a kitchen with guestrooms above was added. Employees of the Consumer Coal & Ice Company and the railroads occupied the majority of the rooms. Bungalows, boat docks, a poultry farm, and a swimming area were all included on this large estate.

Prior to Prohibition, Patrick A. Callaghan and his family operated a bar at the Erin House. All bars were required to be registered and to pay a special tax as a retail liquor dealer. The fee of $25 was payable to the Internal Revenue Service. After Prohibition the bar reopened. During the later part of the 1930s, Paul Gruntisch operated the bar. In 1940, Michael and Florence Chabon rented the bar and property, and in 1954, the Chabons started to purchase what is currently known as Floraine Inc. from the Callaghan heirs.

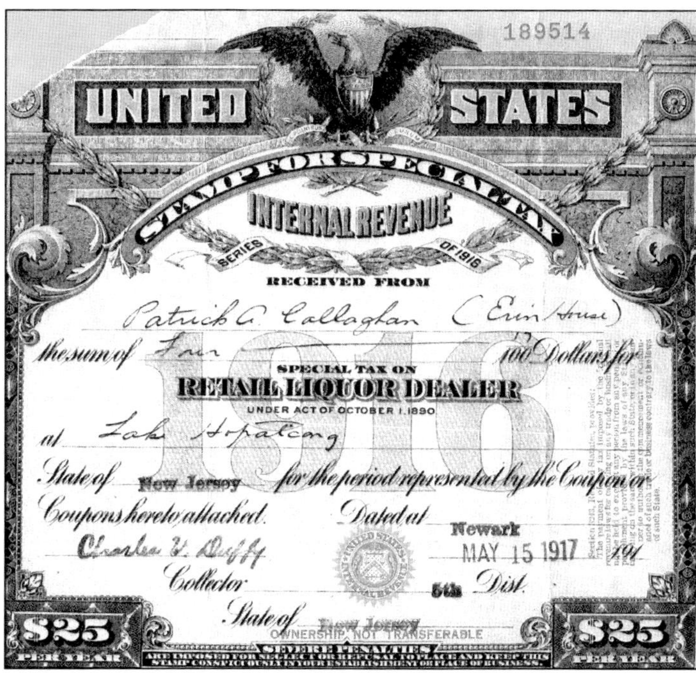

189514

UNITED STATES

INTERNAL REVENUE

SERIES OF 1916

RECEIVED FROM

Patrick A. Callaghan (Erin House)

the sum of ... Dollars for

SPECIAL TAX ON

RETAIL LIQUOR DEALER

UNDER ACT OF OCTOBER 1, 1890

at Lake Hopatcong

State of New Jersey for the period represented by the Coupon or Coupons hereto attached. Dated at Newark MAY 15 1917

Charles V. Duffy

Collector 5th Dist.

State of New Jersey

OWNERSHIP, NOT TRANSFERABLE

$25 PER YEAR

SEVERE PENALTIES

$25 PER YEAR

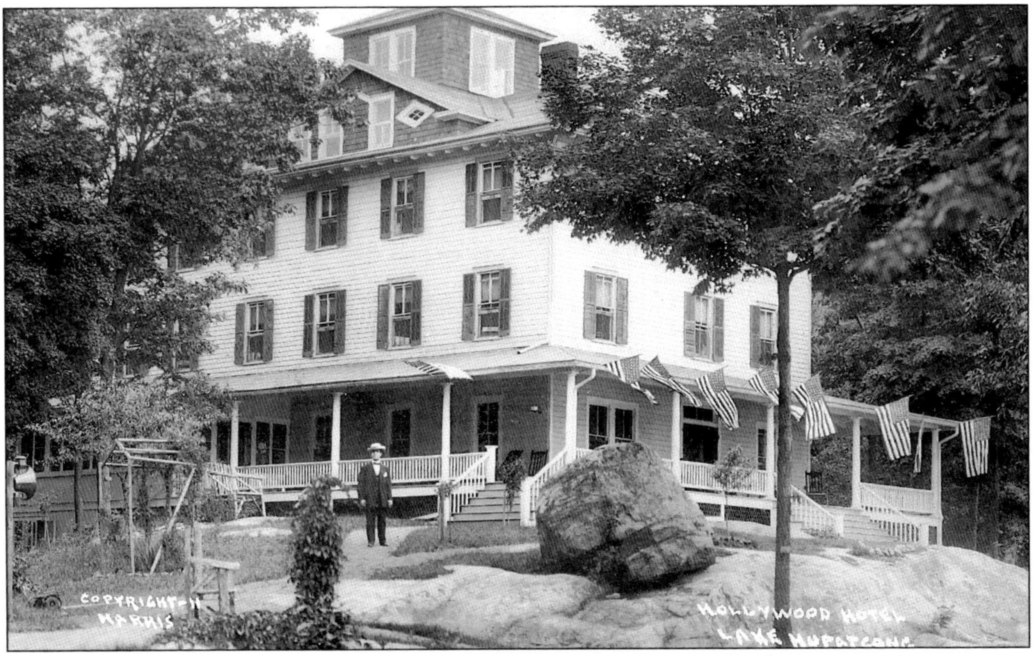

The Raccoon Island Hotel was built and became operational in the late 1880s. Since it was located on an island accessible only by boat or by bridge, the hotel was used solely during the summer months. By 1896, the hotel had been renamed the Hollywood Hotel. In addition to the hotel, the site included cottages, a grocery store, a boat dock, and a swimming and fishing area. Unfortunately, the hotel burned in November 1912 and was never rebuilt.

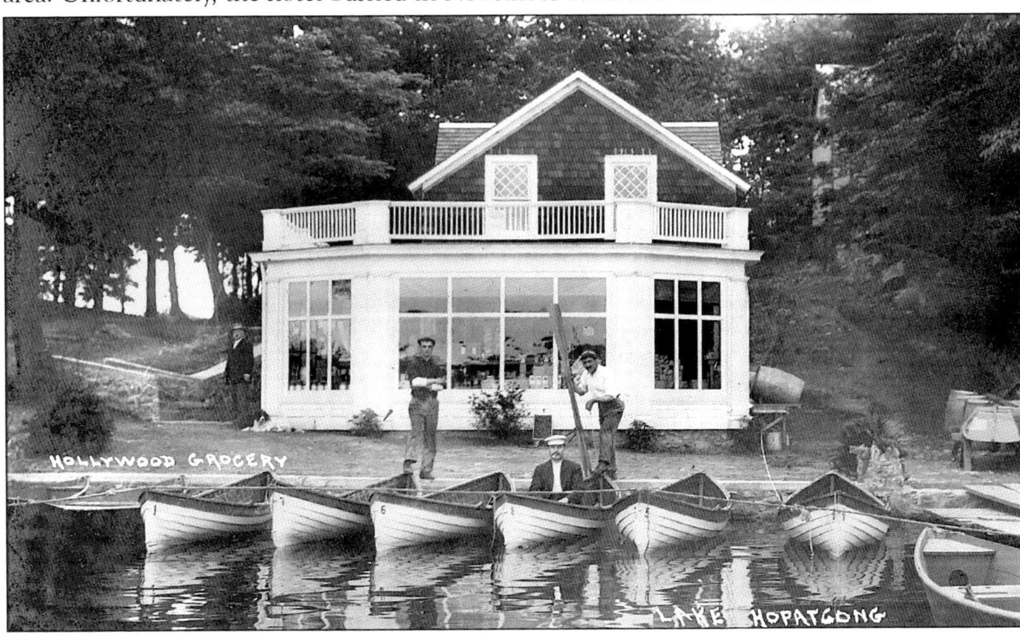

Mr. Rizzi operated the Hollywood Store, which was located next to the hotel. It was a small convenience store for the hotel and local residents. In addition to buying groceries and fuel, hotel and island guests could rent rowboats. This building is still in existence; however, it is a private residence.

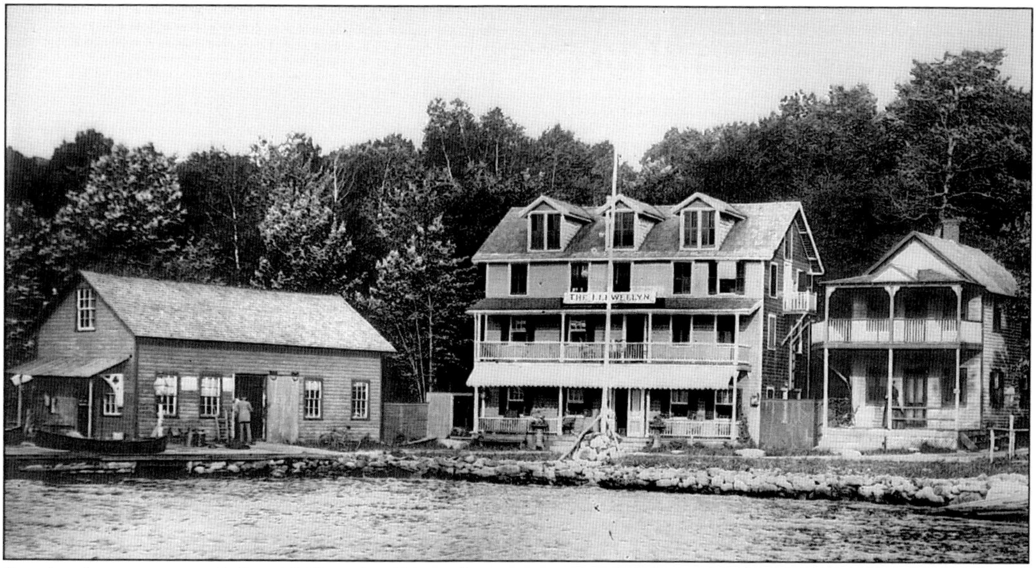

By the latter part of the 1880s, the Llewelyn was owned by Mr. and Mrs. Walter J. Knight. It consisted of one large building and a two-story cottage. This small annex called the Llewelyn Cottage had yellow pine throughout. Both structures were located on the southern shore of Great Cove near the American House Pier.

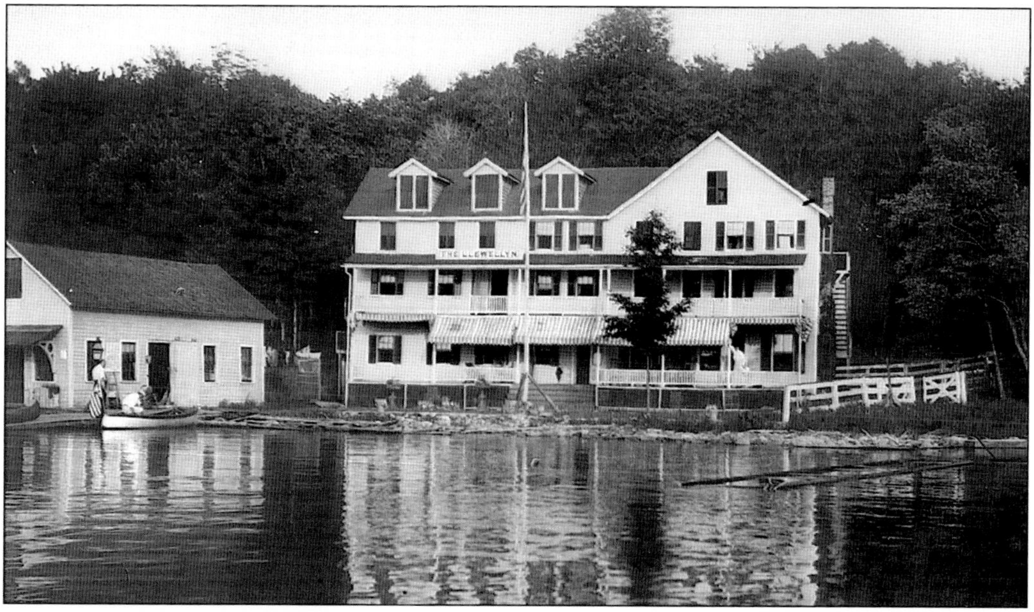

The two buildings of the Llewelyn were connected *c.* 1906. The expanded hotel could now accommodate 50 people under one roof. Fishing, swimming, dancing, boating, and hunting were among the offered activities. In 1912, the name was changed to the Villa Gerard and, by the 1920s, the hotel was no longer in existence.

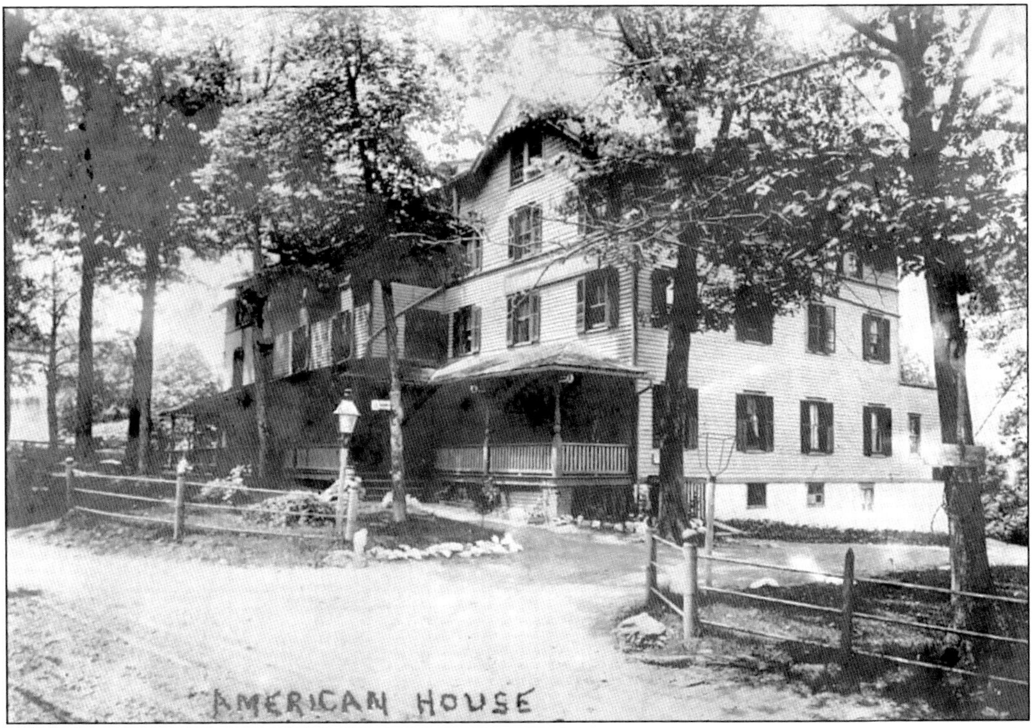

The American House, located above the Llewellyn House in Great Cove, was built in the early 1880s. It was surrounded by woods and had modern conveniences and large cheerful rooms. In 1919, the hotel was renamed the Ellsworth Hotel.

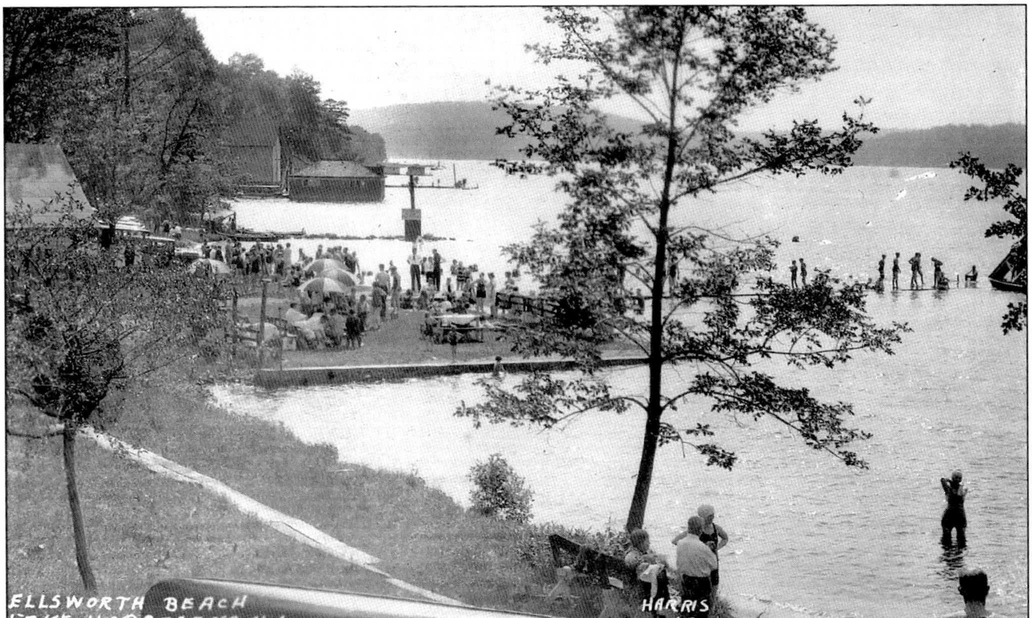

The Ellsworth Hotel had not only a large dock for boating and fishing but also a large, sandy bathing beach. The hotel was situated on five acres and was advertised as "the coolest place on the lake." Near the water's edge, picnic facilities were also available.

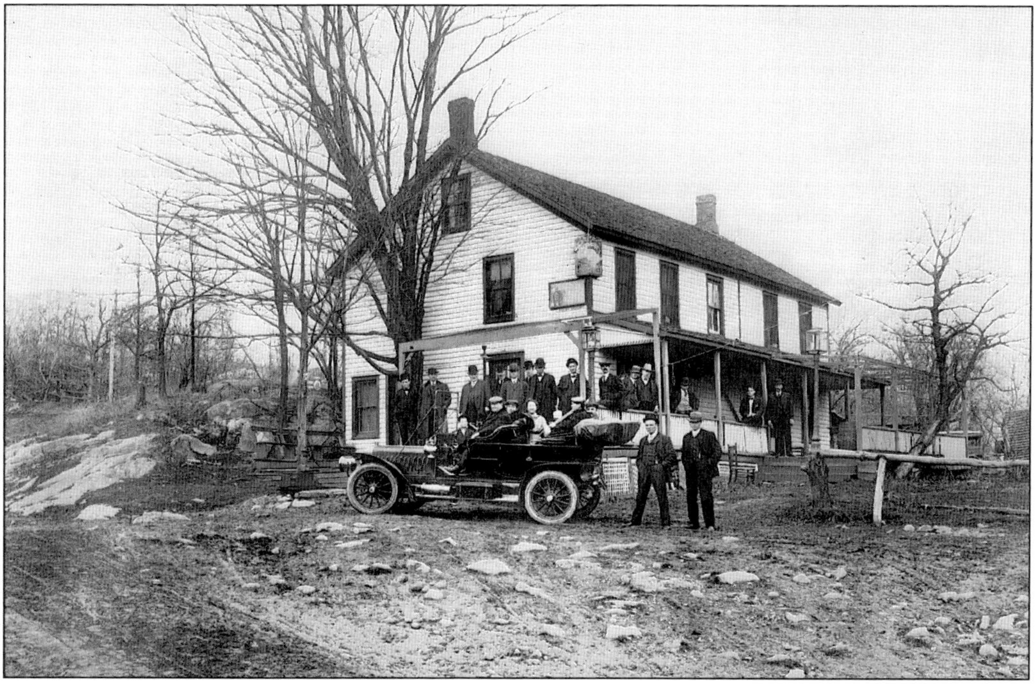

What became the Chamberlain Hotel was originally a farmhouse that belonged to the Chamberlain family *c.* 1880. Around 1906, the John Robinson family purchased it. Robinson, a former theater manager, catered to the theater group.

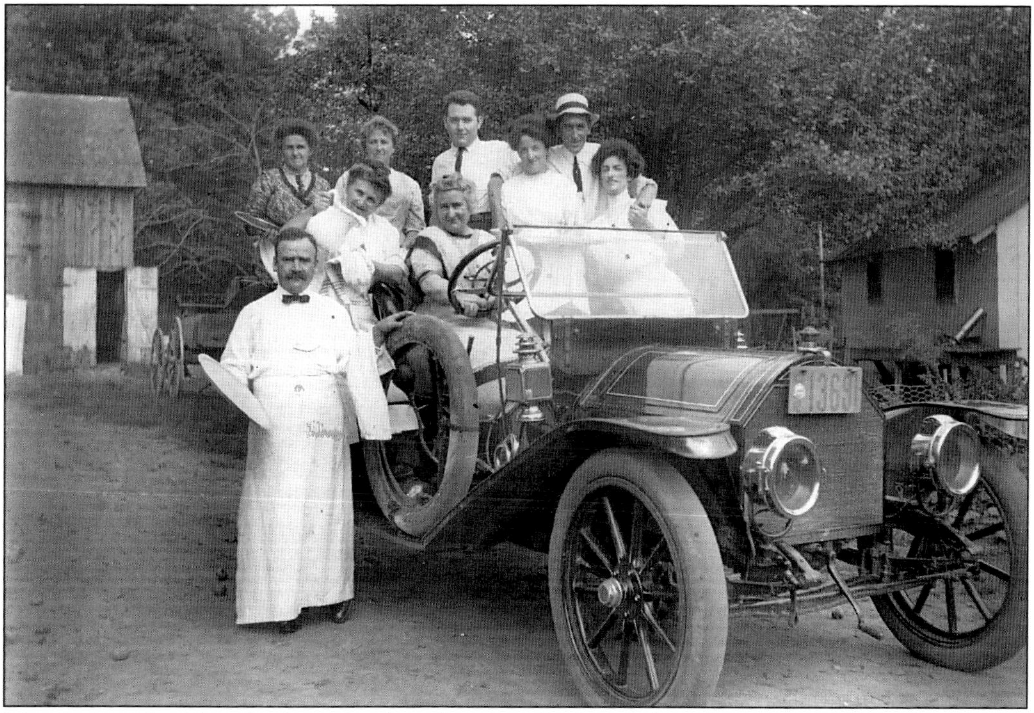

Members of the Chamberlain Hotel staff pose with Mrs. Robinson, seated behind the wheel of the family's touring car.

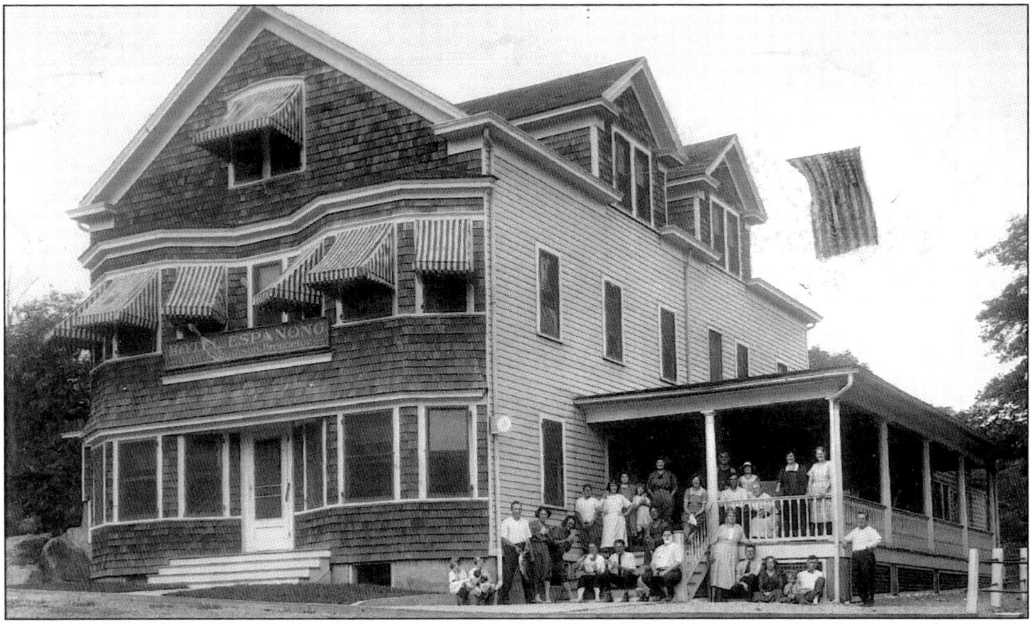

As the popularity of the lake increased, it became necessary to build a replacement hotel. The new one was called the Espanong Hotel. The area was often referred to as 42nd and Broadway because of the great influx of theatrical people, such as Bert Lahr, Walter Donaldson, and the Rose Midgets.

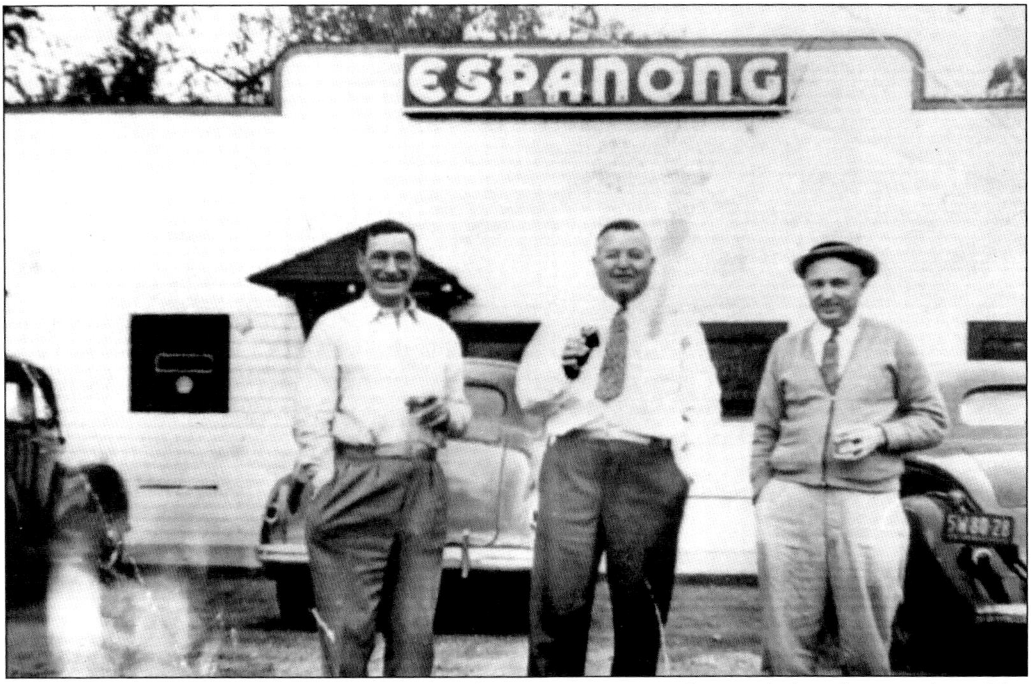

Edward Mewing purchased the Espanong but, in 1929, an electrical fire destroyed it. The carriage house became the New Espanong, which housed a tavern. This building did not last for long because it was too drafty. So, the icehouse was converted and used. The name was later changed to the Espanong Chateau.

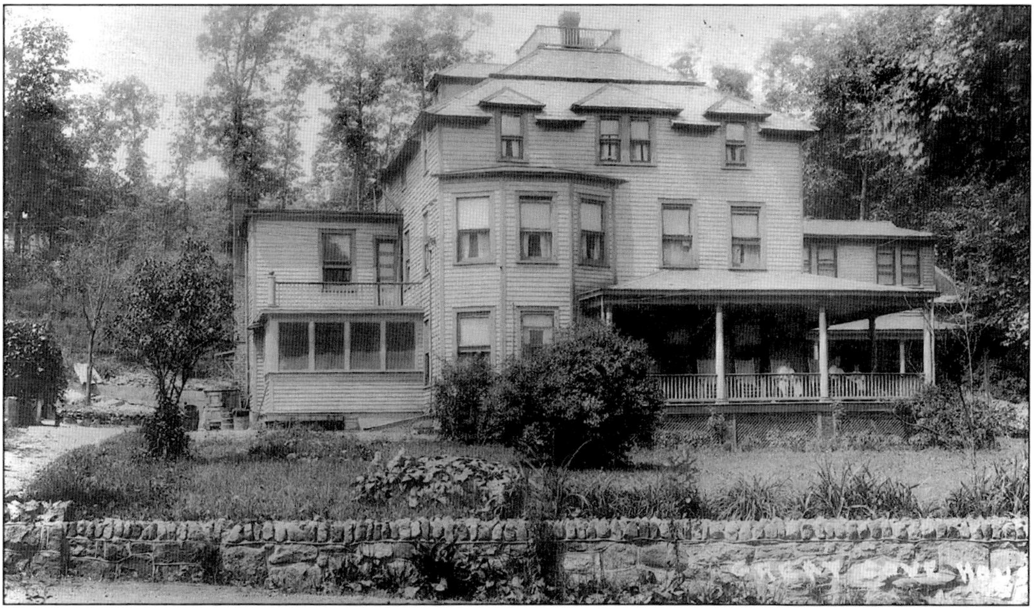

The Van Over House, built in 1884, could accommodate 75 guests. Mr. Apgar, who owned the Woodstock in Mount Arlington, managed the Van Over House for Mr. and Mrs. Van Over. In addition to the hotel, the Van Overs maintained their own icehouse, annex, and pump house.

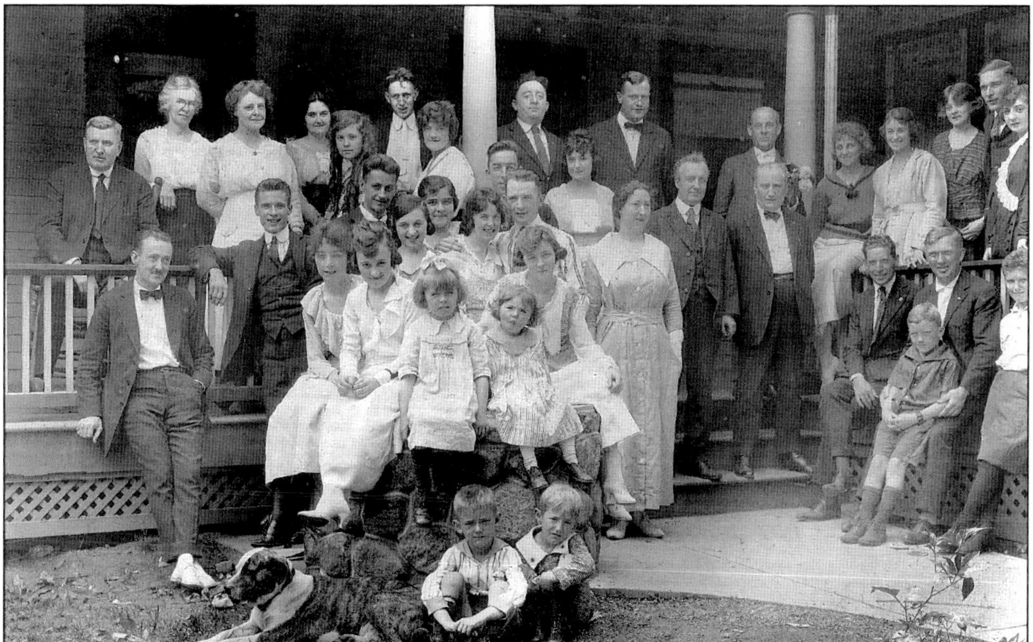

In 1918, the name of the Van Over House was changed to the Great Cove House. The George M. Tolton family purchased it in the early 1920s. It became known for its "best jazz orchestra." By 1937, two Finnish women rented the Great Cove House in order to accommodate Picatinny Arsenal employees. However, in 1938, the women neglected to take the ashes from the coal furnace outside and the hotel burned to the ground. Luckily, no one was injured.

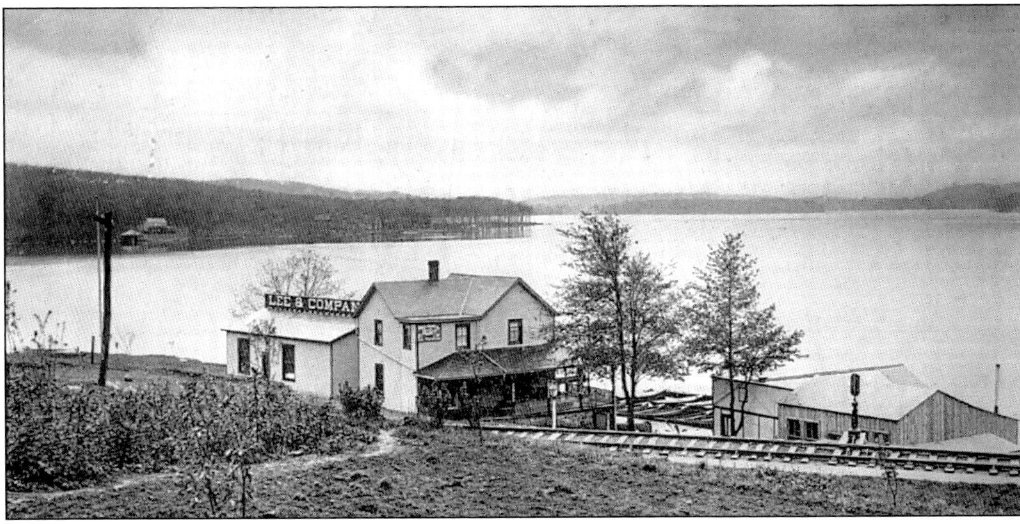

Lee and Company was built by John Lee during the early 1890s. It was a small family hotel, which was serviced by the Central Railroad. Boating, swimming, and fishing were available.

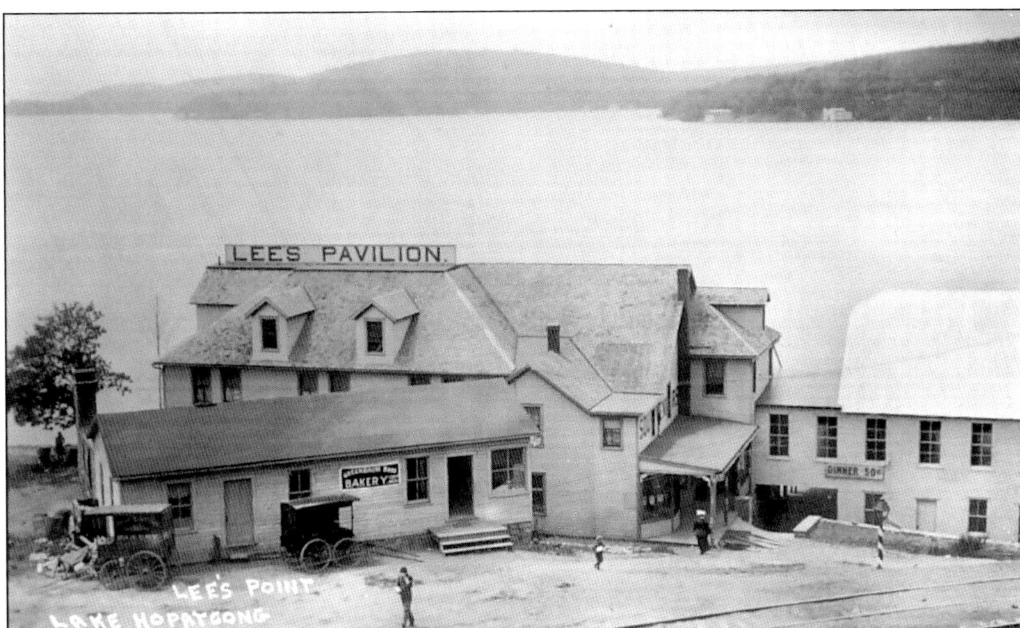

Additions to Lee and Company included Greenbaum Brothers Bakery, a souvenir shop, a dining room, a department store, a pool parlor, a barbershop, a steam laundry, an icehouse, and a drugstore. The hotel also sold beer, liquor, groceries, meat, and gasoline. The final addition to Lee's was a sleeping facility. This was called a dormitory and was one of the first located on Lake Hopatcong. By 1910, Harris Photo Studio and the Idle Hour moving picture theater had been built.

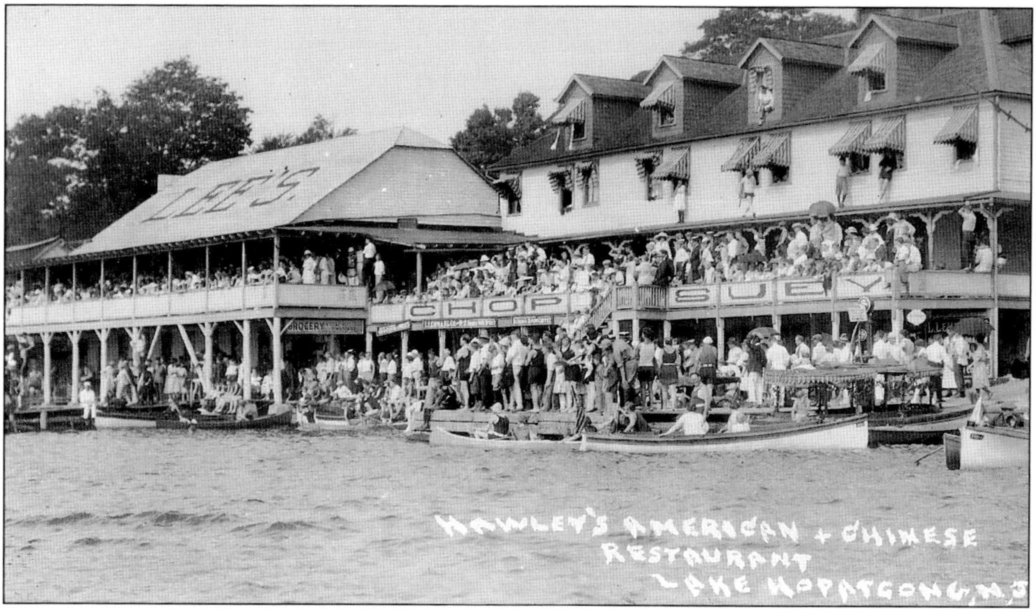

The 1920s brought some new changes to Nolan's Point. Hawley's American and Chinese restaurant introduced a "blue plate dinner" for $1 and up. His restaurant, called the Oriental, was located on the lower floor of Lee's Pavilion. Unfortunately, it was destroyed when Lee's burned in 1924.

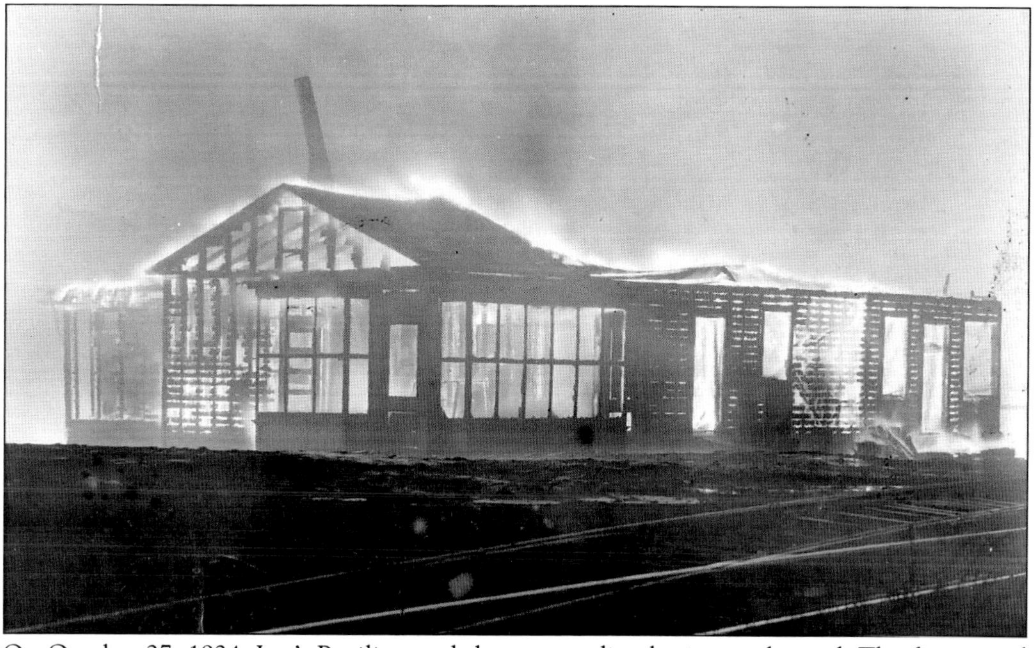

On October 27, 1924, Lee's Pavilion and the surrounding businesses burned. The fire started in the main building at approximately 11:00 p.m. It quickly spread to the annex that housed the dance floor, department store, and adjoining icehouse. Surrounding buildings that were also destroyed included the Harris Photo Studio, the movie theater, which was being used as sleeping quarters for the 1924 season, the bakery (seen here), an ice cream parlor, a restaurant, and a barbershop.

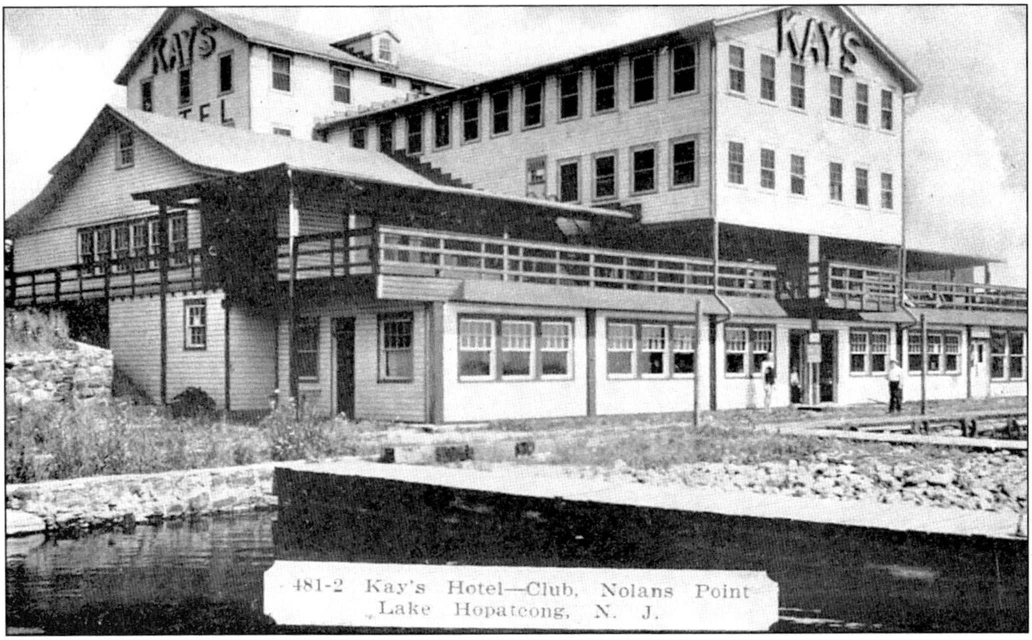

After the fire Lee's was rebuilt but, by the mid-1930s, the name and ownership had changed. It became Kay's and was known to be "smart but informal." Bathing beauty contests, amateur night, and boxing exhibitions occurred during the summer seasons. In 1938, Kay's became the Colony Club, which allowed only Christian members.

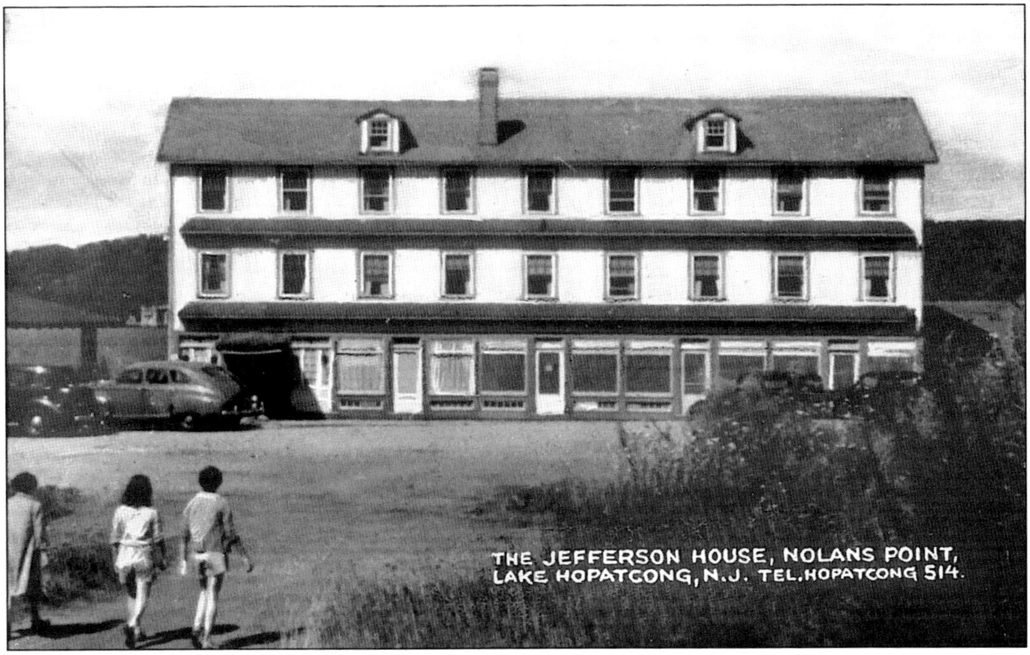

By 1941, the Colony Club was sold and renamed the Jefferson House, a high-class establishment. Today, the Jefferson House is owned by the Orths, who arrived *c.* 1973 and have made major renovations.

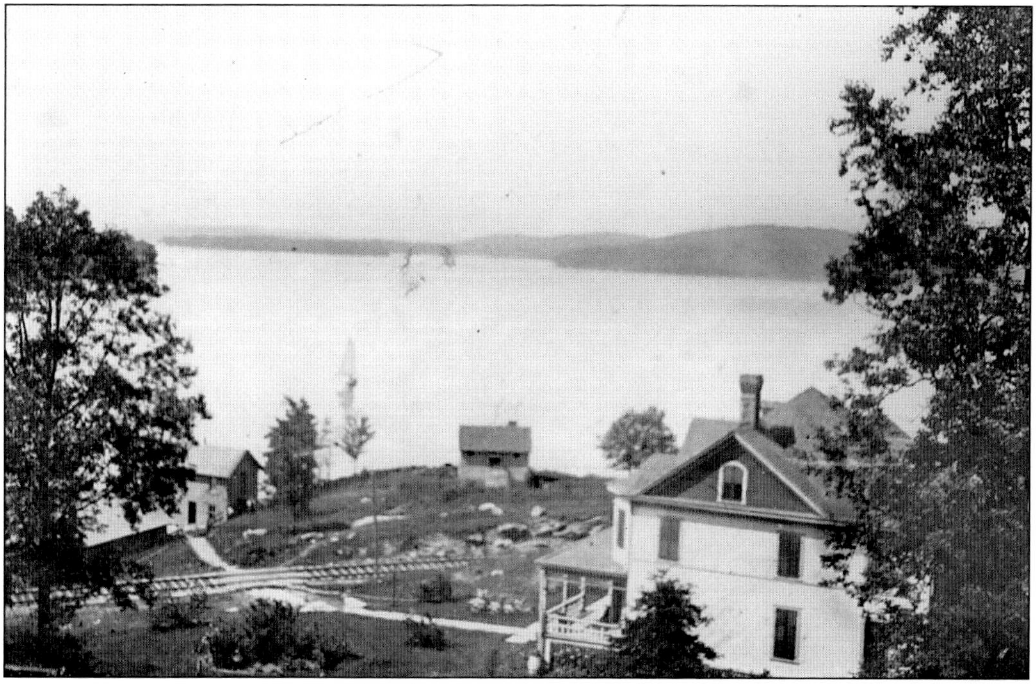

Mahlon Smith built the Sunnyside in the 1880s. It was originally a two-story structure with only nine rooms. Unlike other hotels, the Sunnyside was open all year because the Smith family resided there.

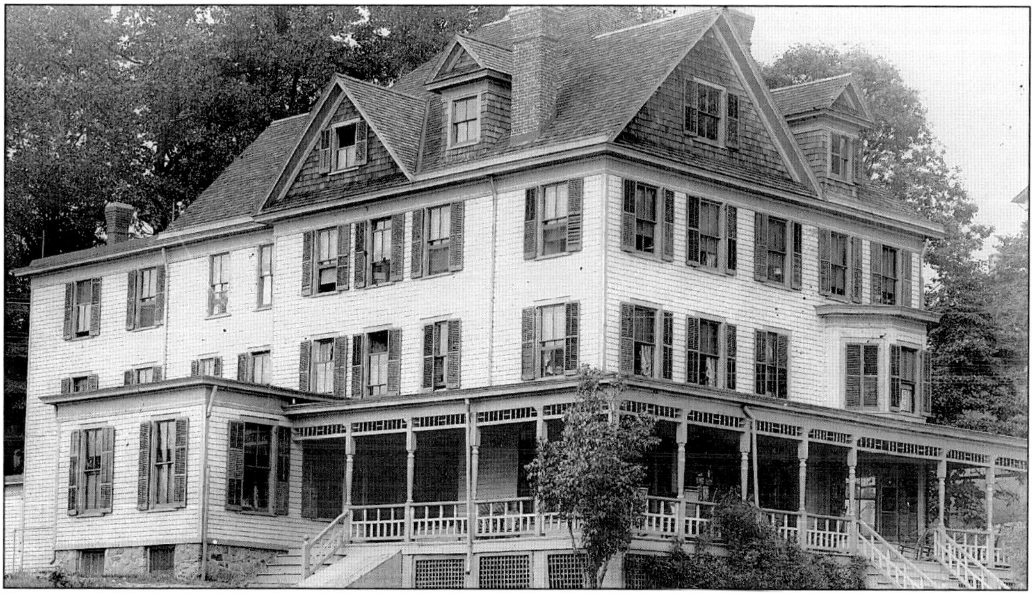

As business increased, the roof of the Sunnyside was lifted and a third floor was added. The additions made it possible to accommodate 100 guests in 48 rooms. After the death of Mahlon Smith, Charlotte Flemly Smith married Jack Lake, and they continued to operate the Sunnyside until they lost it during the Great Depression. In the 1940s, it was purchased by the owners of the Soumi Hovi and was used as an annex. This building is still in existence, although currently uninhabited, and plans for renovation are under way.

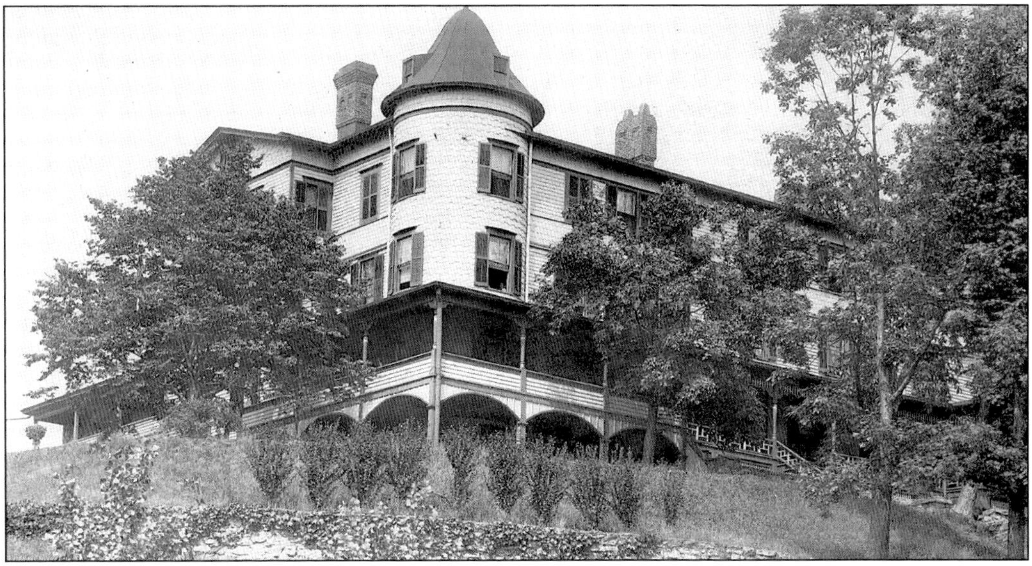

Nolan's Point Villa was erected during the early part of the 1880s. It was built by George Bryant, who was also the manager of the Central Railroad of New Jersey located in Nolan's Point. Originally it was a private dwelling but, as the lake became better known, large additions were added and it became a popular hotel.

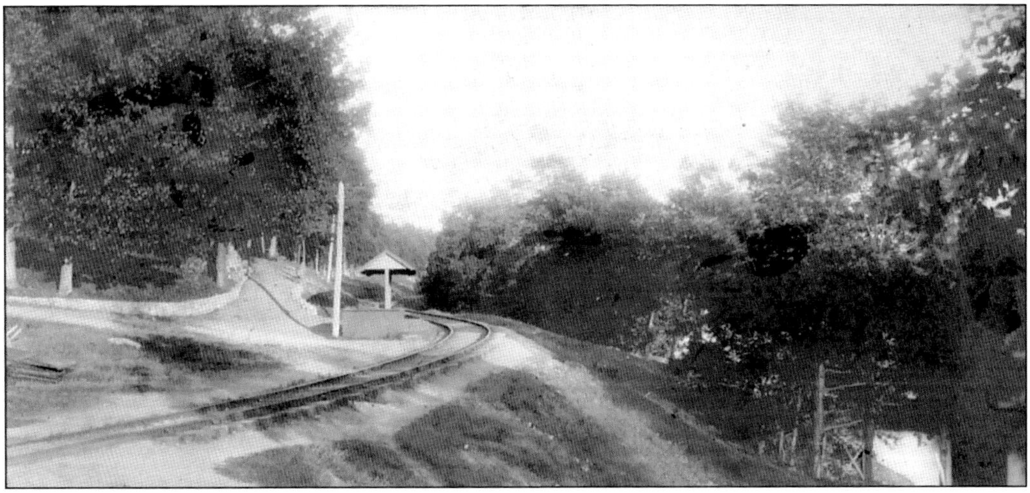

Bryant Villa maintained its own private railroad stop at the base of its steep terrain on the Lake Hopatcong side of the hotel. The Central Railroad stopped to pick up and drop off hotel patrons.

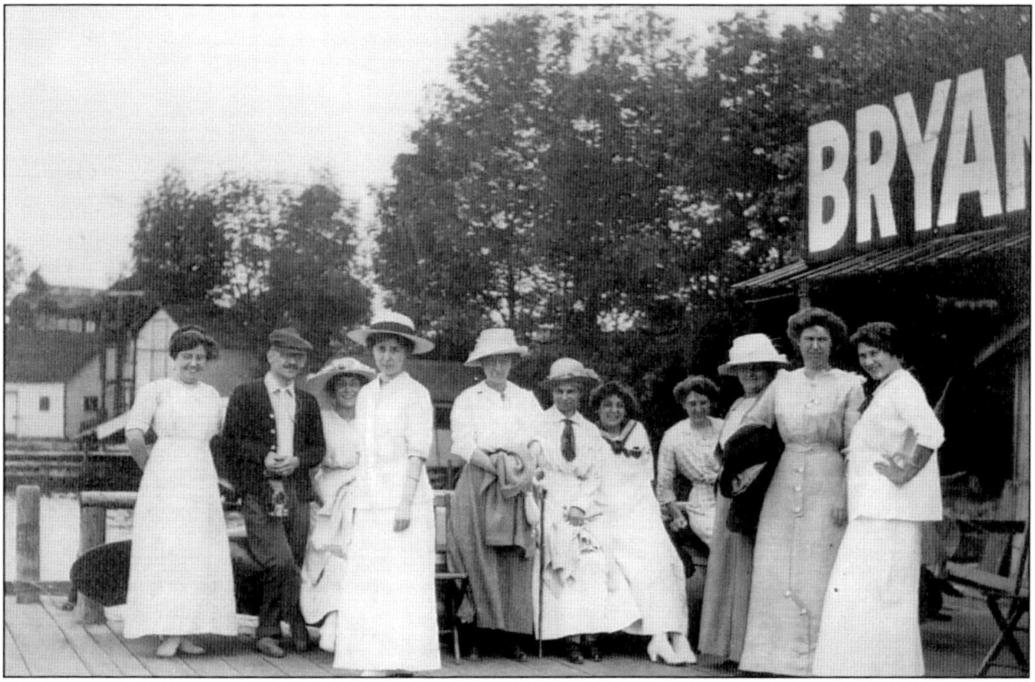

By 1909, the Nolan's Point Villa was sold to the John Frederick Muller family. Unlike the Nolan's Point Villa, the Bryant Villa was open only during the summer season. Guests were able to enjoy fishing, boating, tennis, bowling, dancing, and a scenic view of Great Cove, also called Chamberlain Cove, from the large veranda.

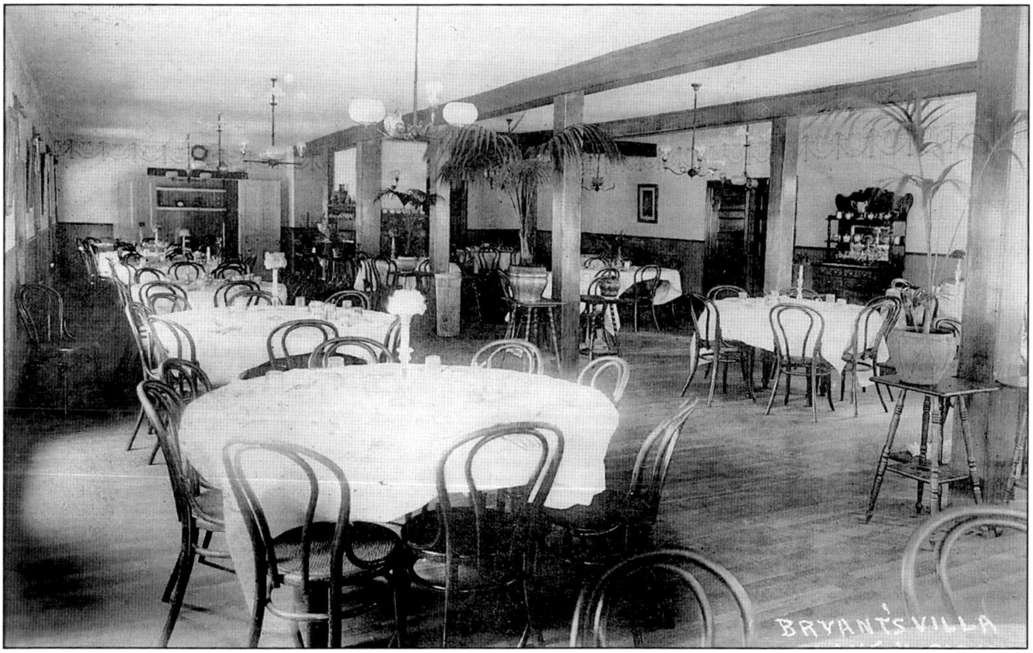

Women in long dresses and men in proper evening attire gathered in Bryant Villa's formal dining room, where home-cooked meals were served. Homegrown vegetables, fresh fish, and baked goods were abundant.

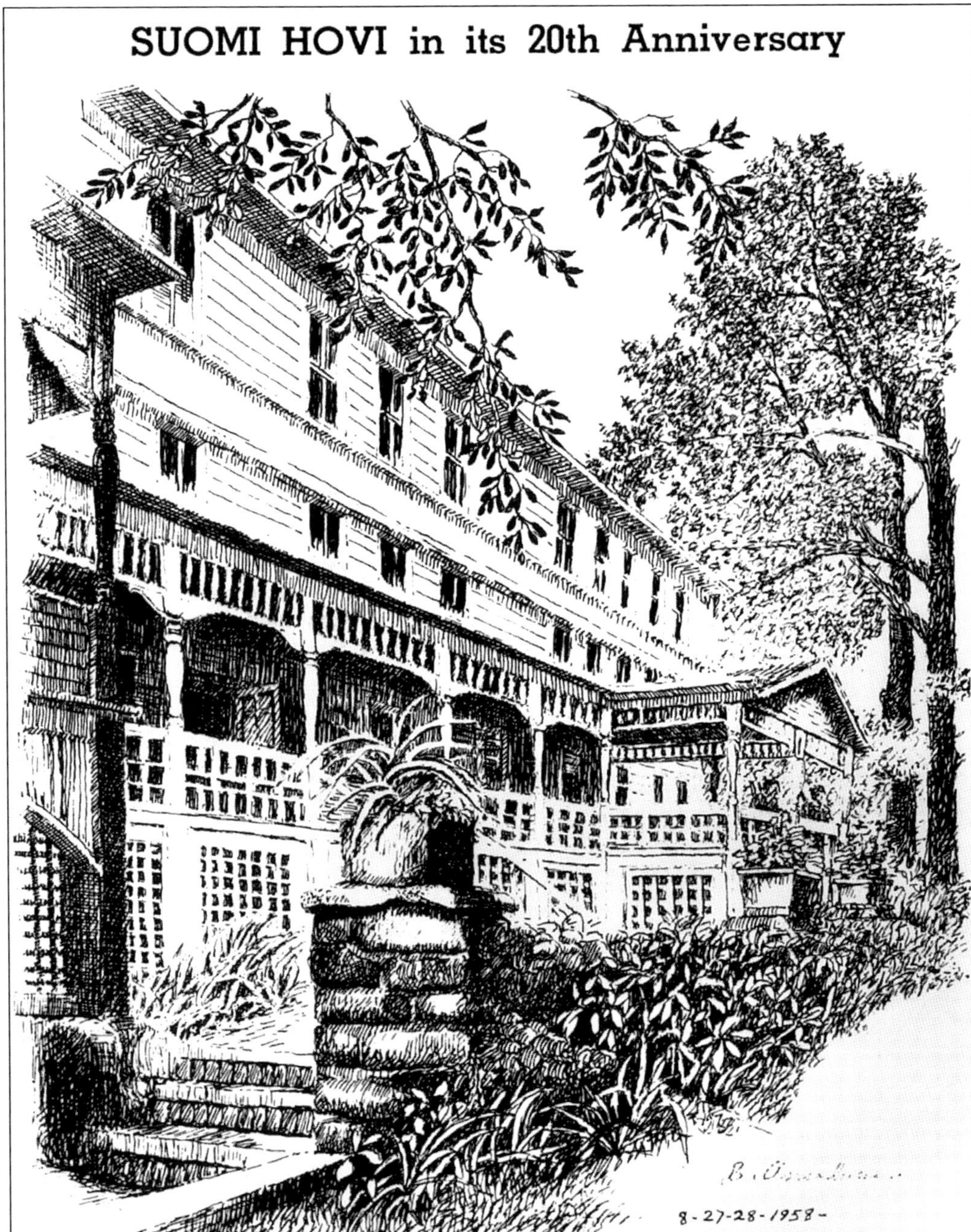

Unfortunately, the Mullers were unable to maintain Bryant Villa, and it was closed due to the Great Depression. In 1938, Selma Lemming bought the hotel and named it Suomi Hovi, meaning "Finnish manor or mansion." It became a Scandinavian-style resort, complete with sauna. The Suomi Hovi burned to the ground in 1976.

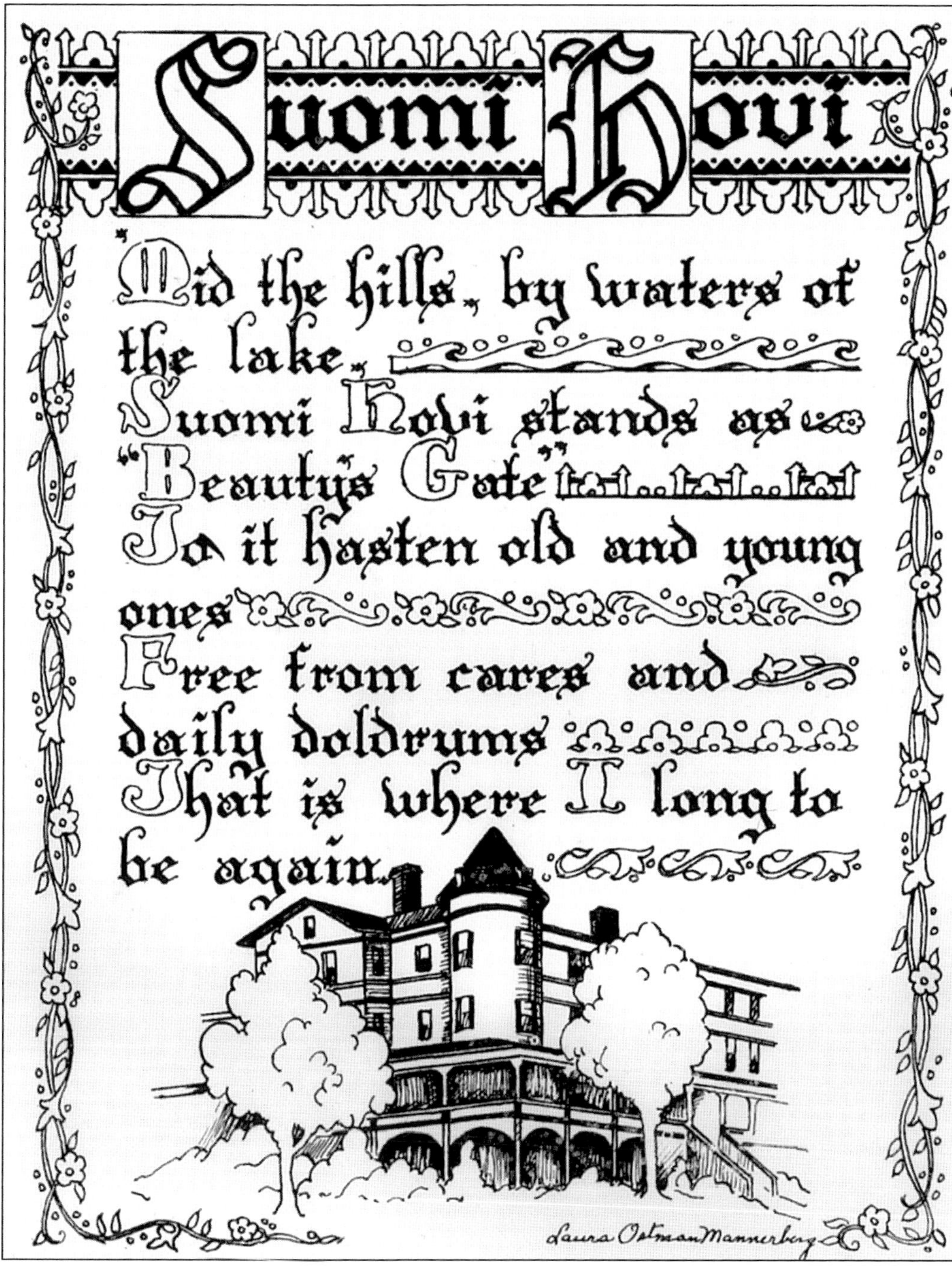

The 20th anniversary booklet of September 1950 for the Suomi Hovi contained this poem, written by hotel employee Laura Mannerberg, whose family still resides in Jefferson Township.

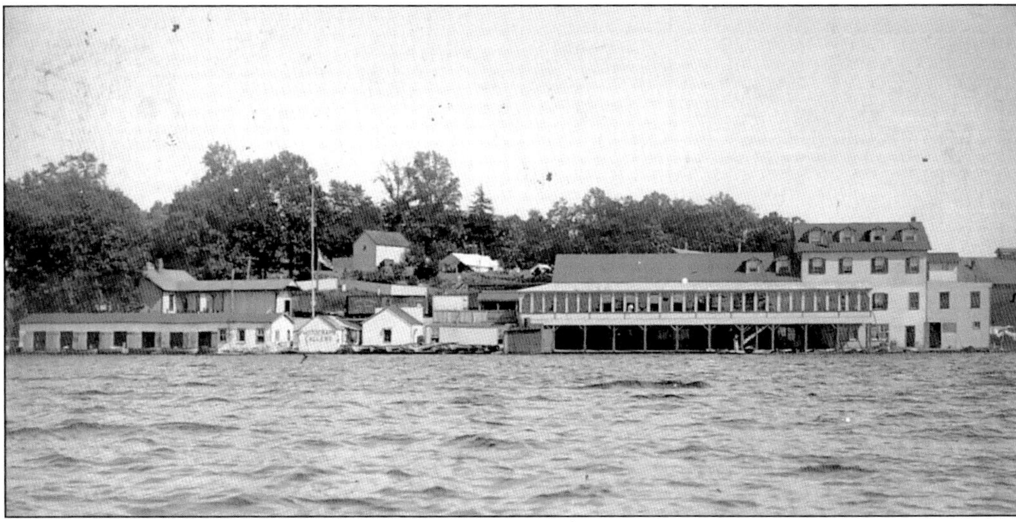

Allen's No. 1 was originally known as the Lake Pavilion Hotel. John L. Allen built it in 1887. It was three stories high, with dormers on the roof. The boathouses were located on the left, and the Central Railroad train station was located above the boathouses. The hotel was destroyed by fire in the fall of 1894. In addition to the hotel, the Nolan's Point icehouse, located next to Allen's, was also destroyed.

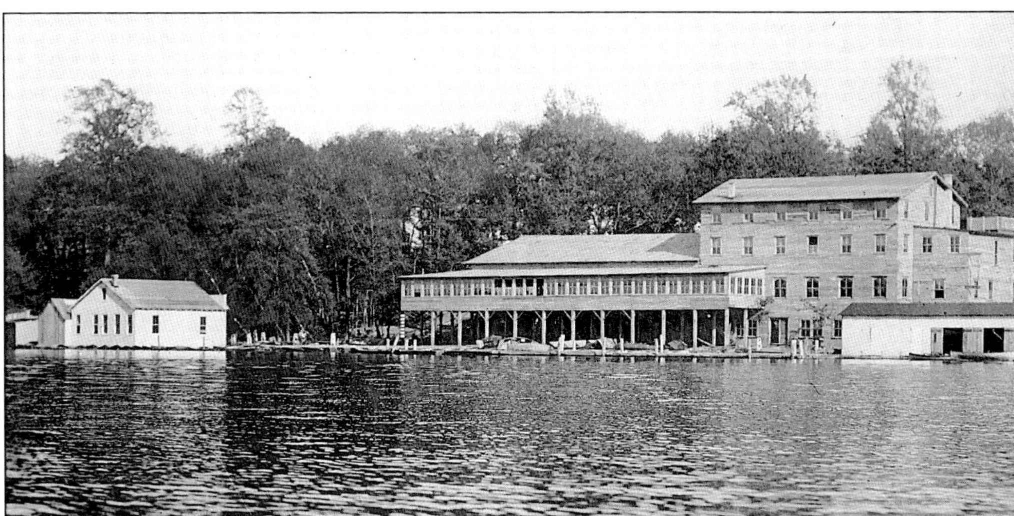

Allen's No. 2 was built in 1895. Unlike No. 1, it had four floors and no dormers. The boathouses were located to the right of the pavilion. This establishment contained a hotel, soda fountain, dance area, general store, post office, barbershop, and bar.

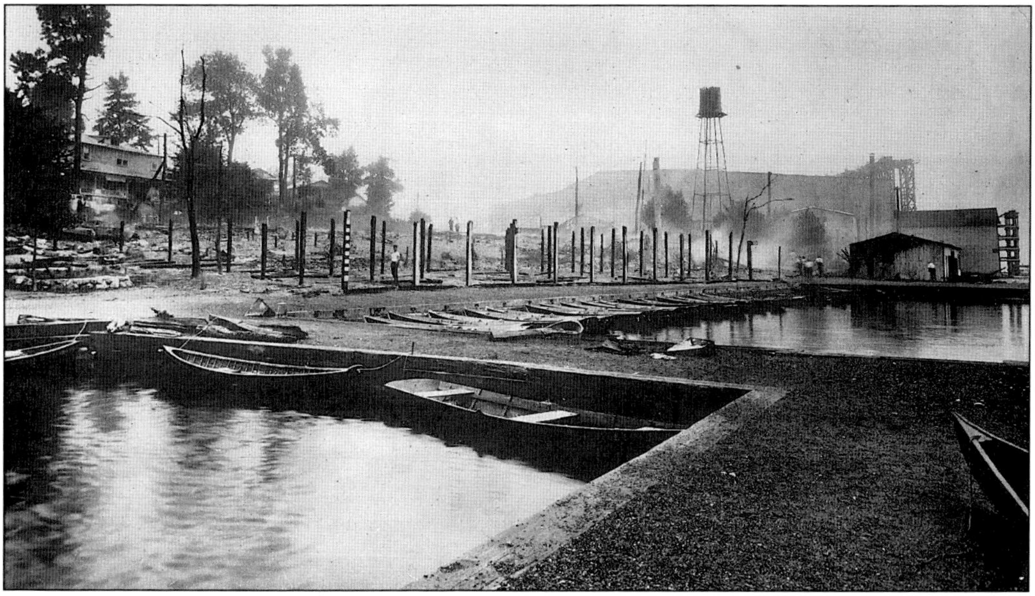

Unfortunately, Allen's No. 2 burned to the ground on September 8, 1919. This fire did not affect the icehouse and the Bellevue Hotel, on the left.

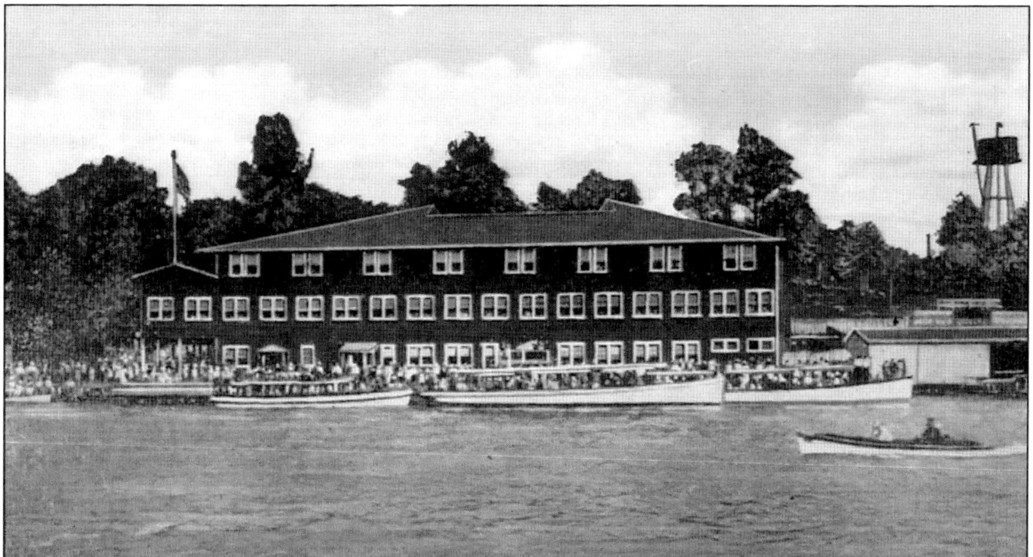

Allen's No. 3 was built during the winter of 1919. Joseph Allen, the son of John L. Allen, purchased the wood from Fort Dix. The building contained bedrooms, a bar and grill, a roller-skating rink and dance floor, and a post office. During the late 1930s, Frank R. Crater bought the establishment.

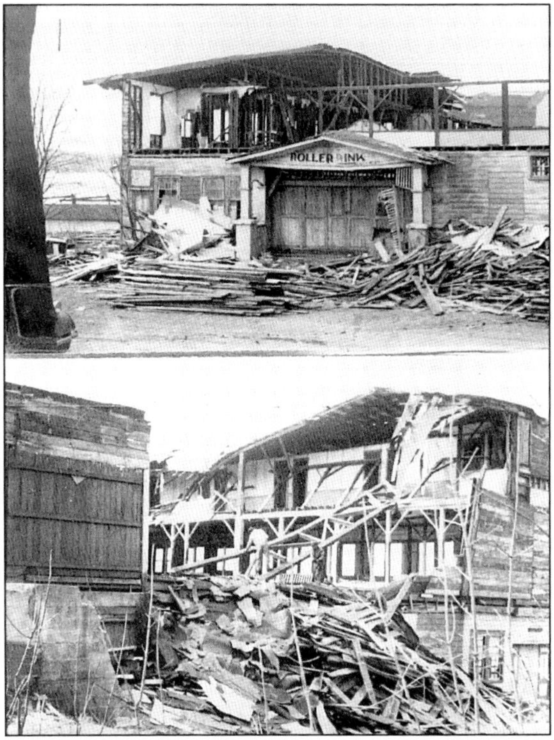

In the late 1940s, a major blizzard caused the center of Allen's No. 3 to collapse. The roof gave way under six feet of snow. The right-hand portion of the building was salvaged. Mr. Crater renovated the building and eventually sold it. What remained of Allen's No. 3 is now the Windlass Restaurant.

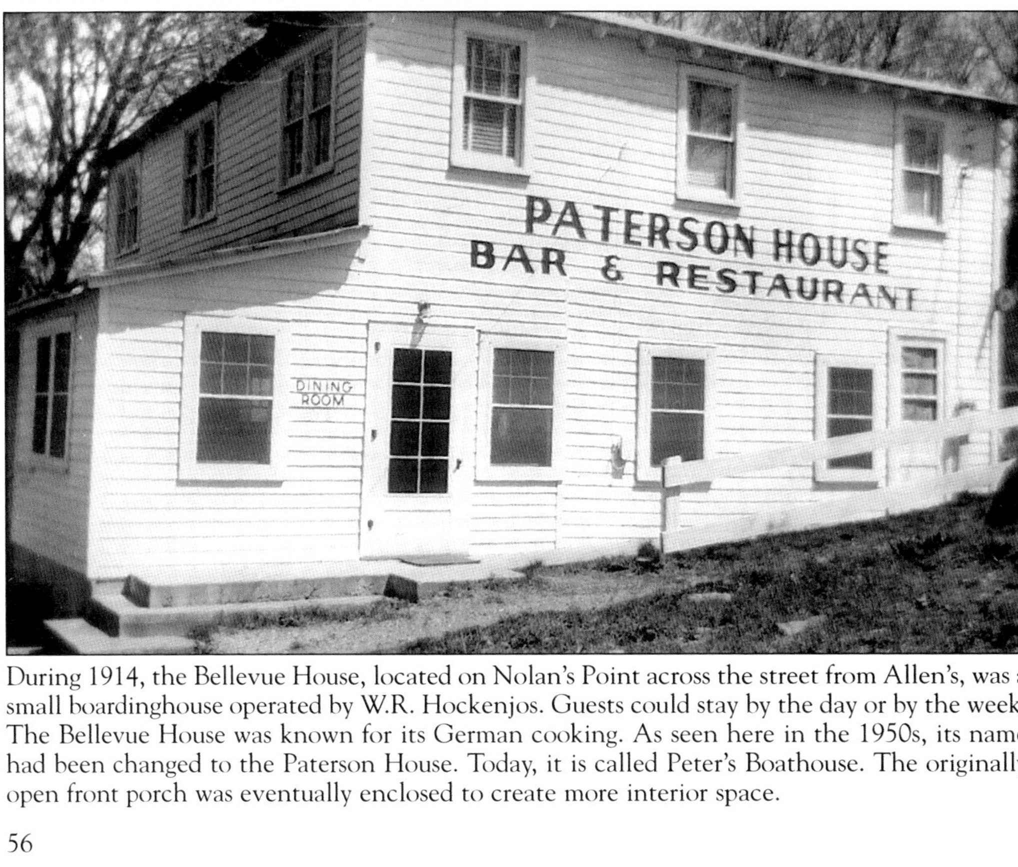

During 1914, the Bellevue House, located on Nolan's Point across the street from Allen's, was a small boardinghouse operated by W.R. Hockenjos. Guests could stay by the day or by the week. The Bellevue House was known for its German cooking. As seen here in the 1950s, its name had been changed to the Paterson House. Today, it is called Peter's Boathouse. The originally open front porch was eventually enclosed to create more interior space.

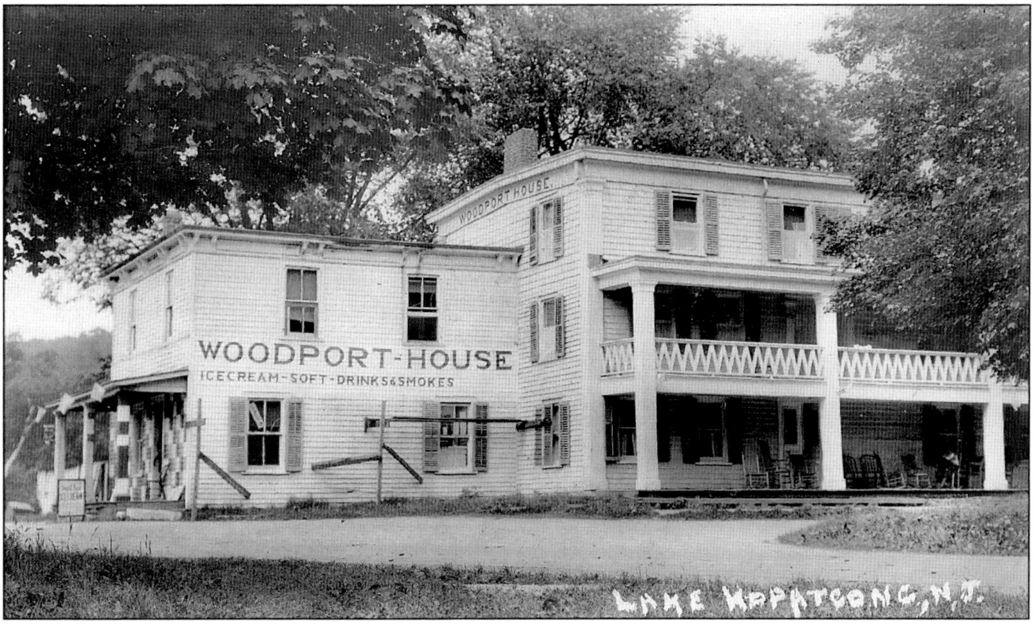

Thomas Bright, who worked for the Glenden Iron Company in Hurdtown, moved to the Woodport area and, by 1872, had purchased the first Woodport House, located on what is currently Bright's Point. In the early 1880s, Bright built the second Woodport House, which was located on the other side of Union Turnpike, now Route 181. This was not only the Brights' residence but also a hotel for summer guests.

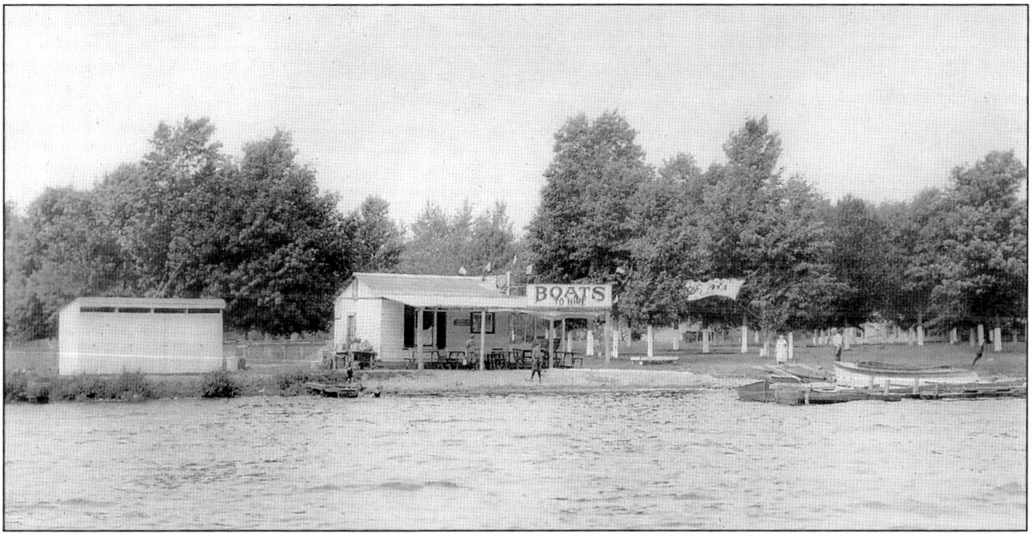

In addition to the hotel, a bathing beach, boating area, and fishing area were enjoyed by its guests. Since Woodport was in a remote location, guests coming to the Woodport House arrived from Nolan's Point and Landing by means of the hotel's launch, the *Emily*.

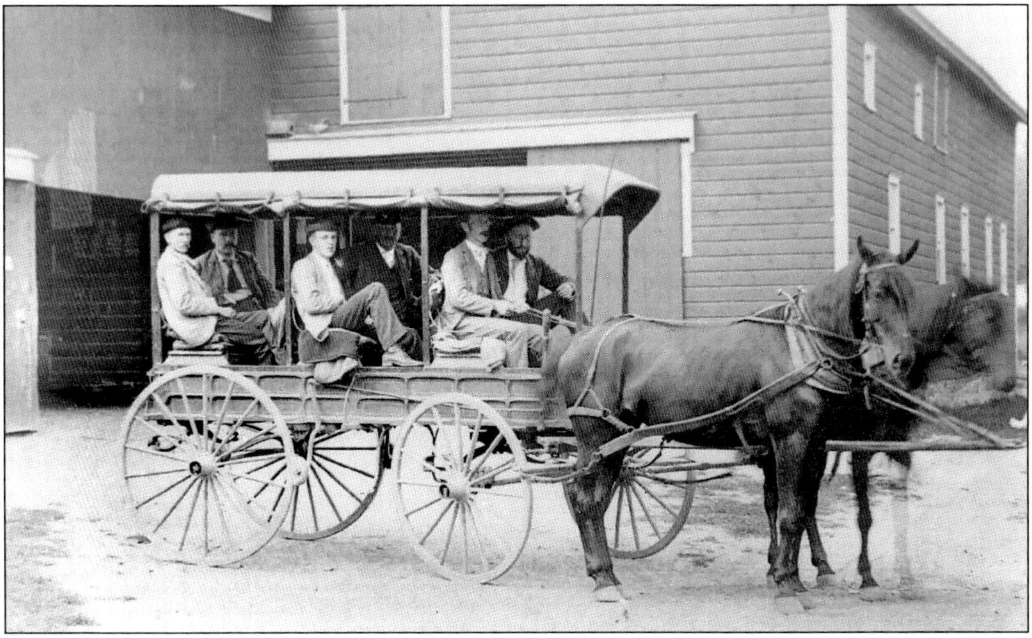

In addition to managing the hotel and bathing area, the Bright family had an apple orchard and a produce garden on what is today Bright's Point. By 1880, a new barn had been built to house chickens, horses, livestock, and a modern buggy. This was located on what is today Lorettacong.

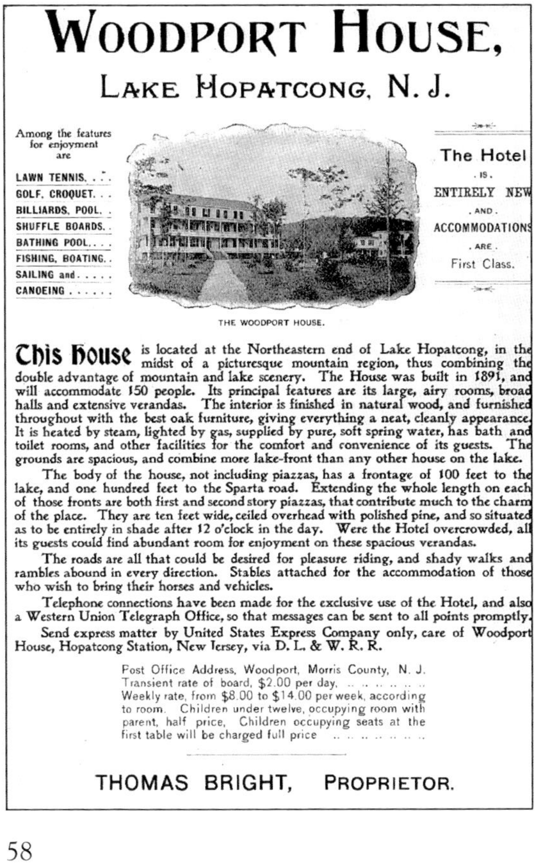

WOODPORT HOUSE,

LAKE HOPATCONG, N. J.

Among the features for enjoyment are

LAWN TENNIS, . . .
GOLF, CROQUET. . .
BILLIARDS, POOL. .
SHUFFLE BOARDS. .
BATHING POOL. . . .
FISHING, BOATING. .
SAILING and . . . . .
CANOEING . . . . . .

The Hotel . IS . ENTIRELY NEW . AND . ACCOMMODATIONS . ARE . First Class.

THE WOODPORT HOUSE.

This House is located at the Northeastern end of Lake Hopatcong, in the midst of a picturesque mountain region, thus combining the double advantage of mountain and lake scenery. The House was built in 1891, and will accommodate 150 people. Its principal features are its large, airy rooms, broad halls and extensive verandas. The interior is finished in natural wood, and furnished throughout with the best oak furniture, giving everything a neat, cleanly appearance. It is heated by steam, lighted by gas, supplied by pure, soft spring water, has bath and toilet rooms, and other facilities for the comfort and convenience of its guests. The grounds are spacious, and combine more lake-front than any other house on the lake.

The body of the house, not including piazzas, has a frontage of 100 feet to the lake, and one hundred feet to the Sparta road. Extending the whole length on each of those fronts are both first and second story piazzas, that contribute much to the charm of the place. They are ten feet wide, ceiled overhead with polished pine, and so situated as to be entirely in shade after 12 o'clock in the day. Were the Hotel overcrowded, all its guests could find abundant room for enjoyment on these spacious verandas.

The roads are all that could be desired for pleasure riding, and shady walks and rambles abound in every direction. Stables attached for the accommodation of those who wish to bring their horses and vehicles.

Telephone connections have been made for the exclusive use of the Hotel, and also a Western Union Telegraph Office, so that messages can be sent to all points promptly.

Send express matter by United States Express Company only, care of Woodport House, Hopatcong Station, New Jersey, via D. L. & W. R. R.

Post Office Address, Woodport, Morris County, N. J.
Transient rate of board, $2.00 per day, ...
Weekly rate, from $8.00 to $14.00 per week, according to room. Children under twelve, occupying room with parent, half price, Children occupying seats at the first table will be charged full price .. ..

THOMAS BRIGHT, PROPRIETOR.

This Woodport House advertisement appeared in the *Breeze*, a Lake Hopatcong publication.

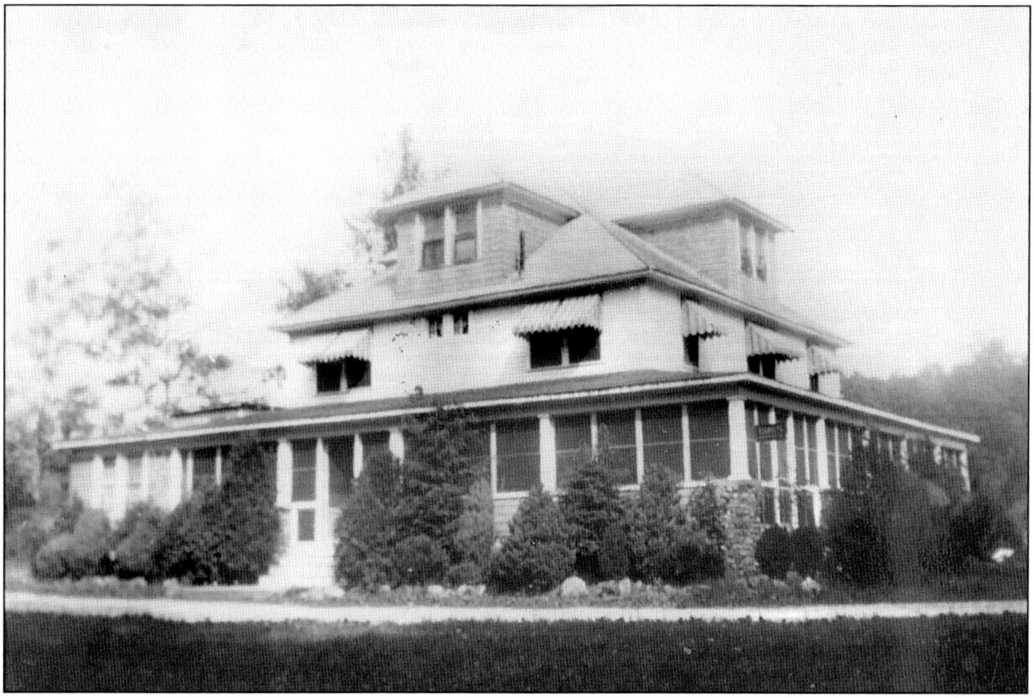

The original Woodport House burned in 1924 and was replaced by this Victorian-looking Woodport Hotel. Although it was not as large as the other hotels, it was very comfortable and was known for its warmth and hospitality. After leaving Camp Village, the Gerhardt family, originally from Paterson, took over managing the Woodport House. Eventually, the hotel was sold to J. Ferrio and it was destroyed by fire in the mid-1900s.

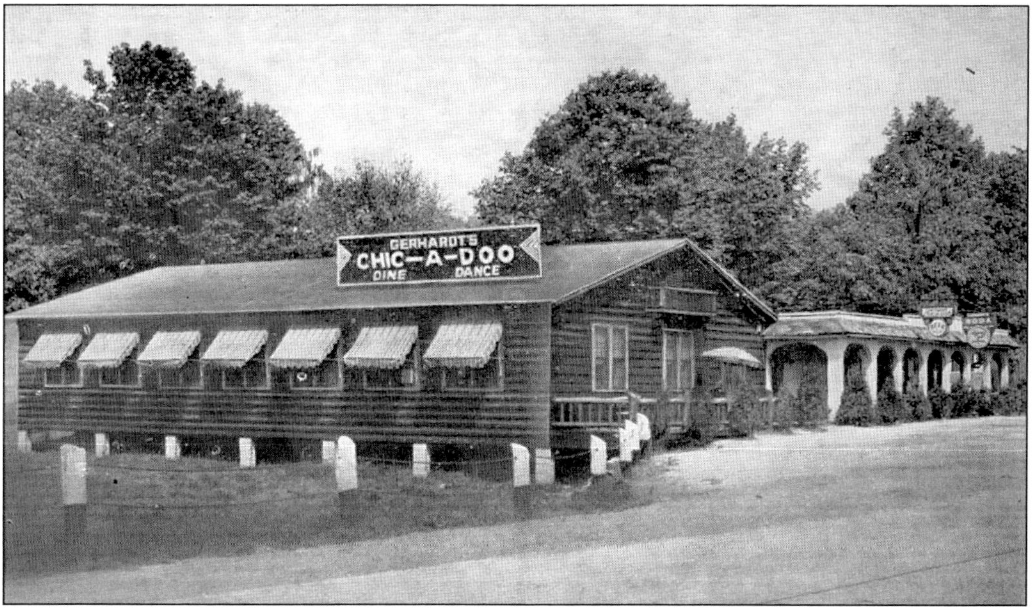

By the mid-1930s, the Chic-a-doo had been built next to the Woodport house. At first it was a snack bar, store, and gas station managed by Mr. Gerhardt. Within a short time, the large log cabin area was added. This area served as a dining room and dance hall.

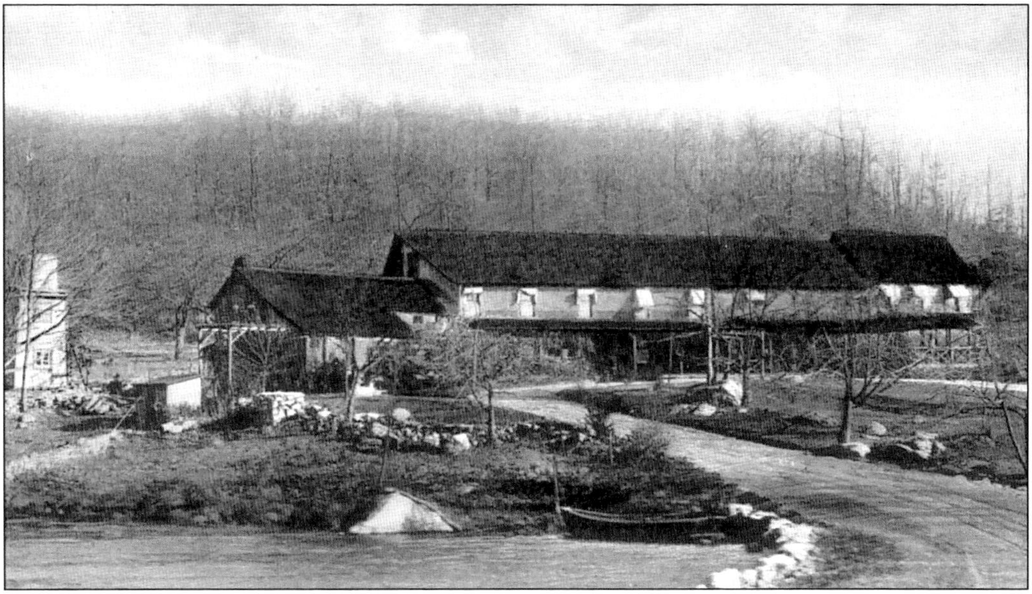

The Old Orchard Inn was located in the Woodport section of Jefferson. Bradley J. Bloodgood built the hotel *c.* 1910. This hotel was surrounded by apple trees, hence its name, Old Orchard Inn. The hotel was situated on 27 acres and had its own private lake. The building stands today and is on the Willow Lake Day Camp property.

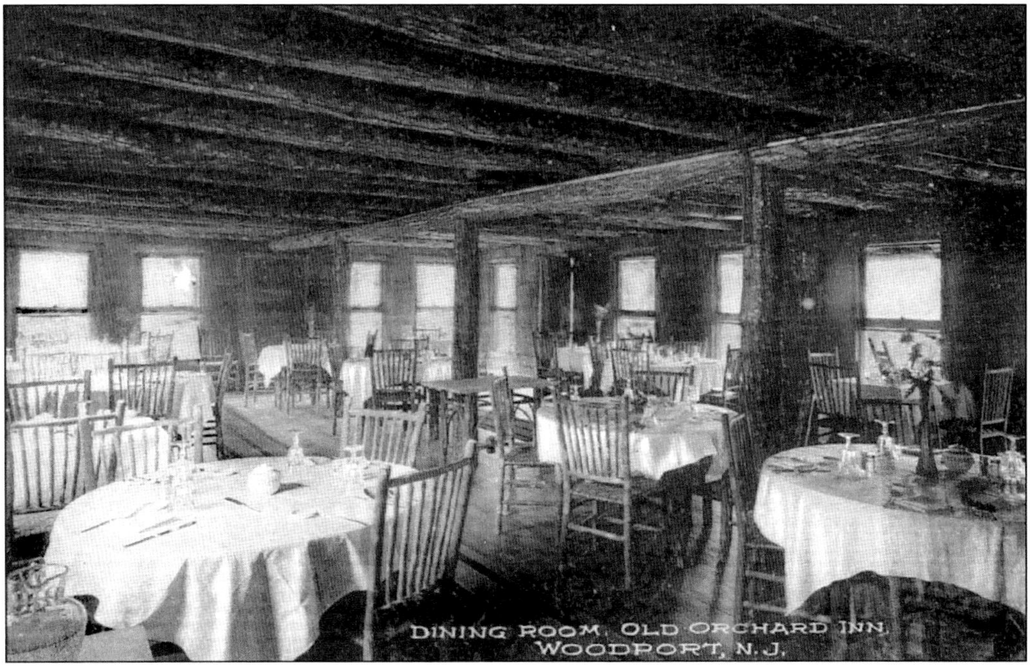

Seen here is the dining room of the Old Orchard Inn. The building was of rustic appearance. The timbers came from the surrounding area. Other rooms included the parlor, billiard room, and dancing parlor.

Four

THE FAMOUS LEND A HAND

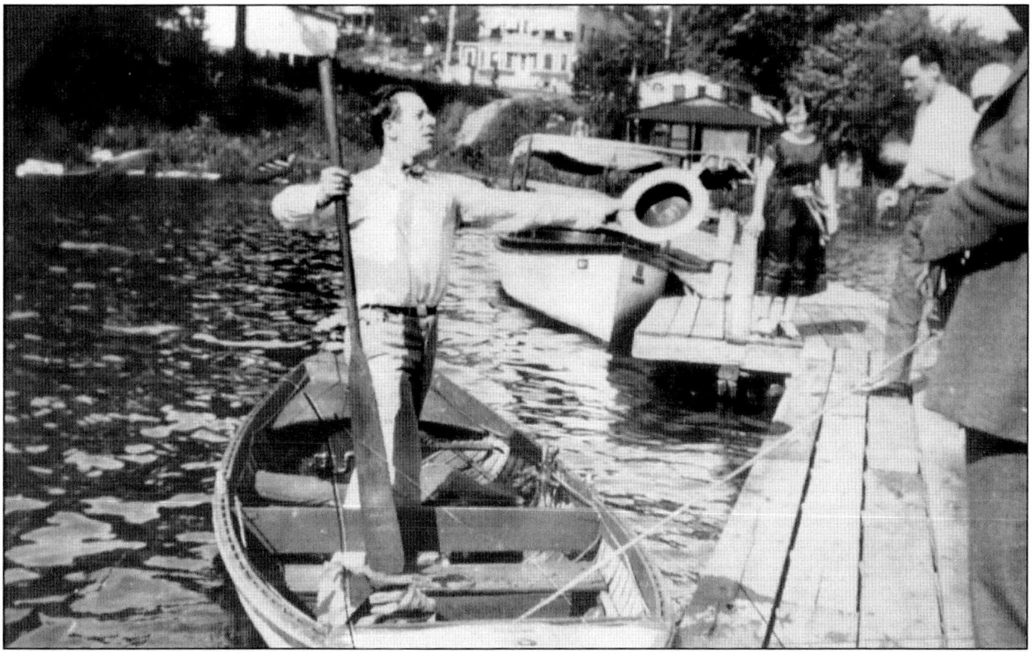

Bert Lahr, a vaudeville comedian and later the Cowardly Lion from the *Wizard of Oz*, is seen here entertaining an audience by the Espanong Hotel dock. He owned a home in Northwood but, during the summers of the 1920s, he was readily available to lend his talents to help raise funds for improvements around Nolan's Point and Jefferson Township.

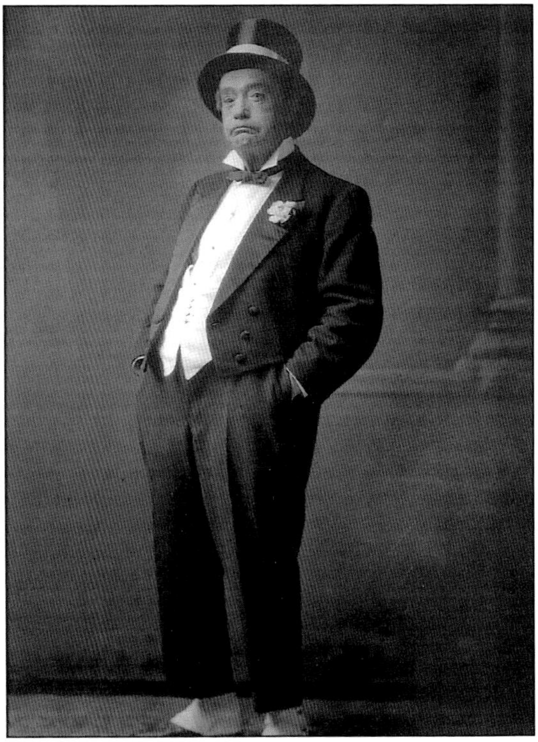

By 1914, Johnnie Jess, a vaudeville favorite, was a familiar sight around the Espanong Hotel and Minisink Road. He is best known for a burlesque routine that was adopted from the comic strip *Maggie & Jiggs–Bringing up Father*, by George McManus. Jiggs was fashioned after "a fat little Irish comic," who enjoyed his carefree ways until his wife caught up with him.

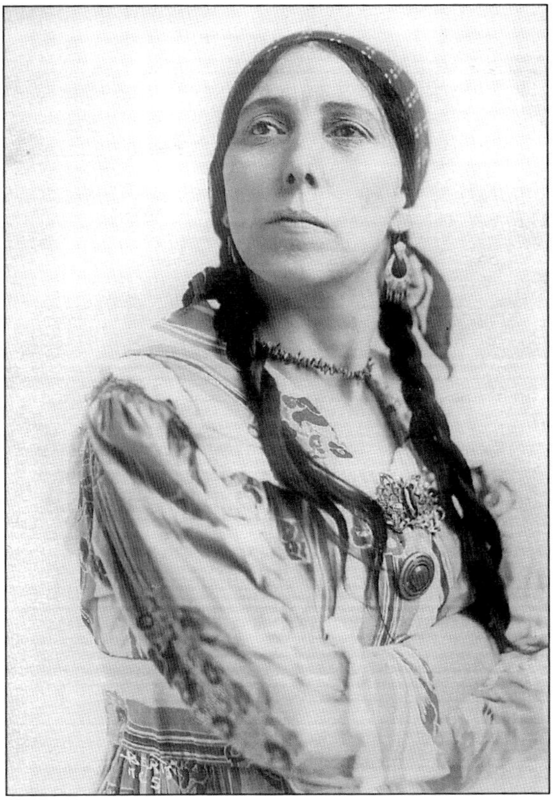

Blanche Jess, wife and vaudeville partner of Johnnie Jess, played Maggie, who "ruled the roost." She was best known for her free-swinging rolling pin and stern ways. Johnnie and Blanche Jess were both very popular at the Lyceum Theater in Paterson.

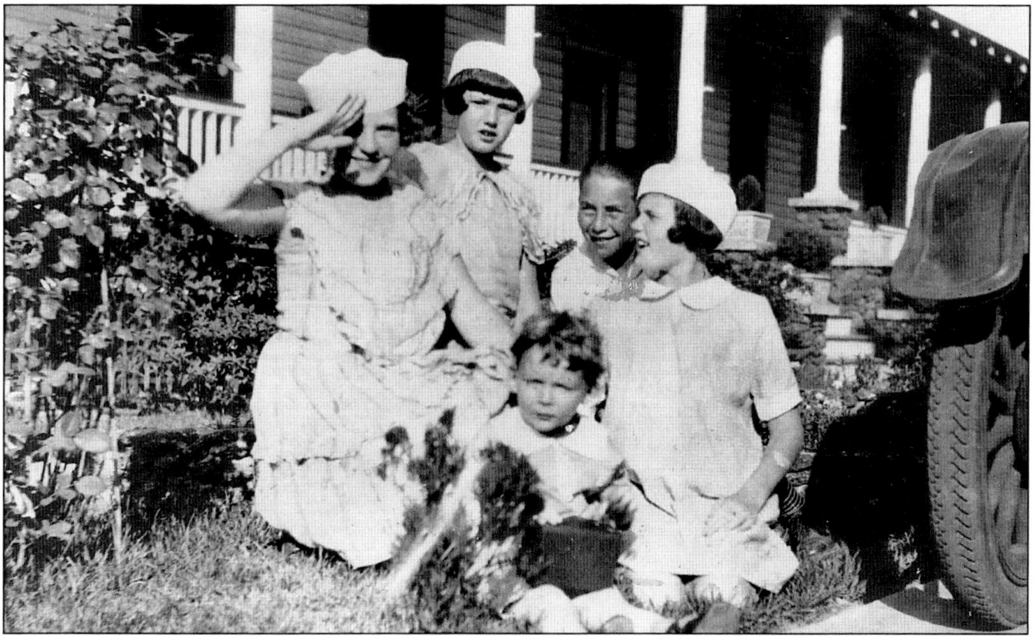

Prior to buying a home in Northwood, vaudeville performer Vinnie Phillips vacationed at the Chamberlain Hotel with her family *c.* 1915. The Chamberlain was later replaced by the Espanong Hotel. Phillips' daughter "Buster" also became a vaudeville entertainer.

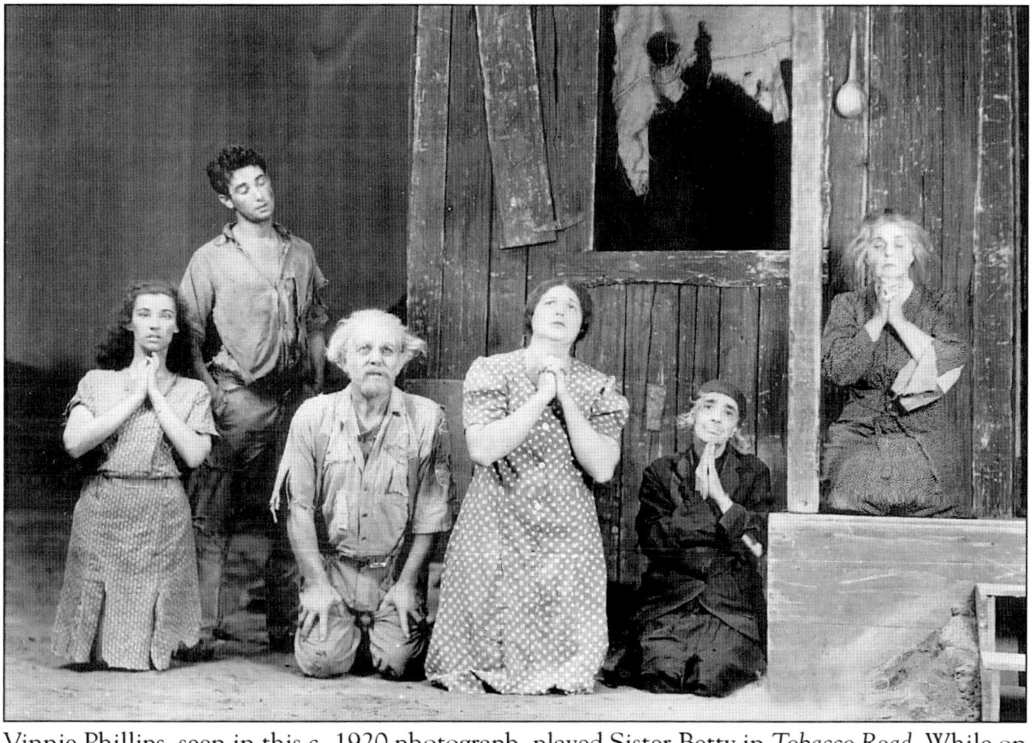

Vinnie Phillips, seen in this *c.* 1920 photograph, played Sister Betty in *Tobacco Road.* While on tour, this popular and long-running play was also viewed at the Lakeside Theatre in Landing, which is currently the Leber Lakeside Funeral Home.

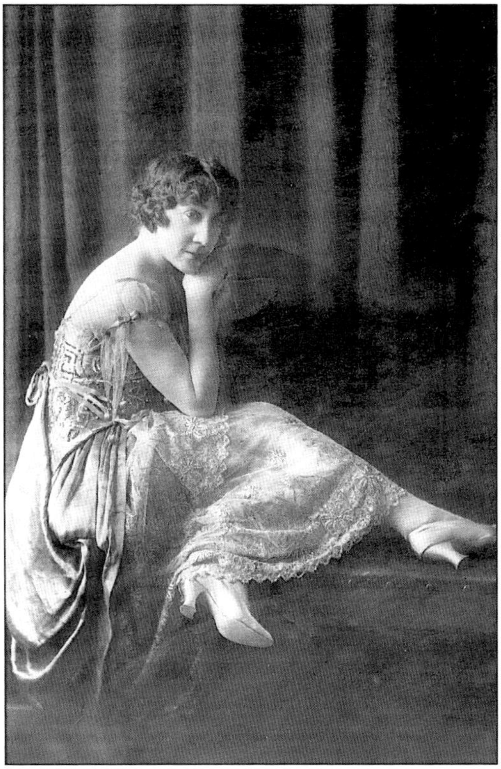

During the early to late teens, Lillian and George Gardner were familiar faces at the Espanong Hotel and throughout Nolan's Point. They were "xylophone wizards" who participated in many fund-raisers to help improve the community. Some of the funds went to improve the churches, roads, and amusement park. George Gardner also played the accordion and the piano. The Gardners also performed in the Beer Garden at Bertrand Island *c.* 1933.

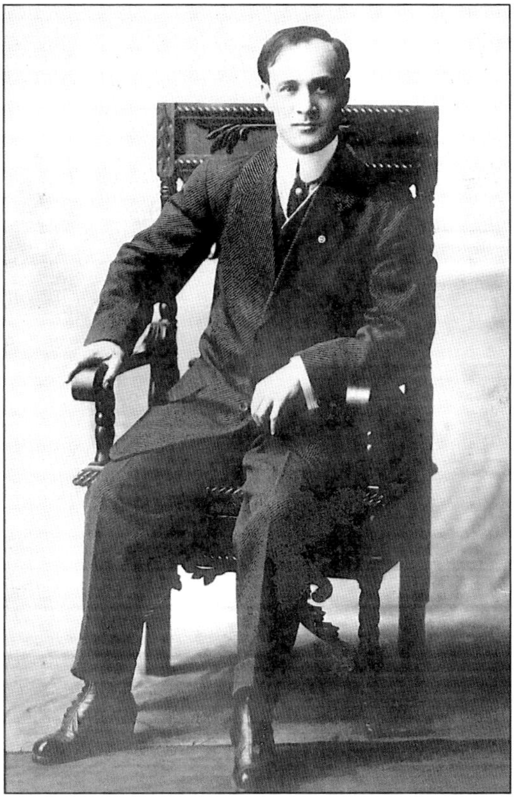

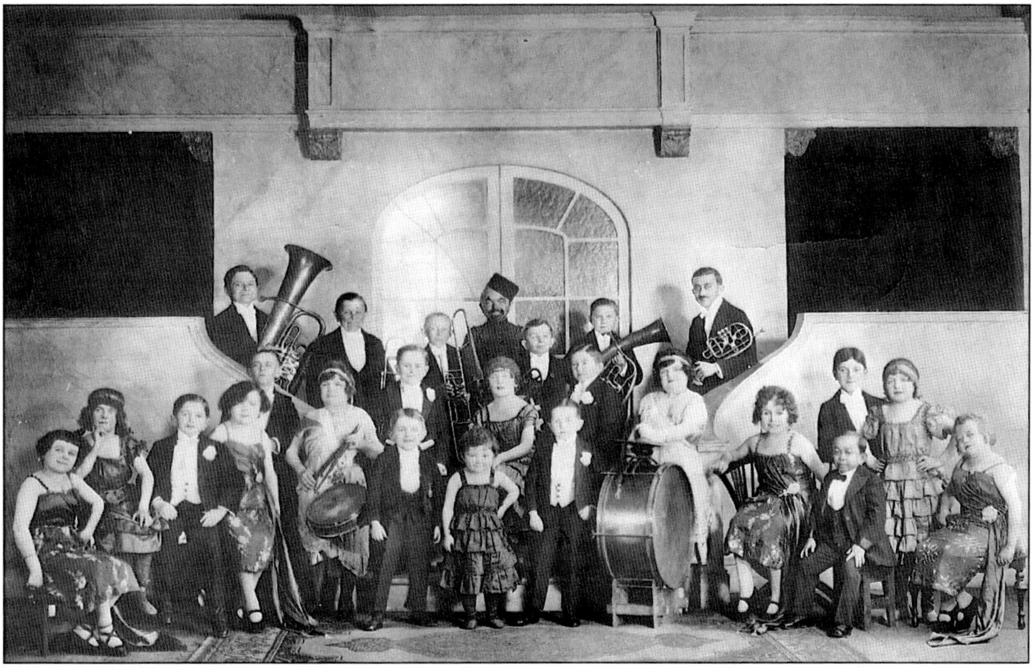

In July 1922, Rose's Royal Midgets arrived in the United States from Germany. Ike Rose was their theatrical agent who introduced them to the local vaudeville houses. There were 9 females and 15 men in the troop, and their act included dancing, a violin solo, acrobatics, juggling, and magic tricks. During the mid-to-late 1920s, the group frequented the Espanong Hotel.

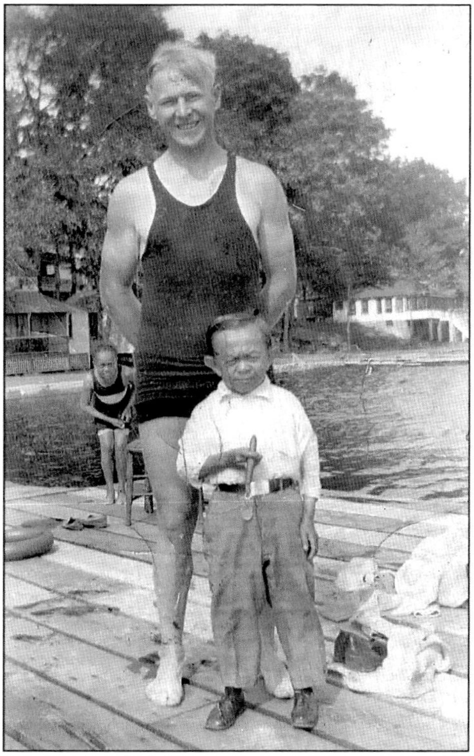

Because he smoked a large cigar, Penny was always the most visible of Rose's Midgets, as in this c. 1923 photograph with Whitey Fastnackt on a dock in Great Cove.

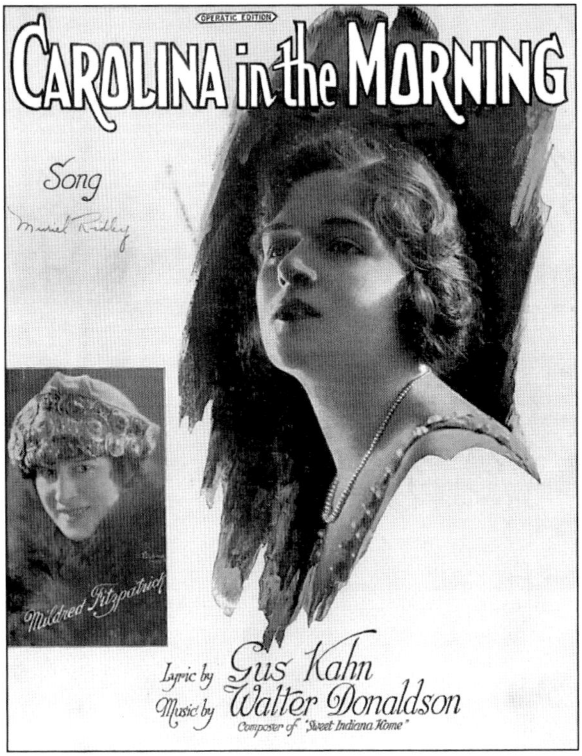

Walter Donaldson was born in 1893 in Brooklyn, New York. He originally started out on Wall Street with a brokerage firm but joined the staff of the Irving Berlin Music Publishing Company and, in 1929, moved to Hollywood, where he wrote songs and music for various films. Donaldson died in California in 1947.

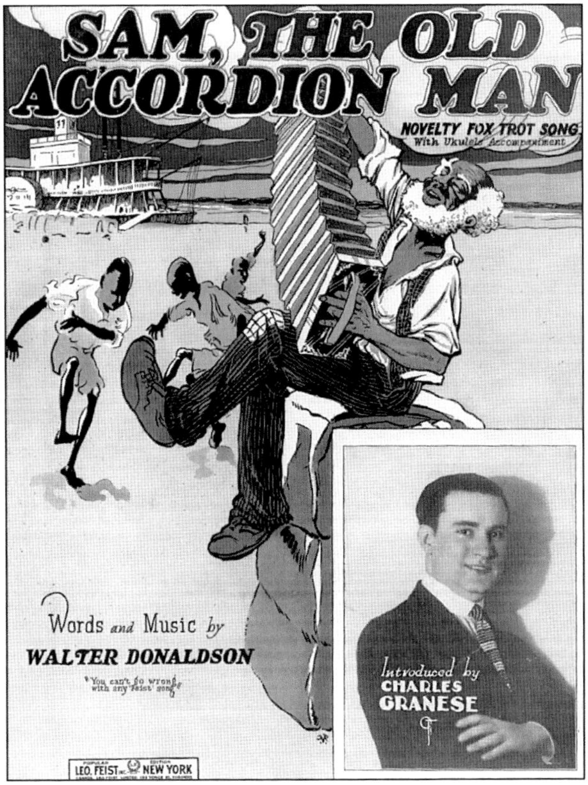

Like so many other famous performers, Walter Donaldson was well known at the Espanong Hotel. During the summer of 1923, he often played the piano and entertained the guests. "Carolina in the Morning," "Sam, the Old Accordion Man," "Sweet Indiana Home," and "Georgia," are some of his most popular pieces. Many times, Donaldson wrote not only the music but also the lyrics. He is considered one of Tin Pan Alley's greats.

Prior to 1923, when he teamed up with Gracie Allen, George Burns was regularly seen at Lake Hopatcong. He was a personal friend of Senator Thompson, who vacationed in Castle Rock. Burns also helped organize shows at Nolan's Point. He had a well-known reputation for being a vaudeville comic producer. In earlier years, he was also known for being a trick roller-skater and dance instructor.

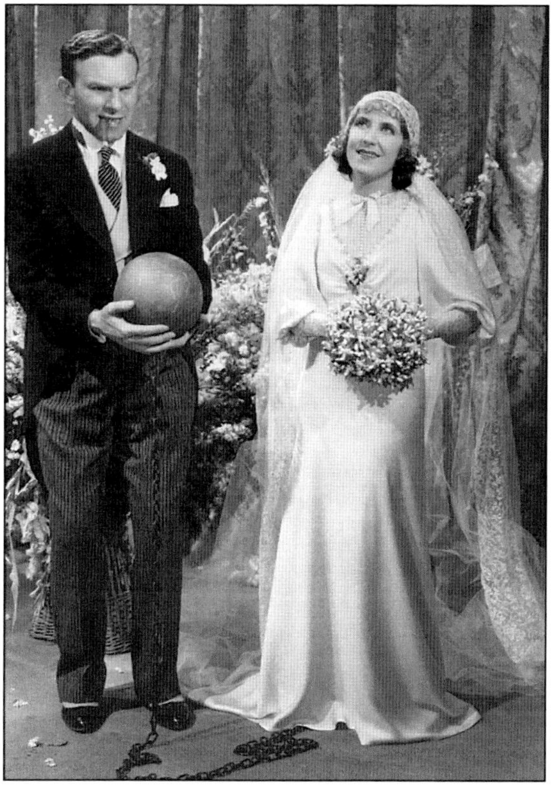

All Star Minstrel Show

FRIDAY, JULY 17

On open lot next to Espanong House

Benefit CITIZENS IMPROVEMENT ASSOCIATION

Admission 50 Cents

Tickets for sale at all hotels and Richards' Souvenir Store

LOOK at the Cast!

JOHNNIE JESS	BILLY WATSON
ARTHUR WHITELAW	VIOLET HILSON
TOM McKENNA	BABE LA TOUR
JOHN COPE	ZELLA RUSSELL
CHARLES RAYMOND	LUCELLIE MANNION
EDDIE B. COLLINS	BARNES & ROBINSON
BERT BAKER	THE GARDNERS
JACK GOLDIE	AND THE VERDENS

And a Real Live Chorus of 50 Girls

By 1914, many vaudeville performers had flocked to the Espanong Hotel, where all-star minstrel shows were not uncommon and were organized to help local organizations. These shows earned money for lights, roads, and sidewalks.

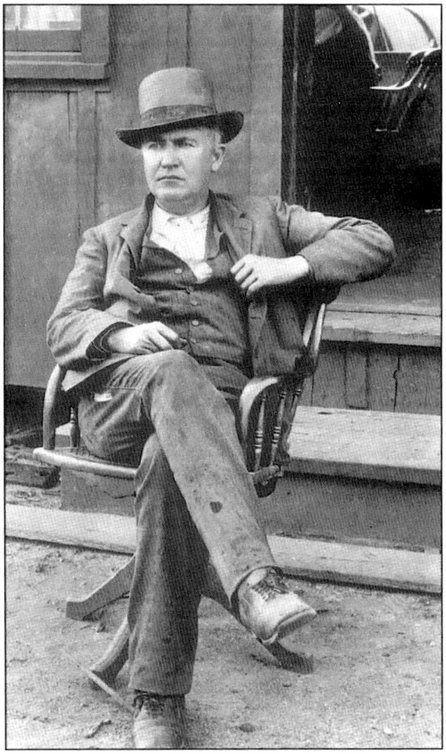

Between the late 1890s and 1900, inventor Thomas Alva Edison was a frequent visitor at the Nolan's Point Villa. He stayed there when he visited his mine and processing plant in Sussex County.

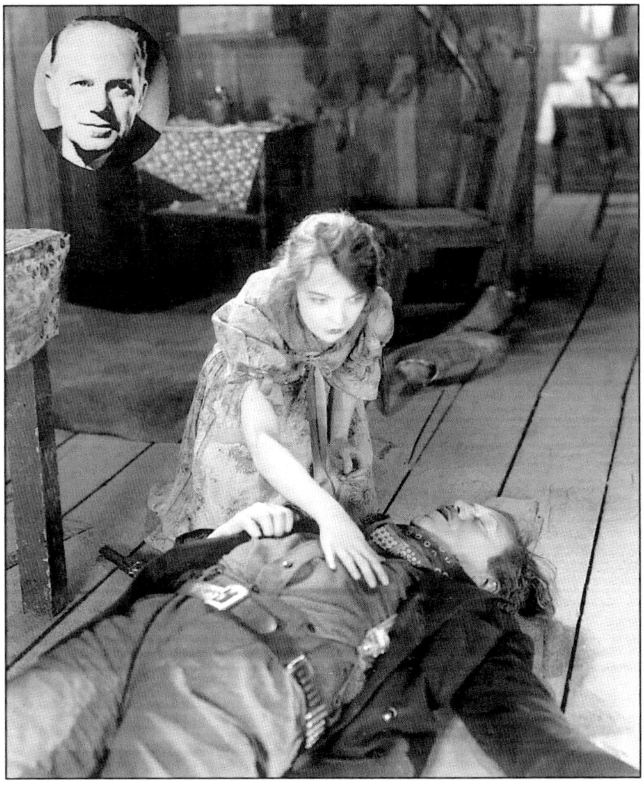

Montague Love and Lillian Gish starred in the film *The Wind* c. 1927. Born in England in 1877, Love came to the United States in 1913 and started his film career in 1915 at the New Jersey World Studio. He was thought to be the "finest villain of the silent movies." During the summer of 1923, while recuperating at the Sunnyside Hotel, he became a familiar sight around Nolan's Point.

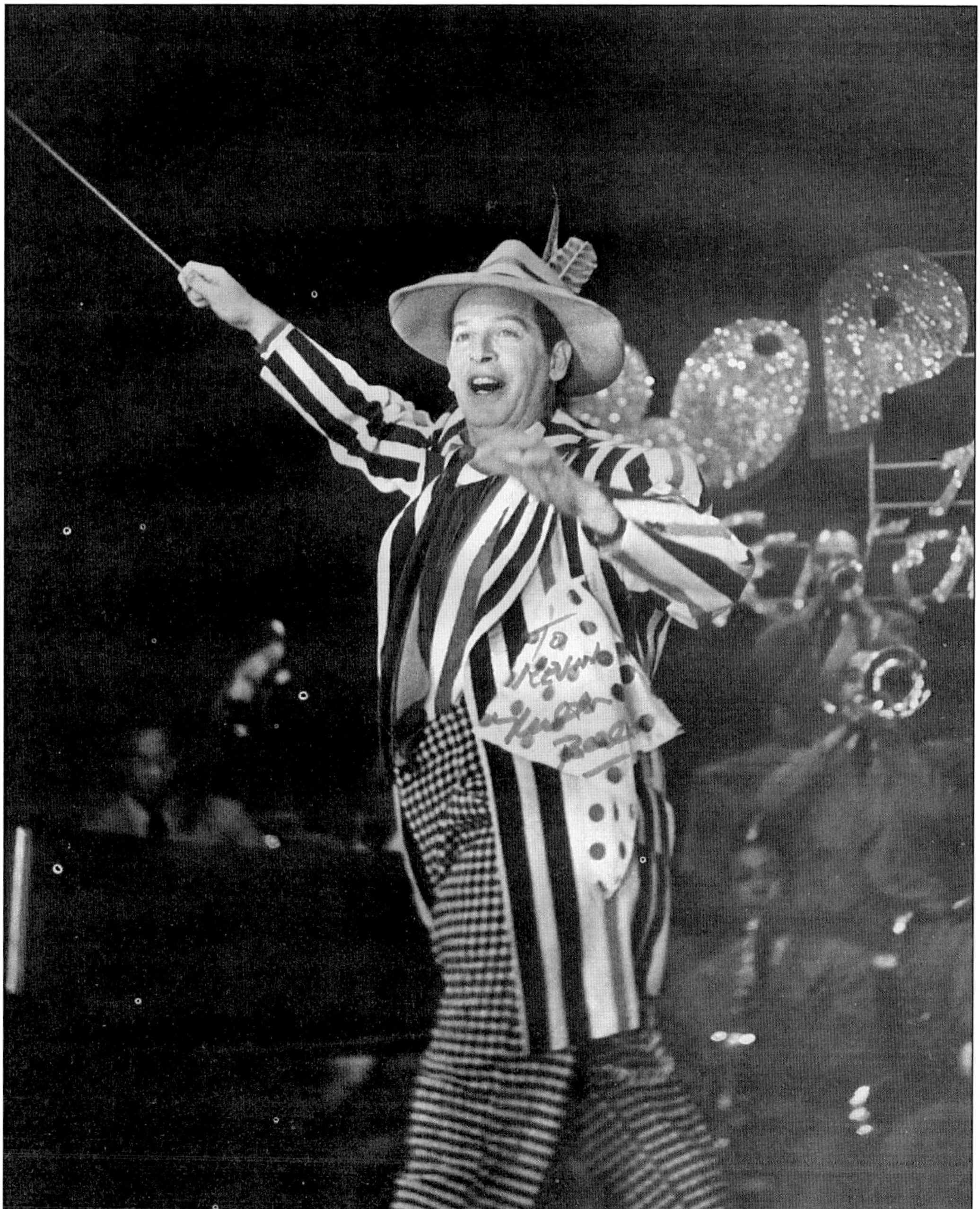

Milton Berle, best known as "Uncle Miltie," seen here portraying "the Clown Prince" one of his many comic characters, was often seen vacationing and entertaining at the Alamac in Mount Arlington. Emma Robinson, daughter of John Robinson, who owned the Espanong Hotel, recalled visits that Berle made to her family's establishment.

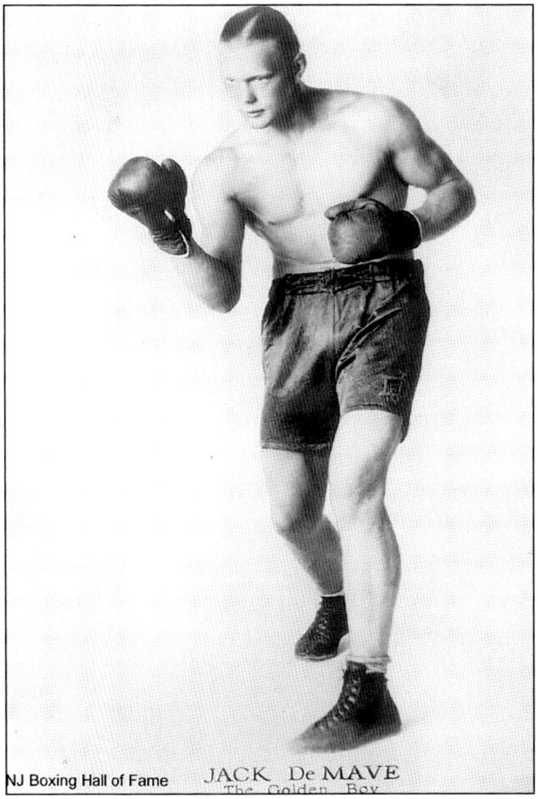

Jack DeMave, a heavyweight prizefighter born in Amsterdam, Holland, on March 30, 1904, came to the United States in 1908. He was a familiar face at the Sunnyside Hotel on Nolan's Point. During the summer of 1927, he was in training and fought practice bouts in the ring located between the Sunnyside and the Lake.

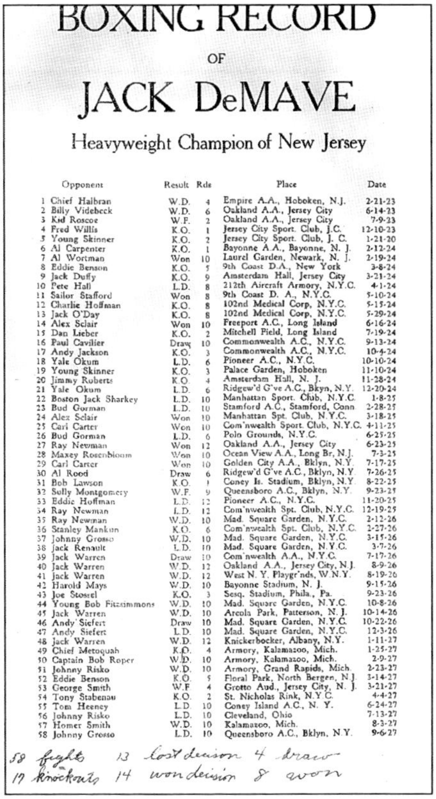

BOXING RECORD

OF

JACK DeMAVE

Heavyweight Champion of New Jersey

	Opponent	Result	Rds	Place	Date
1	Chief Halbran	W.D.	4	Empire A.A., Hoboken, N.J.	2-21-23
2	Billy Videbeck	W.D.	6	Oakland A.A., Jersey City	6-14-23
3	Kid Roscoe	W.F.	2	Oakland A.A., Jersey City	7-9-23
4	Fred Willis	K.O.	1	Jersey City Sport. Club, J.C.	12-10-23
5	Young Skinner	K.O.	2	Jersey City Sport. Club, J. C.	1-21-20
6	Al Carpenter	K.O.	1	Bayonne A.A., Bayonne, N. J.	2-12-24
7	Al Wortman	Won	10	Laurel Garden, Newark, N. J.	2-19-24
8	Eddie Benson	K.O.	5	9th Coast D.A., New York	3-8-24
9	Jack Duffy	K.O.	9	Amsterdam Hall, Jersey City	3-21-24
10	Pete Hall	L.D.	8	212th Aircraft Armory, N.Y.C.	4-1-24
11	Sailor Stafford	Won	8	9th Coast D. A., N.Y.C.	5-10-24
12	Charlie Hoffman	K.O.	8	102nd Medical Corp, N.Y.C.	5-15-24
13	Jack O'Day	K.O.	8	102nd Medical Corp, N.Y.C.	5-29-24
14	Alex Sclair	Won	10	Freeport A.C., Long Island	6-16-24
15	Dan Lieber	K.O.	2	Mitchell Field, Long Island	7-19-24
16	Paul Cavilier	Draw	10	Commonwealth A.C., N.Y.C.	9-13-24
17	Andy Jackson	K.O.	3	Commonwealth A.C., N.Y.C.	10-4-24
18	Yale Okum	L.D.	6	Pioneer A.C., N.Y.C.	10-10-24
19	Young Skinner	K.O.	3	Palace Garden, Hoboken	11-10-24
20	Jimmy Roberts	K.O.	4	Amsterdam Hall, N. J.	11-28-24
21	Yale Okum	L.D.	6	Ridgew'd G've A.C., Bkyn, N.Y.	12-20-24
22	Boston Jack Sharkey	L.D.	10	Manhattan Sport. Club, N.Y.C.	1-8-25
23	Bud Gorman	L.D.	10	Stamford A.C., Stamford, Conn	2-28-25
24	Alex Sclair	Won	10	Manhattan Spt. Club, N.Y.C.	3-18-25
25	Carl Carter	Won	10	Com'nwealth Sport. Club, N.Y.C.	4-11-25
26	Bud Gorman	L.D.	6	Polo Grounds, N.Y.C.	6-25-25
27	Ray Newman	Won	12	Oakland A.A., Jersey City	6-23-25
28	Maxey Rosenbloom	Won	10	Ocean View A.A., Long Br, N.J.	7-3-25
29	Carl Carter	Won	10	Golden City A.A., Bklyn, N.Y.	7-17-25
30	Al Rood	Draw	6	Ridgew'd G've A.C., Bklyn, N.Y.	7-26-25
31	Bob Lawson	K.O.	1	Coney Is. Stadium, Bklyn, N.Y.	8-22-25
32	Sully Montgomery	W.F.	9	Queensboro A.C., Bklyn, N.Y.	9-23-25
33	Eddie Hoffman	L.D.	12	Pioneer A.C., N.Y.C.	11-20-25
34	Ray Newman	L.D.	12	Com'nwealth Spt. Club, N.Y.C.	12-19-25
35	Ray Newman	W.D.	10	Mad. Square Garden, N.Y.C.	2-12-26
36	Stanley Mankun	K.O.	6	Com'nwealth Spt. Club, N.Y.C.	2-27-26
37	Johnny Grosso	W.D.	10	Mad. Square Garden, N.Y.C.	3-15-26
38	Jack Renault	L.D.	10	Mad. Square Garden, N.Y.C.	3-7-26
39	Jack Warren	Draw	10	Com'nwealth A.A., N.Y.C.	7-17-26
40	Jack Warren	W.D.	12	Oakland A.A., Jersey City, N.J.	8-9-26
41	Jack Warren	W.D.	12	West N. Y. Playgr'nds, W.N.Y.	8-19-26
42	Harold Mays	W.D.	10	Bayonne Stadium, N. J.	9-15-26
43	Joe Stossel	K.O.	3	Sesq. Stadium, Phila., Pa.	9-23-26
44	Young Bob Fitzsimmons	W.D.	10	Mad. Square Garden, N.Y.C.	10-8-26
45	Jack Warren	W.D.	10	Arcola Park, Patterson, N. J.	10-14-26
46	Andy Siefert	Draw	10	Mad. Square Garden, N.Y.C.	10-22-26
47	Andy Siefert	L.D.	10	Mad. Square Garden, N.Y.C.	12-3-26
48	Jack Warren	W.D.	12	Knickerbocker, Albany, N.Y.	1-11-27
49	Chief Metoquah	K.O.	4	Armory, Kalamazoo, Mich.	1-25-27
50	Captain Bob Roper	W.D.	10	Armory, Kalamazoo, Mich.	2-9-27
51	Johnny Risko	W.D.	10	Armory, Grand Rapids, Mich.	2-23-27
52	Eddie Benson	K.O.	5	Floral Park, North Bergen, N.J.	3-14-27
53	George Smith	W.F.	4	Grotto Aud., Jersey City, N. J.	3-21-27
54	Tony Stabenau	K.O.	2	St. Nicholas Rink, N.Y.C.	4-4-27
55	Tom Heeney	L.D.	10	Coney Island A.C., N. Y.	6-24-27
56	Johnny Risko	L.D.	10	Cleveland, Ohio	7-13-27
57	Homer Smith	W.D.	10	Kalamazoo, Mich.	8-3-27
58	Johnny Grosso	L.D.	10	Queensboro A.C., Bklyn, N.Y.	9-6-27

58 fights 13 lost decison 4 draw
17 knockouts 14 won decision 8 won

Jack DeMave was named the Golden Boy in 1925 by George B. Underwood, a well-known boxing writer. From 1923 to 1930, DeMave had 90 encounters in the ring and was called a terrific right-hand puncher.

From 1911 to 1918, Rex Beach, the author of adventure novels, owned a home on Chincopee Road. Two of his popular books, *The Spoilers* and *The Silver Hordes*, were made into motion pictures. *The Spoilers* was made into six different versions, one of which starred Marlene Dietrich and John Wayne.

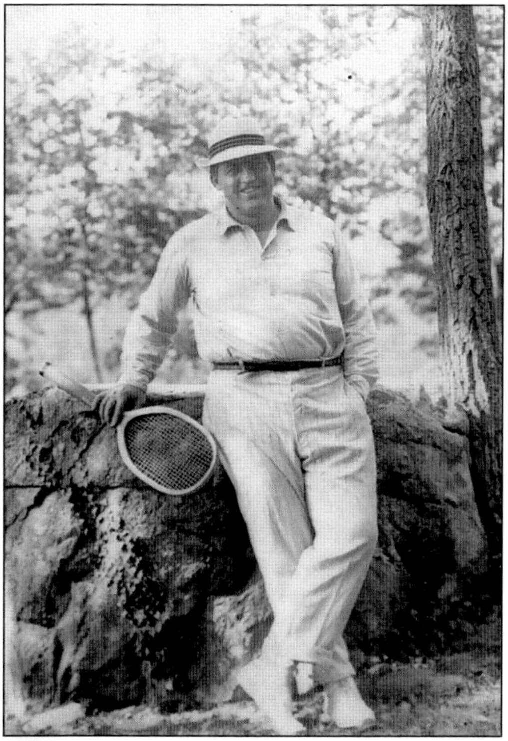

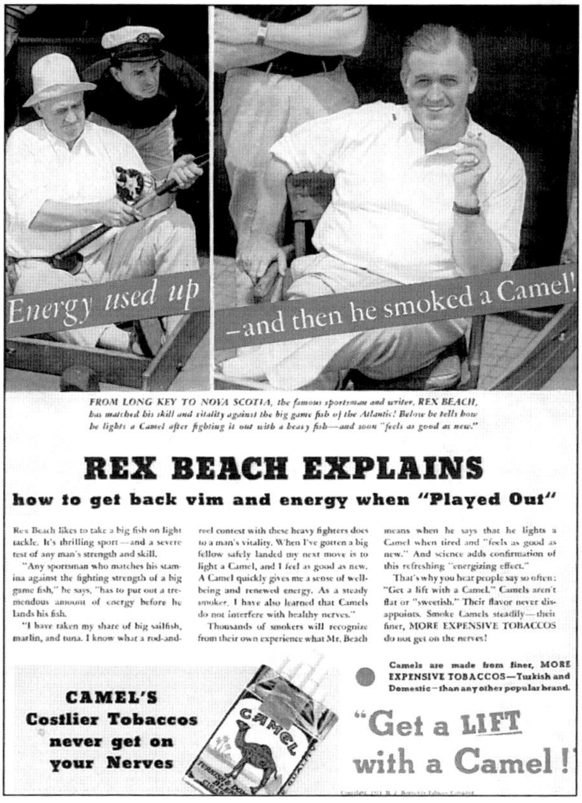

During the 1930s, Rex Beach was often seen in advertisements. In addition to advertising cigarettes, he also posed for Goodyear tires.

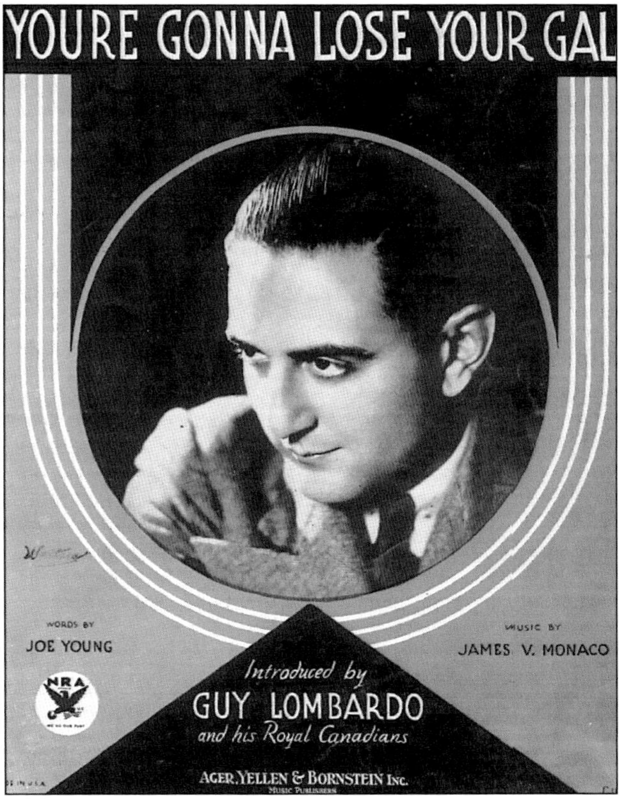

Gaetano Albert Lombardo, better known as Guy Lombardo, was born in Canada in 1902. By the age of 12, he had mastered the violin and he and his brother Carmine Lombardo started a three-member band. Lombardo's band, the Canadians, had their debut in the United States in 1923. The Canadians were renamed the Royal Canadians and, in 1927, CBS gave him his first opportunity at network broadcasting. As the years passed, his band produced "the sweetest music this side of heaven," and his signature song was "Auld Lang Syne."

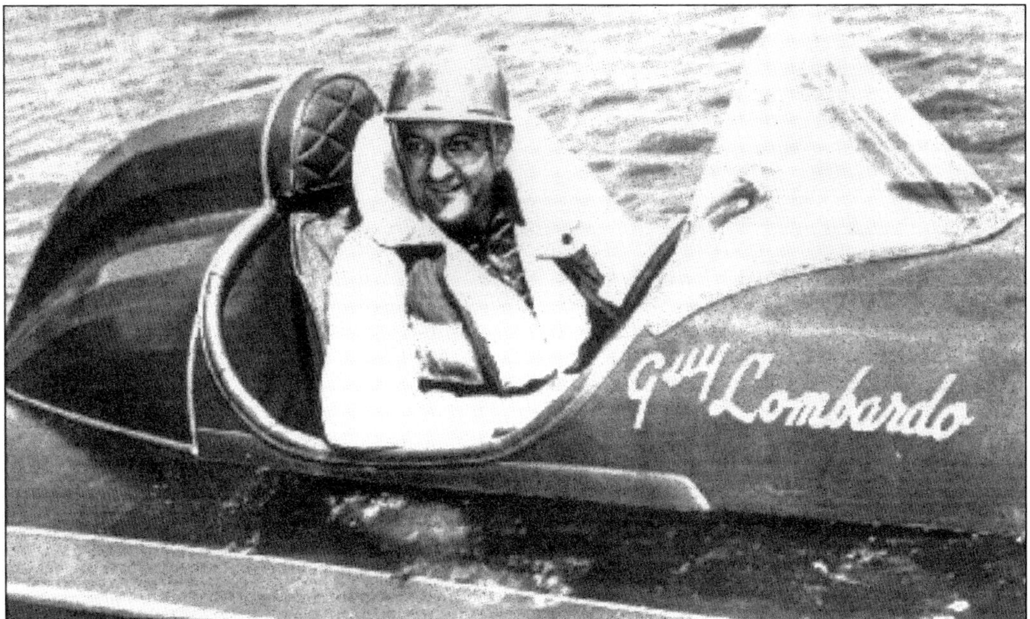

Jefferson Township residents remember Guy Lombardo racing his boat the *Tempo* in Lake Hopatcong in the late 1940s. He was a dedicated speedboat racer and was the national champion from 1946 to 1949. One of his boats, *Tempo IV,* was capable of going 116.8 mph.

Five

Fun and Frolic

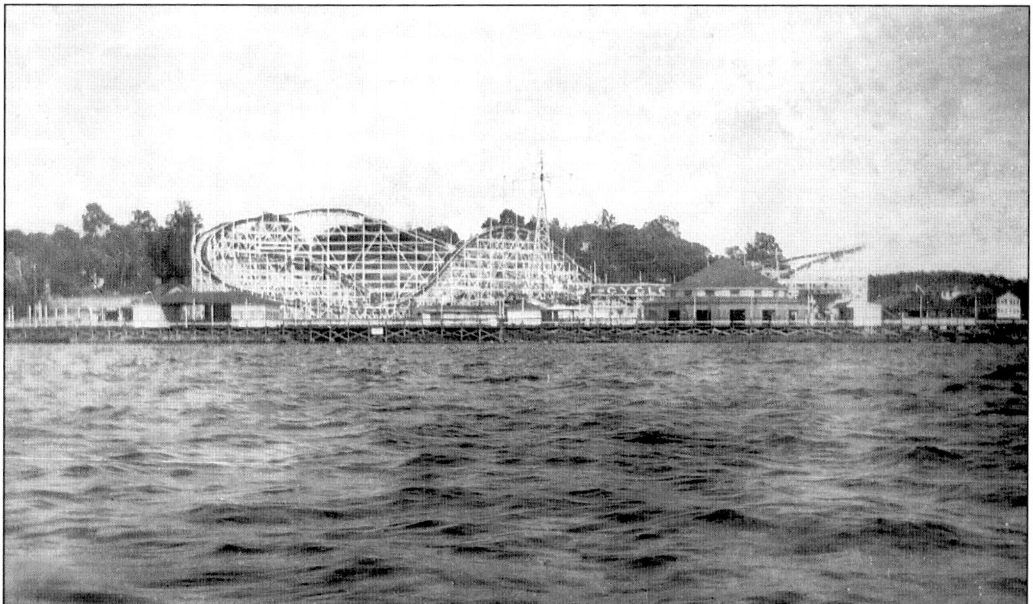

The wooden Nolan's Point Roller Coaster was known to be quite rough because it was confined to a limited amount of space between the lake, railroad, and access roads. The roller coaster sat vacant from the early 1930s until the early 1940s, when it was demolished.

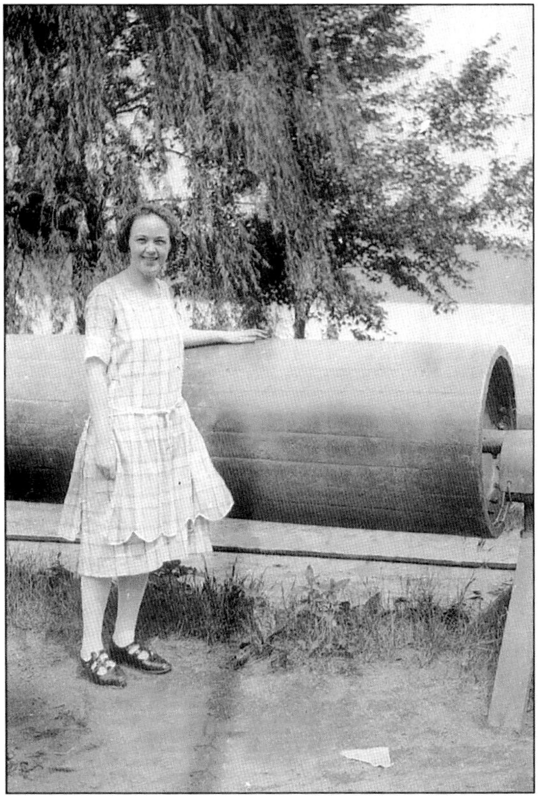

As early as 1905, the Log Roll was one of the most popular amusements at the Nolan's Point Park. This was a portable, self-propelled unit that was moved regularly from season to season. After the motorized rides were added, the Log Roll continued to be a challenge.

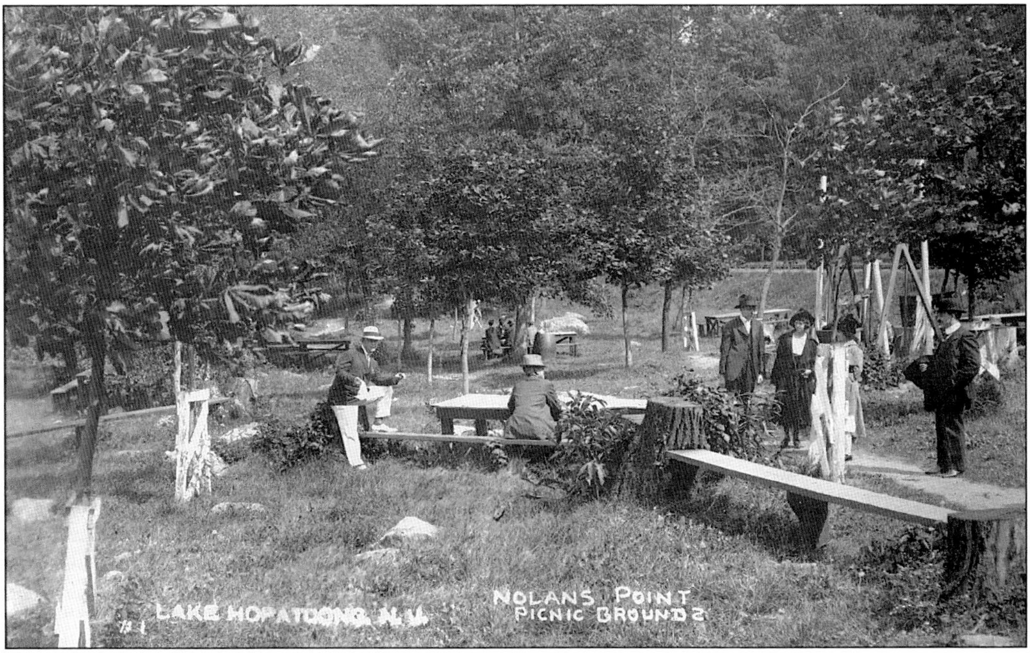

The picnic area was located near the bathing beach and became a social gathering place for residents and tourists. Covered and uncovered picnic tables were available at no charge. This was a very popular area because footpaths traversed the grove.

Dancing bears, pictured *c.* 1905, were often a common sight at the Nolan's Point Amusement Park. Wandering entertainers would put on impromptu shows and then move on.

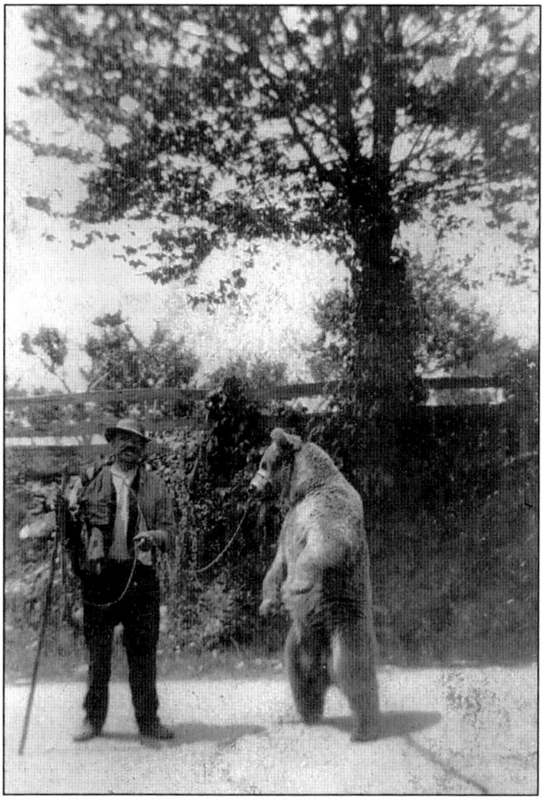

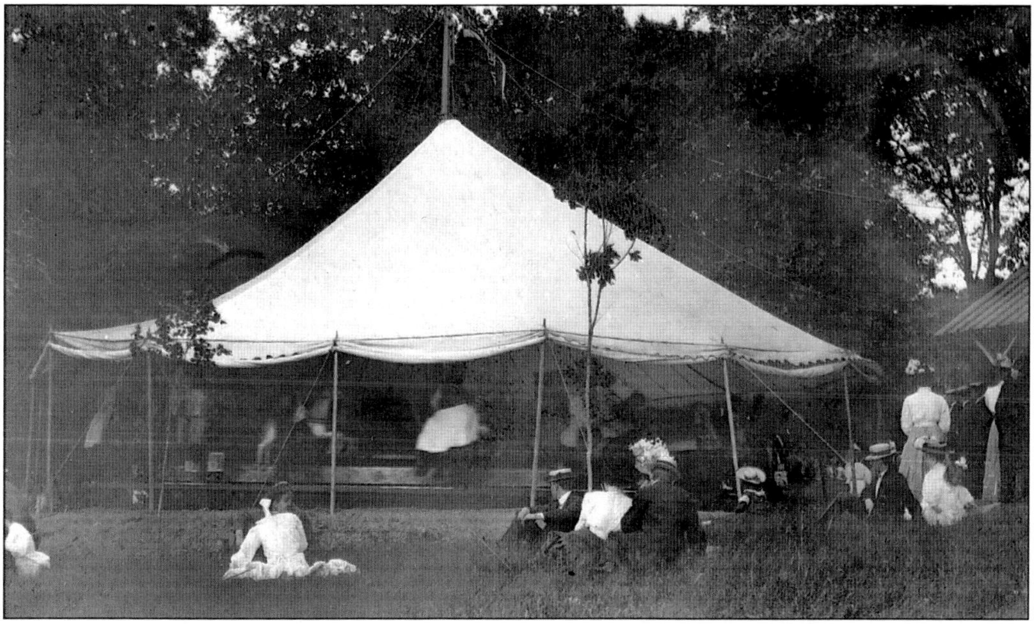

The oldest amusement center in northern New Jersey opened at Allen's on Nolan's Point *c.* 1887. One of its first amusements was a self-propelled merry-go-round. Each winter it was dismantled and put away, and then next season would find it situated in a different location.

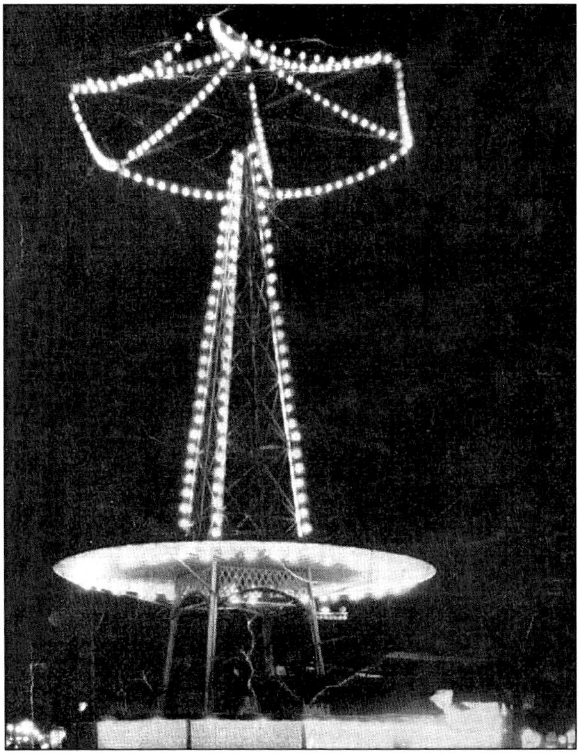

A brightly lit Anderson Aeroplane Swing was added to the modernized Nolan's Point Amusement Park *c.* 1925. This stood 67 feet high and the swings moved in a circular motion out over Lake Hopatcong.

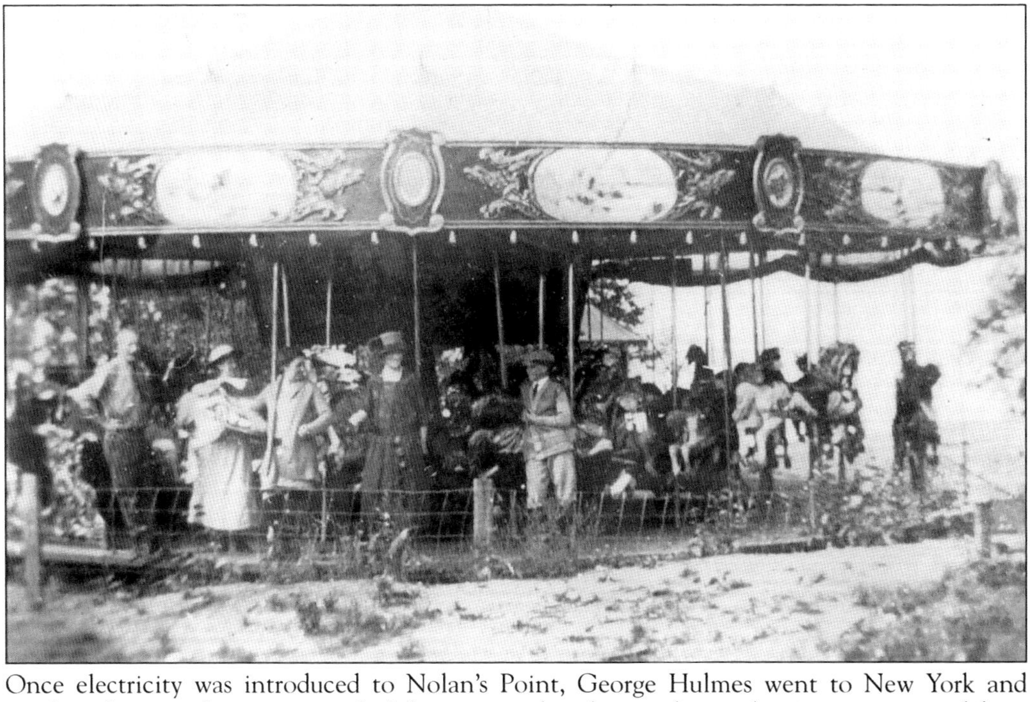

Once electricity was introduced to Nolan's Point, George Hulmes went to New York and purchased a new electric carousel. A house was placed around it so that it was protected from the weather. This carousel was eventually sold to the Bertrand Island Amusement Park; another carousel took the place of Hulmes on Nolan's Point.

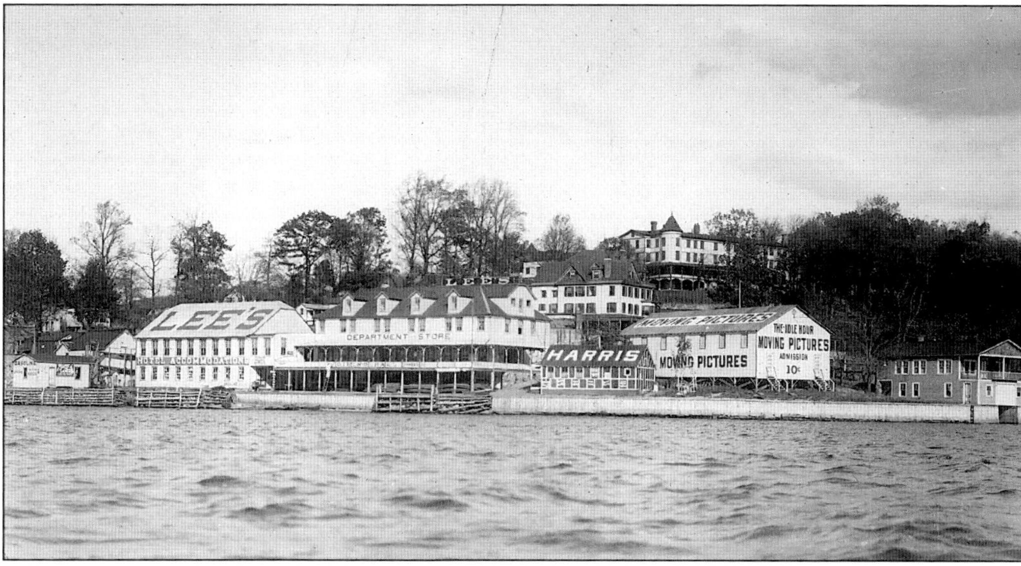

The Idle Hour Theatre was located next to Lee's Pavilion and had continuous moving pictures from 2:30 p.m. to 11:00 p.m. The pictures changed daily, and the admission was only 10¢.

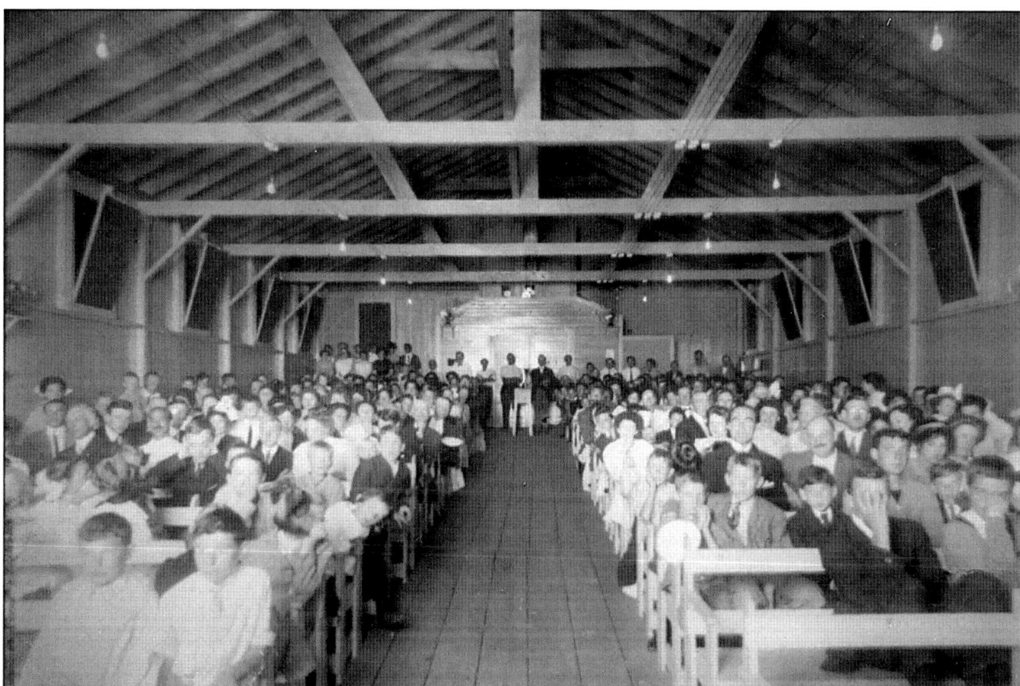
Both young and old enjoyed the Idle Hour Theatre. To assure the clients' comfort, the building seated 400 and was equipped with fans and electric lights. Box seats were available for parties of 8 to 12 people. Arrangements could also be made to transport the clients to and from the theater.

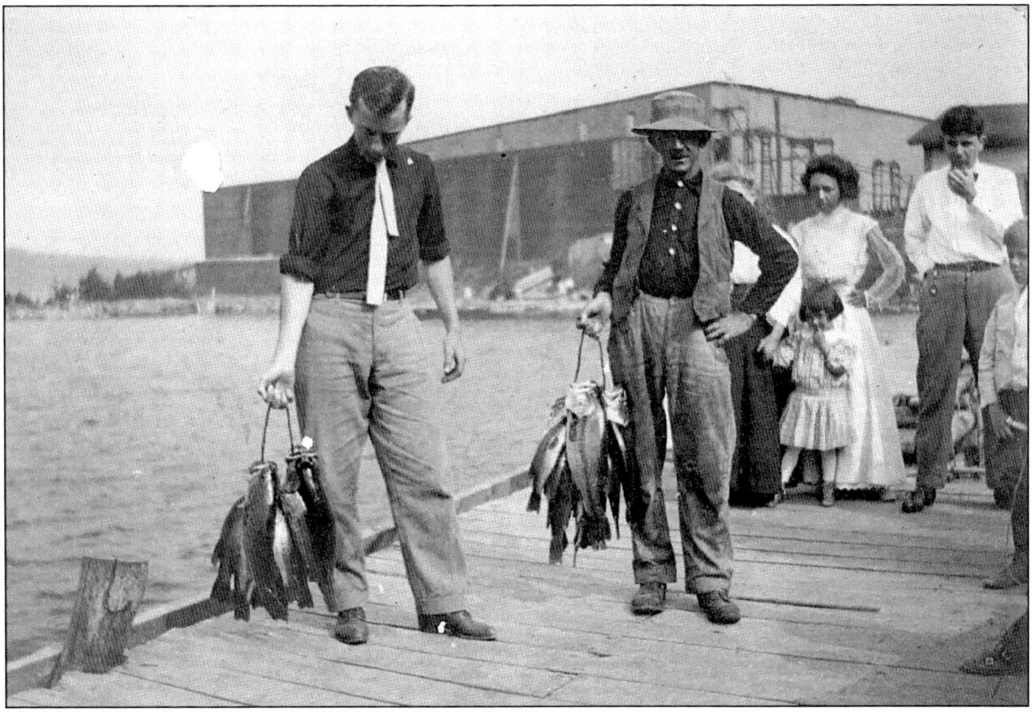

Vacationers are amazed at the number and size of the fish that could be caught in Lake Hopatcong. These fish were not only for private consumption but also for hotels, guesthouses, and restaurants.

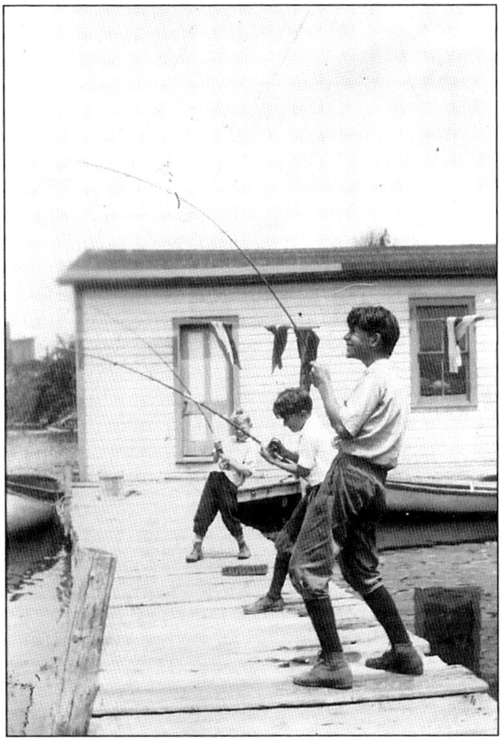

Young men did not always have a fishing boat available, so they would fish off the dock of Lee's Pavilion. Hopefully, bent poles meant big fish.

People who did not mind sitting out in the cold enjoyed ice fishing. Unfortunately, during the icehouse era, fishermen were often restricted as to where they were allowed to fish. No fishing holes were permitted in the ice-harvesting areas because the horses could fall and break a leg.

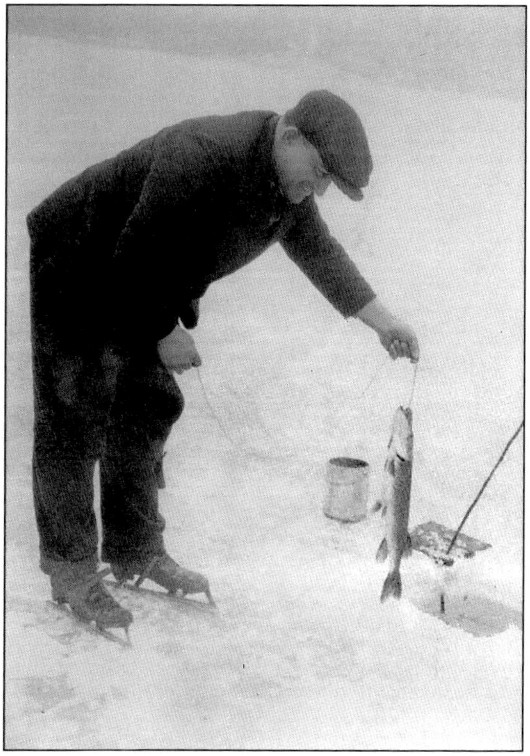

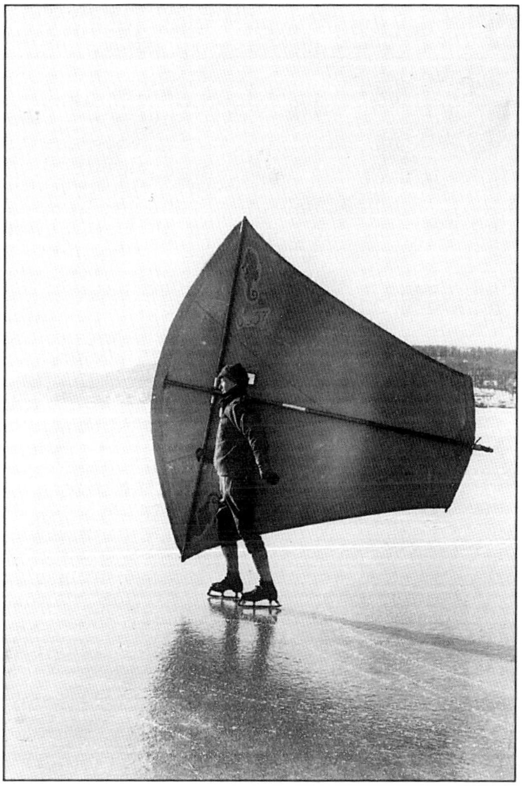

During windy days, skaters often used a sail to propel them across the ice. These sails were usually homemade, and sail plans were printed in the *Breeze*.

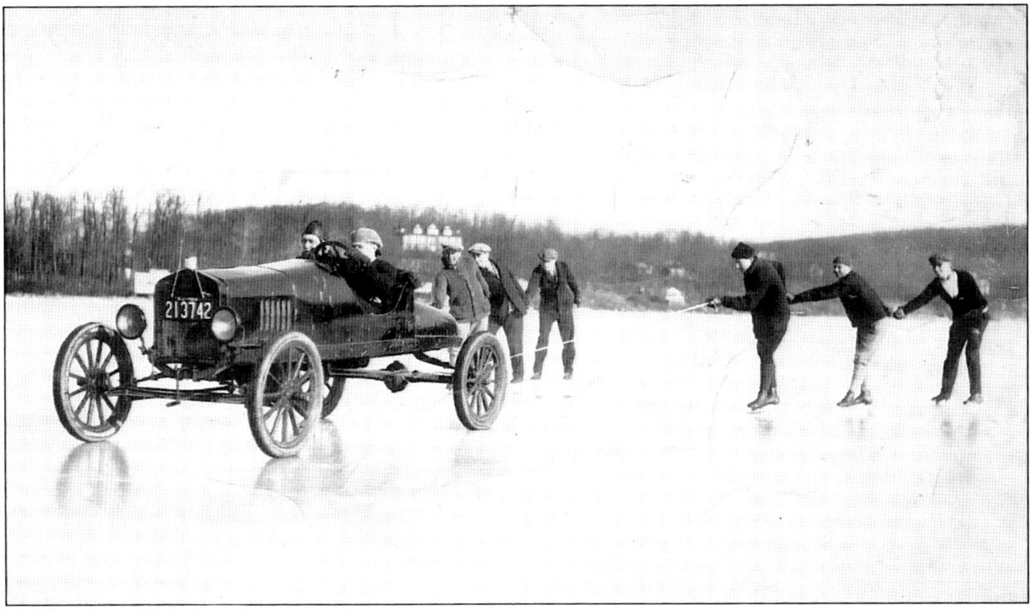

Lake Hopatcong was usually frozen from December through March. Ice-skating was always a popular pastime for locals and visitors. Leo Lauerman (driver) took his friend for a thrill ride behind his red roadster *c.* 1920.

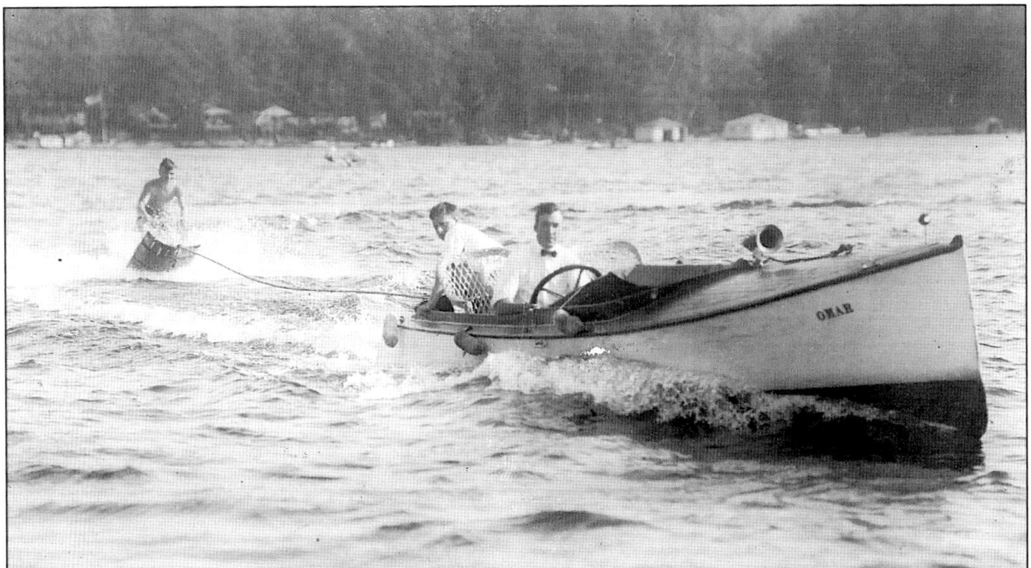

Aquaplaning became a popular watersport with the young. It was introduced to Lake Hopatcong in the early 1930s. A powerboat doing between 10 and 30 mph pulled a flat board with rider over the waters.

Plays and short skits were abundant during the summer season. Professionals and locals performed for many different organizations. Emma Robinson, daughter of the owners of the Espanong Hotel, grew up with theatrical personnel and liked to display her talents. She is seen here acting out a Greek tragedy for the Elks organization.

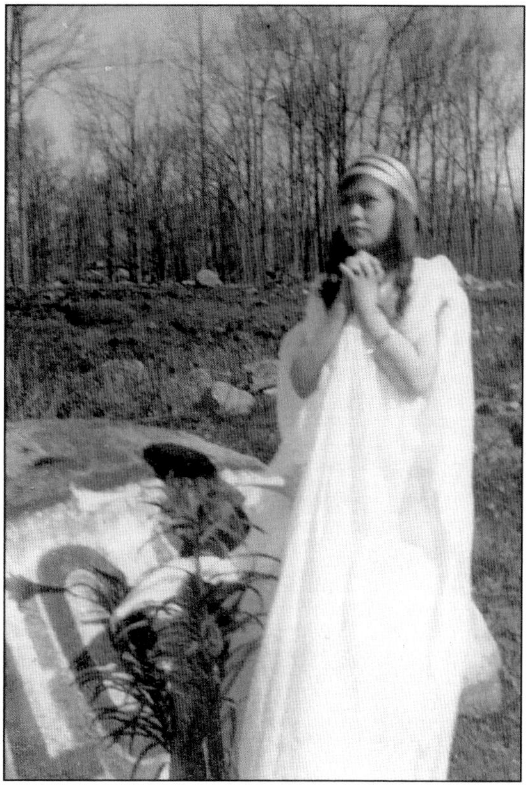

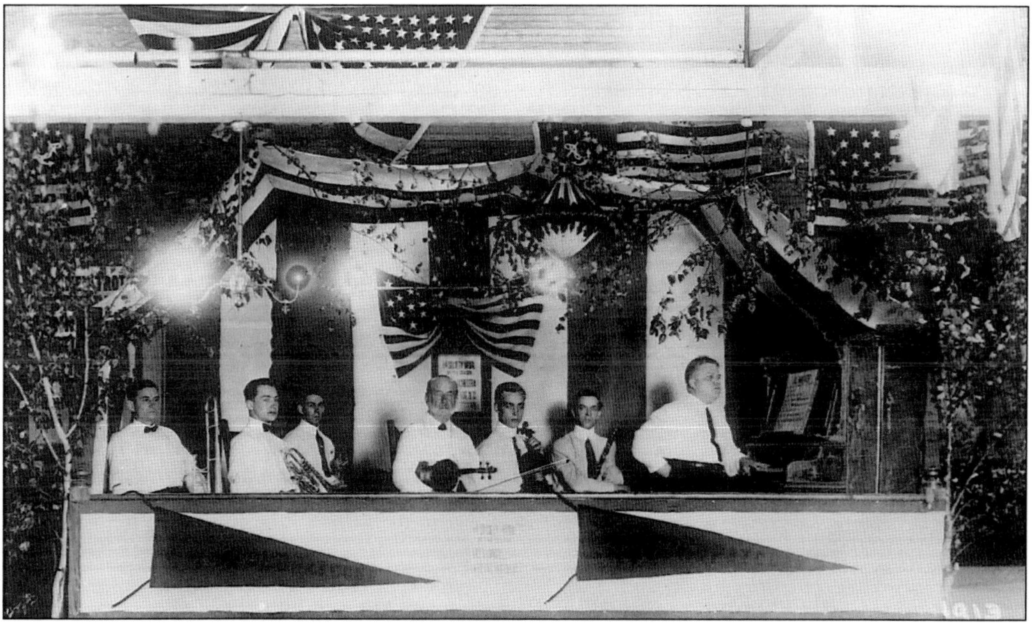

Throughout the summer months, music was in abundance. Hotels and taverns often employed local talent to entertain their guests and patrons. This photograph was taken *c.* 1913.

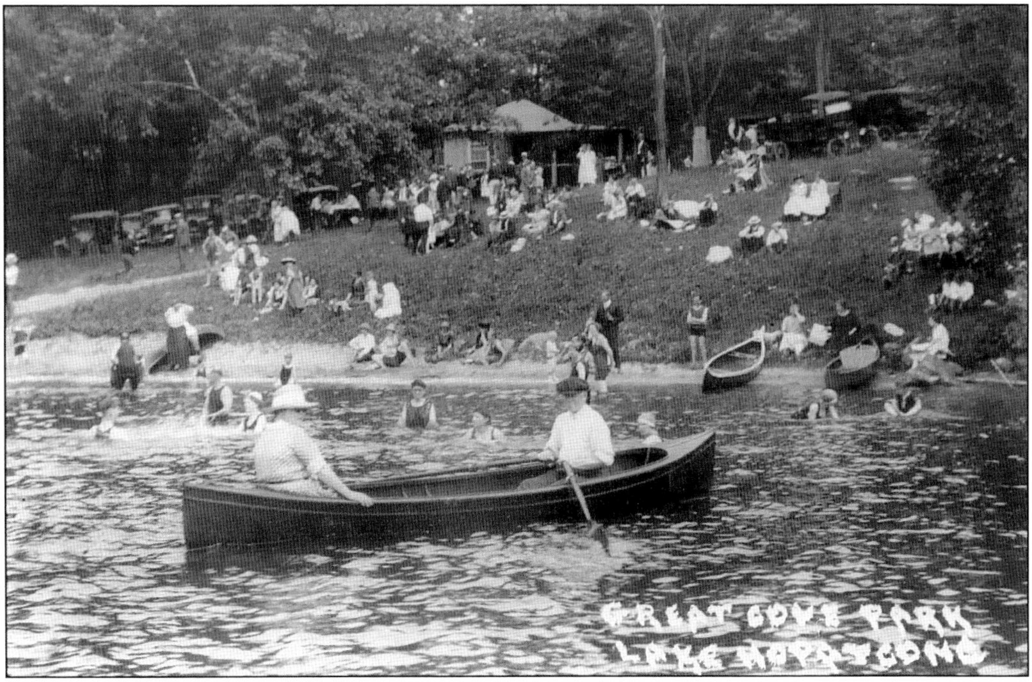

During the 1920s, the Great Cove Park, located in what was Chamberlain Cove, was a very popular bathing area for residents and tourists. A refreshment stand, boat rentals, and a boardinghouse were available on the grounds. Eventually, a swimming dock, diving tower, and waterwheel were added.

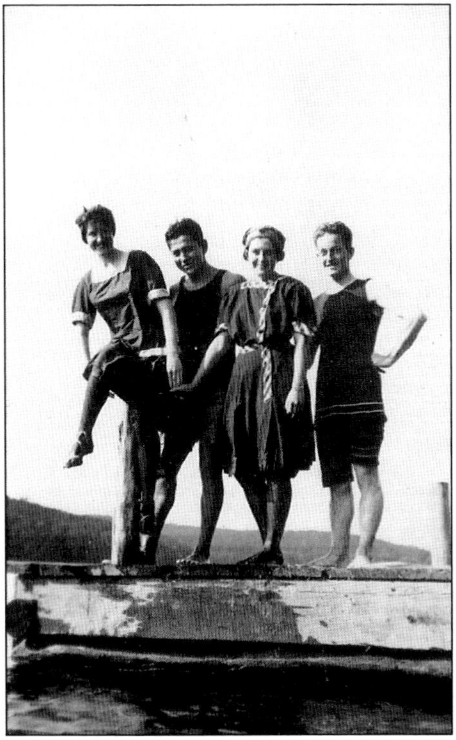

Warm days usually meant it was time to go swimming and cool off. Hopefully these bathing suits did not make swimmers sink.

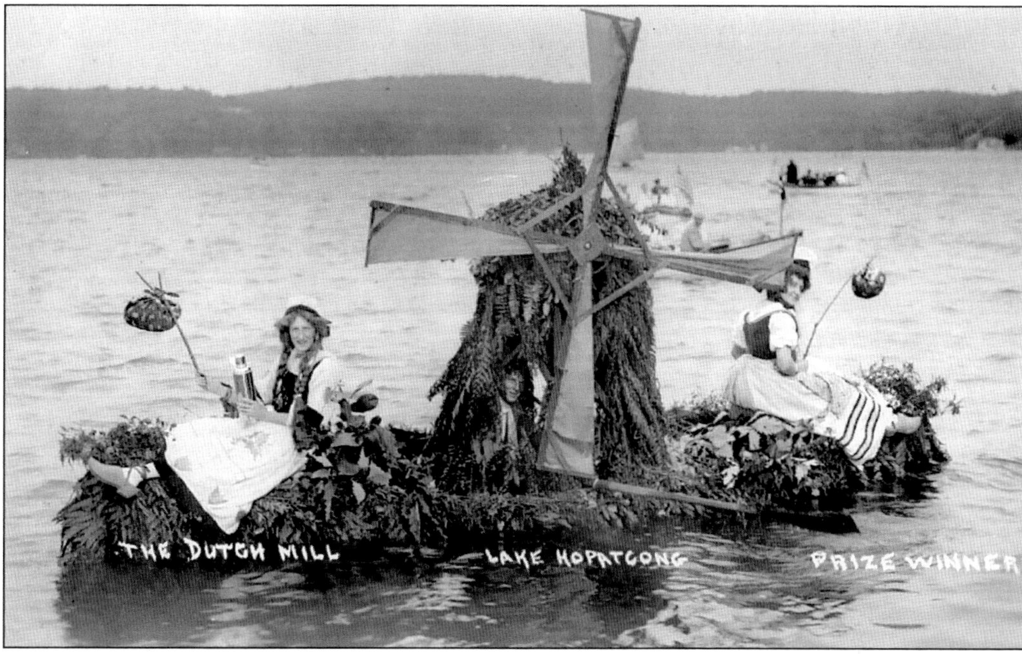

As seen in this *c.* 1910 photograph, many of the boats were elaborately designed and decorated. It did not matter if your boat was small or large, motorized or nonmotorized. People of all ages were encouraged to participate.

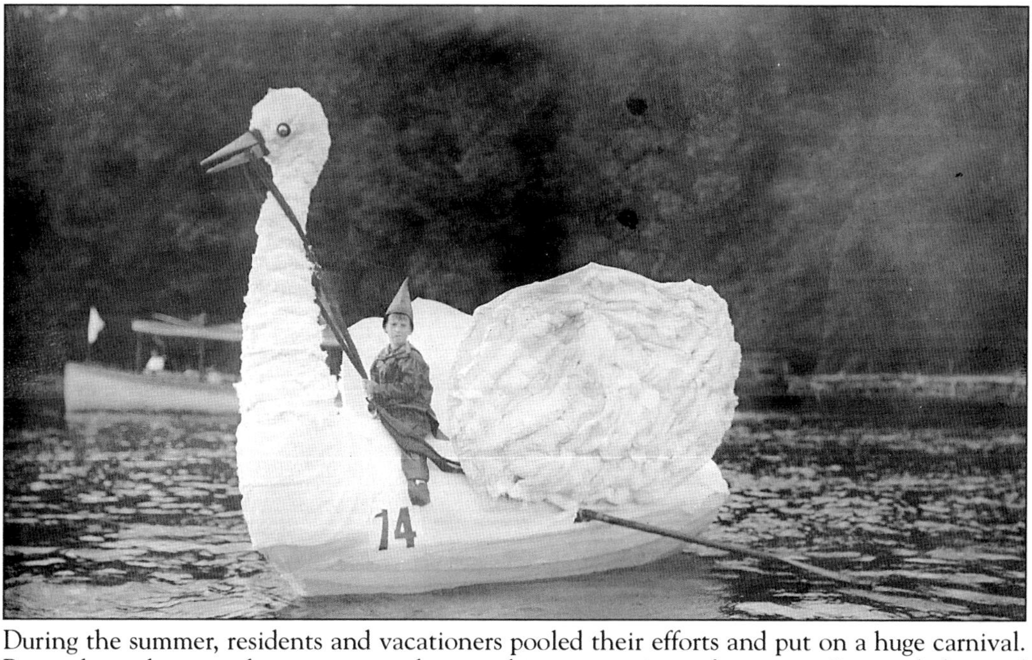

During the summer, residents and vacationers pooled their efforts and put on a huge carnival. Boats, bungalows, and camps were decorated in competition for prizes. Festive lights and campfires lit up the lake.

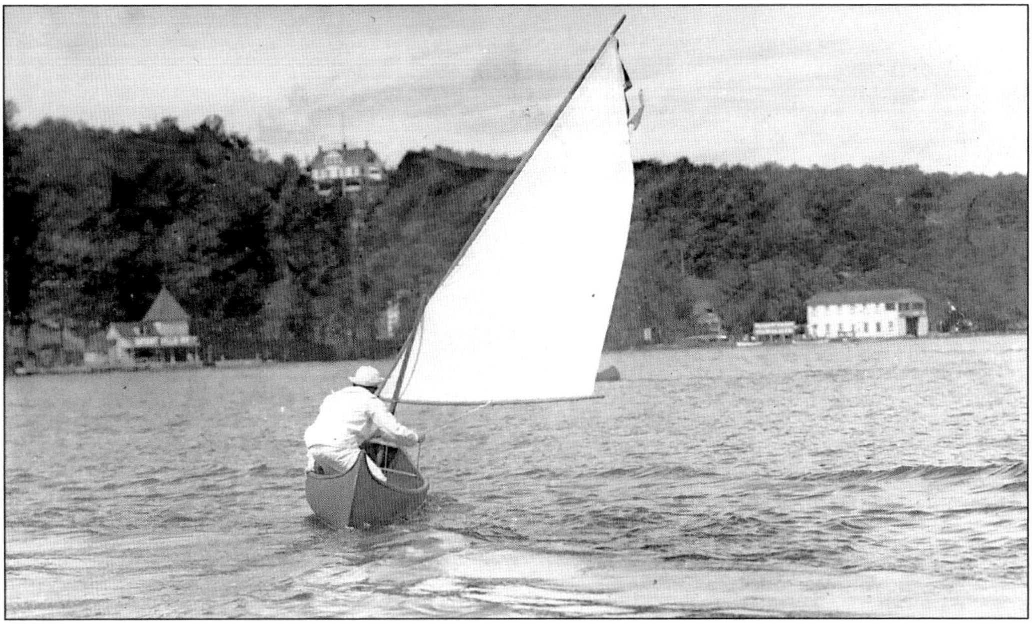

A less expensive way to go sailing was to use a canoe and rig a sail. It was usually a one- or two-man sport because of the lack of space. Canoe sailors felt that it took a lot more skill than sailing a regular sailboat because the canoe was more likely to capsize.

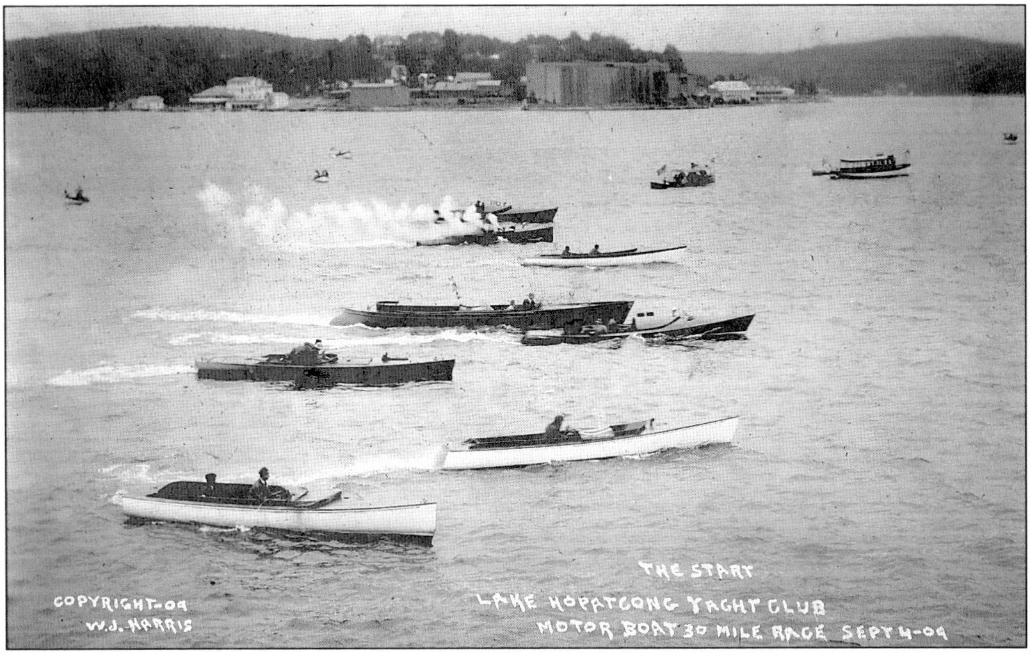

Motorboat racing has been popular on Lake Hopatcong since the early 1900s. The course was in front of Nolan's Point heading to the Lake Hopatcong Yacht Club because the water was deep and it was the longest uninterrupted part of the lake.

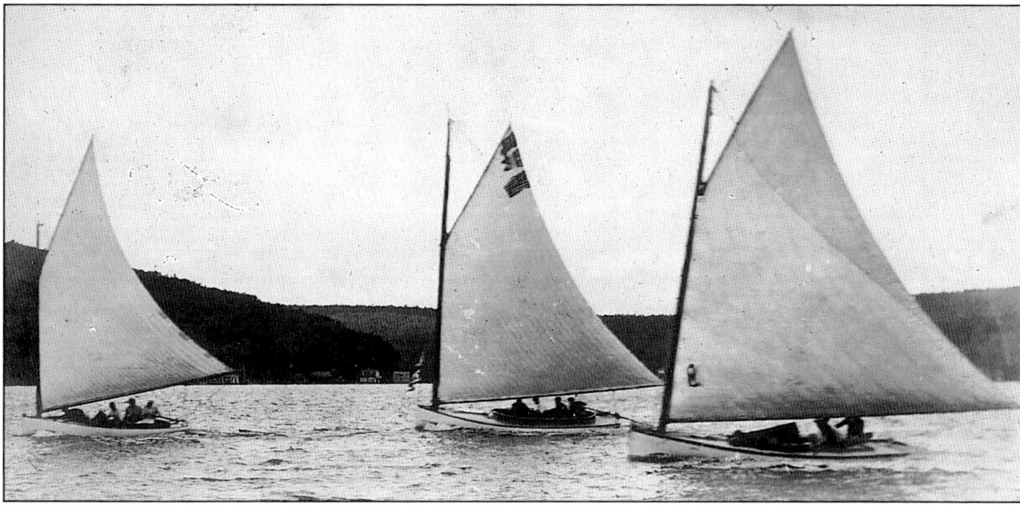

Water, wind, and a sailboat were all that were necessary to engage in a sailing challenge; formal and informal races have been held in abundance every summer since the late 1800s. Different sizes and classes often competed against each other.

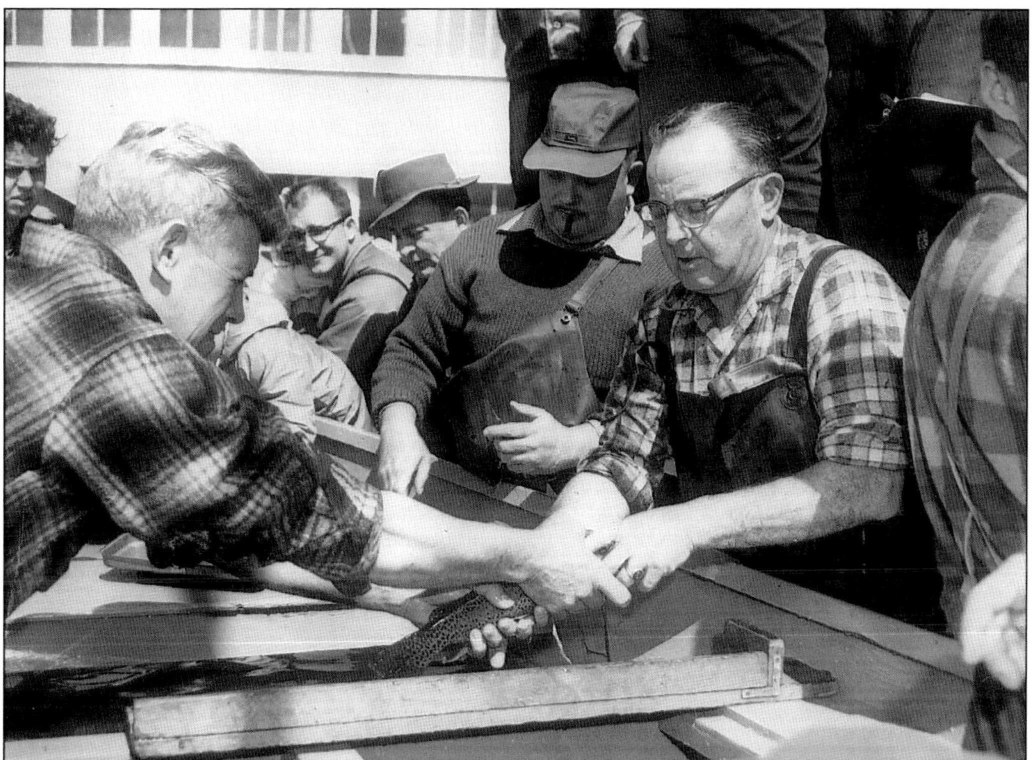

The Knee Deep Hunting and Fishing Club started in 1946. In 1953, it lobbied the state of New Jersey to stock walleye in the lake. After being tagged, the fish were placed in the water. Unfortunately, this program was not successful and was abandoned.

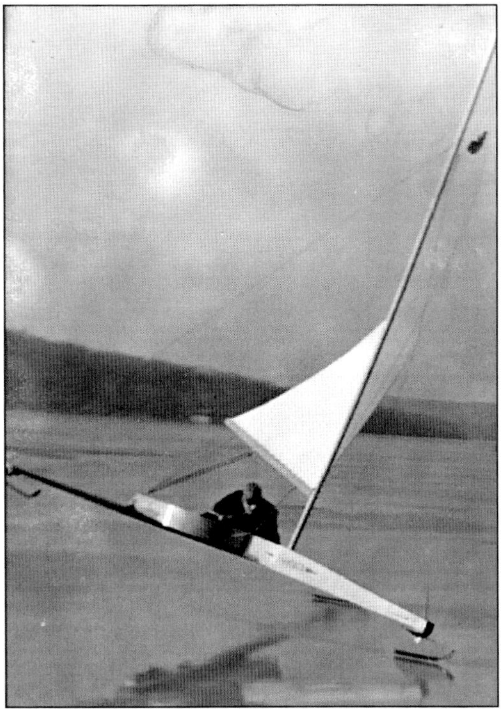

This *c.* 1938 homemade iceboat was owned by Charles T. Shipman II of Montclair, a summer resident of Lake Hopatcong. It has one mainsail and no jib. It was a front-steering iceboat that was manipulated with a steering wheel and not a tiller. This particular type of boat was the forerunner of the Yankee Class.

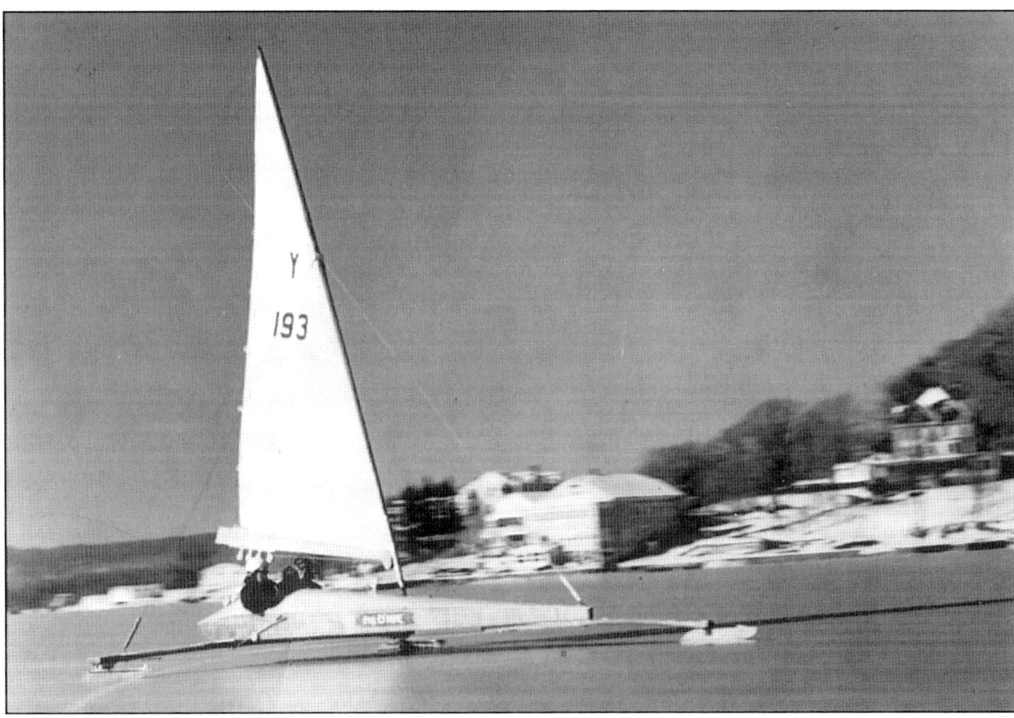

This Y 193 was built *c.* 1950 by Elbie Kronenberg, former owner of Hockenjos Boat Basin, to Yankee Class specifications. It was a front-steering boat with cables that regulated the steering from the cockpit to the runner via the springboard. It held two people and averaged 50 to 60 mph.

Six

Working Hard

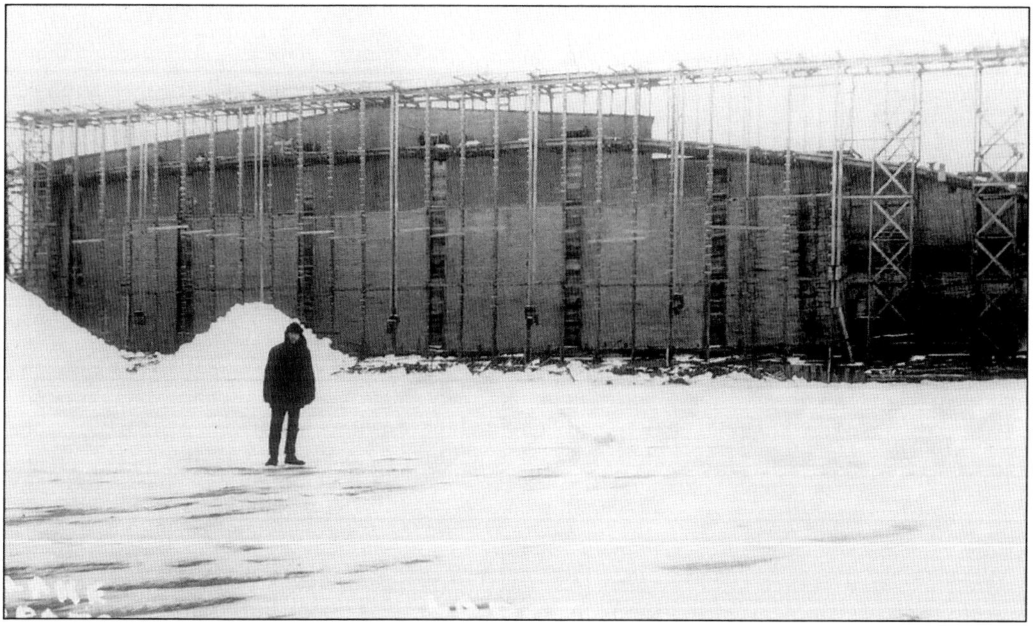

The Consumer Coal & Ice Company was owned by Brady Brothers. By the mid-to-late 1800s, Brady Brothers owned four commercial icehouses, the largest of which was the Nolan's Point Ice House. This icehouse was three stories high and was made of heavy, double-plank walls. The studs in the walls were 18 inches apart, and the space between them was filled with sawdust and seaweed. The large, adjustable wood and metal conveyor ran the height and length of the icehouse.

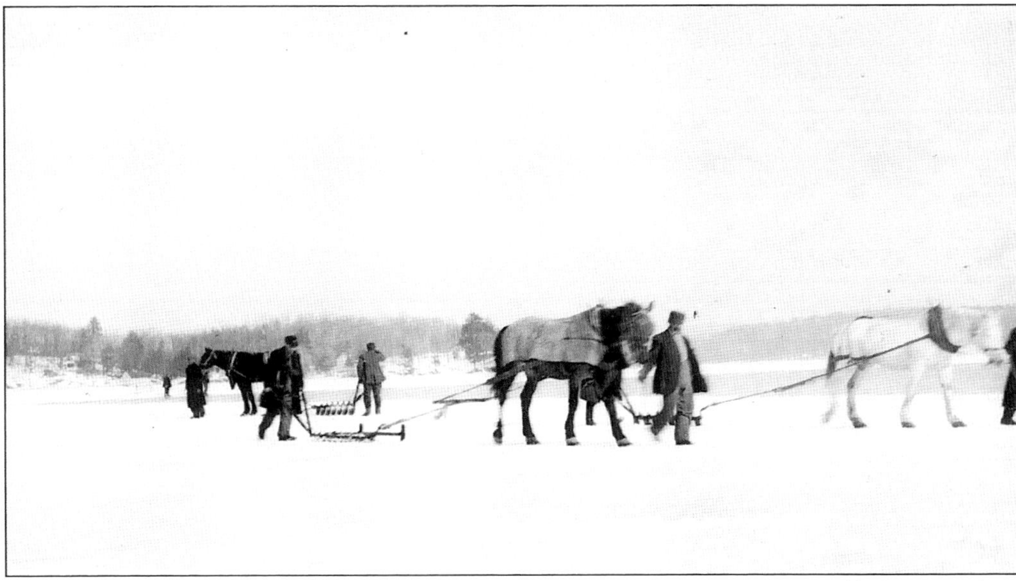

After the snow was cleared, the ice was marked into one-acre fields. Horses pulled an ice plane, which had a handle for each hand and a thick blade with teeth that scored the ice. These teeth cut three inches into the ice. However, prior to scoring the ice, the cutting field was marked by string.

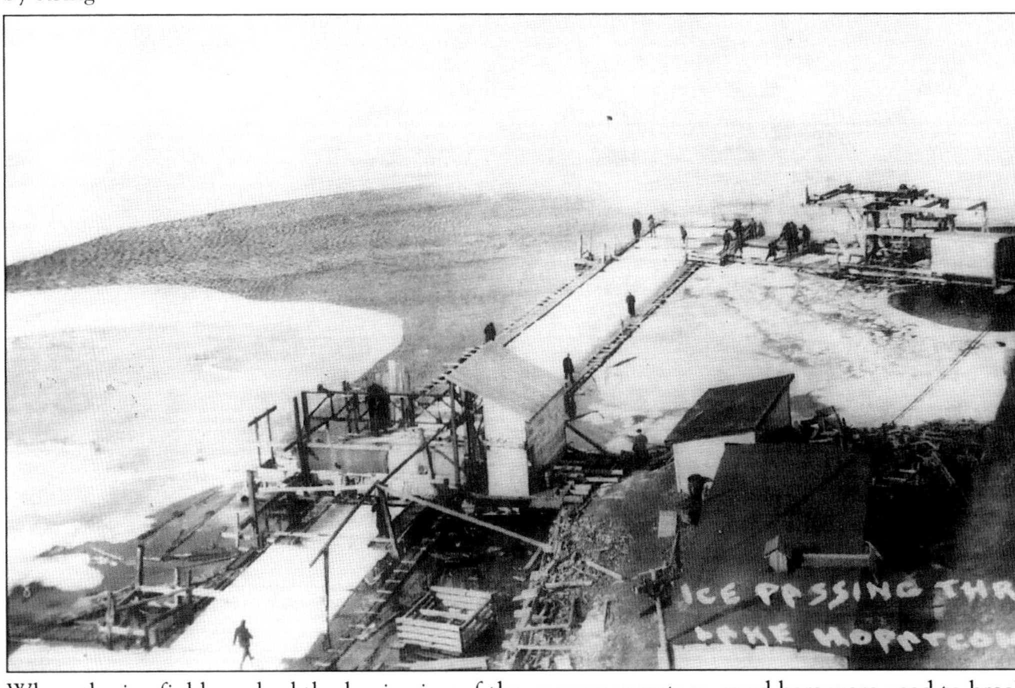

When the ice field reached the beginning of the conveyor system, spud bars were used to break the large pieces of ice into individual cakes. If the cakes were too thick, the top layer was planed off. The ice proceeded up the conveyor and, at the top, a quality control inspector determined if the ice was clear enough to be placed in the icehouse for later shipment. Unclear ice was put off to the side for local residents. The "swinger" would take the ice off the conveyor and "swing" it onto a stack.

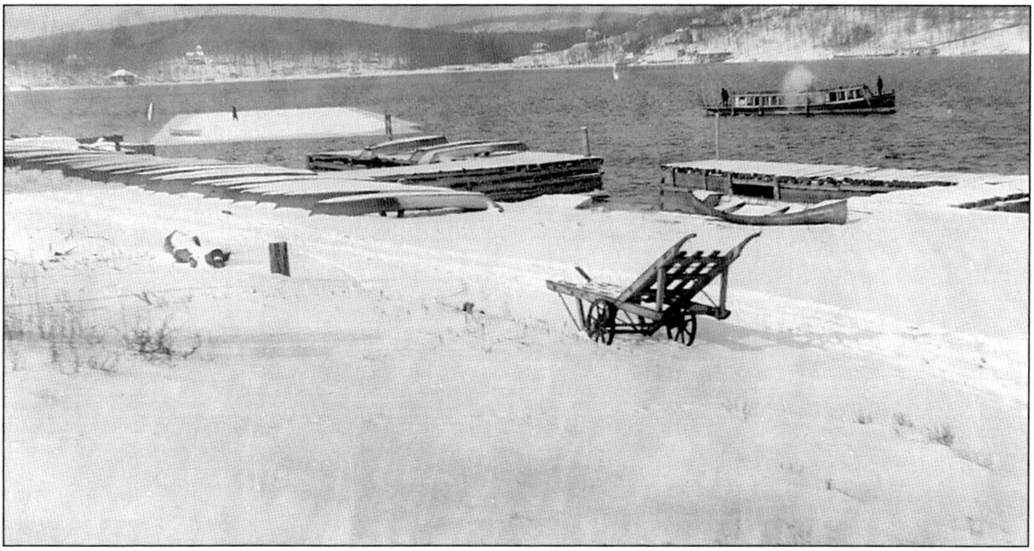

As the lake became cleared of ice, it was necessary to have the ice towed to the conveyor system. The *Mystic Shrine*, a summer passenger boat, would hook onto an ice field and deliver it. Several men would ride on the ice in order to ensure that nothing was damaged en route.

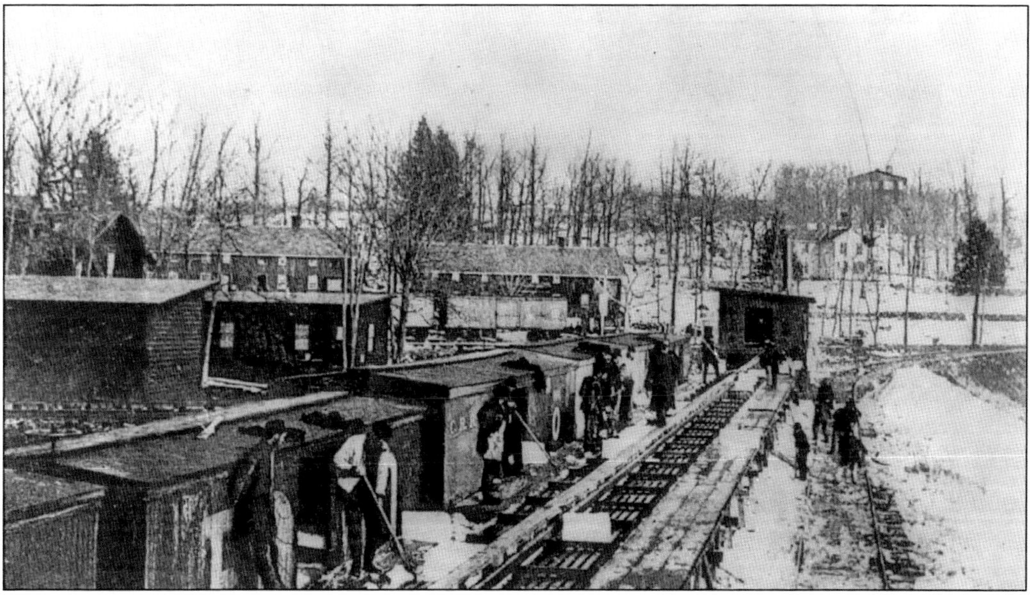

The canal boats of the Morris Canal were used to deliver ice to distant cities during the spring and summer. The ice was packed in sawdust and seaweed to insulate it. Eventually, the Central Railroad took over and delivered the ice to Jersey City, Newark, and even delivered to Florida. The train cars were also insulated.

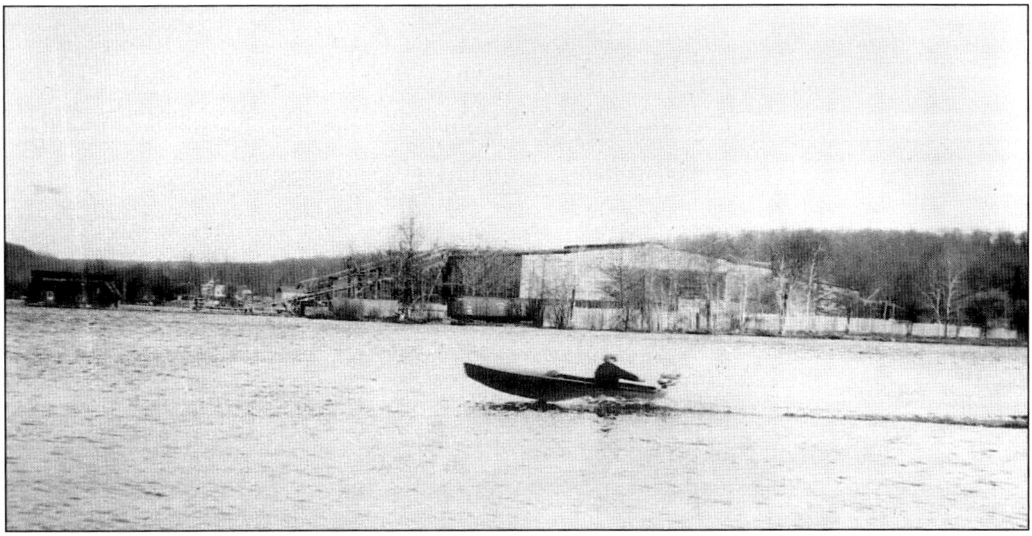

The partner to the Nolan's Point icehouse was Callaghan's Ice House, which was located at the entrance to Callaghan's Cove (Hurd Cove). This icehouse was located on the shallower part of Lake Hopatcong, and it was necessary for Brady Brothers to construct an earthen work dam to hold back the water in order to thicken the ice for harvesting. The same harvesting procedures were used at this icehouse. Boxcars loaded the ice on site and then transported it.

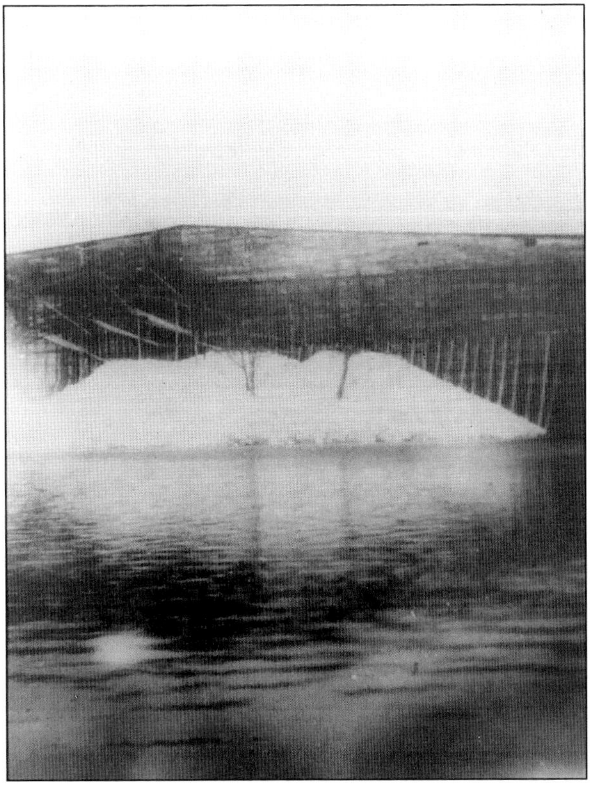

The fourth Consumer Coal & Ice Company icehouse was constructed by accident. Lake Hopatcong did not freeze, so Brady Brothers took its employees to Lake Shawnee (Duck Pond) to harvest ice. Since there was no icehouse, the ice was piled up as high as the on-site engineer would allow. Once they were finished harvesting the ice, the icehouse was built around the piles of ice. This icehouse became known as "the stack."

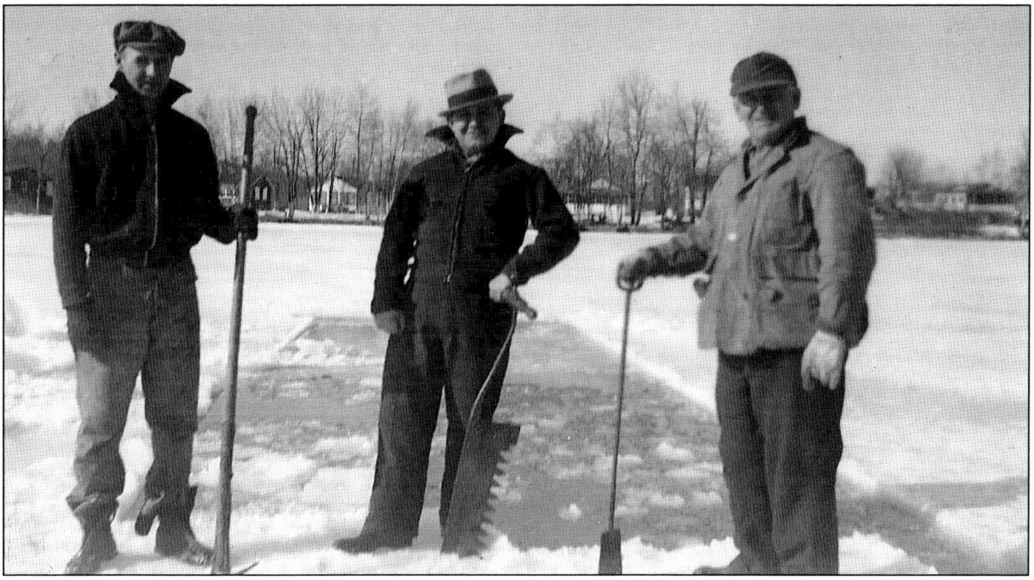

Local business people continued to harvest ice until 1941. Michael Chabon (center) and his friends used the pike pole, saw, and spud bar to harvest ice. The ice was then stored in a cavern behind the Erin House (Callaghan's Hotel) until it was needed in the hotel.

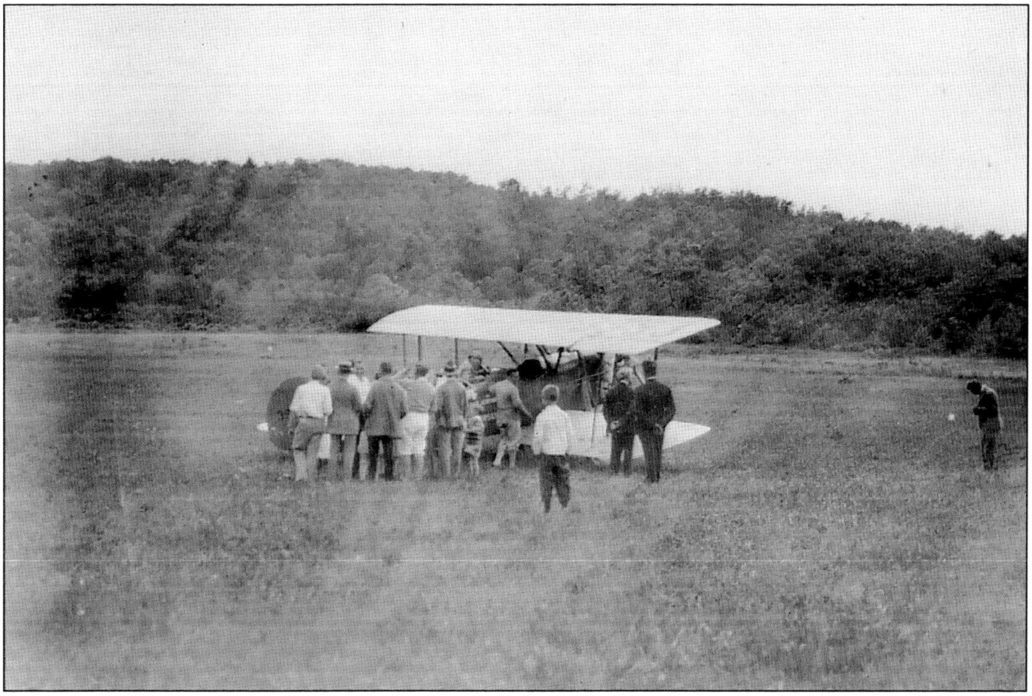

The private airport for Brady Brothers (Consumer Coal & Ice Company) was located behind the Airport Inn (Doc's) on Route 15. Brady Brothers used this airport when checking in on the ice business. Eventually, airshows and private flying clubs began to use the airport. Lakeside and firemen's fields occupy the area today.

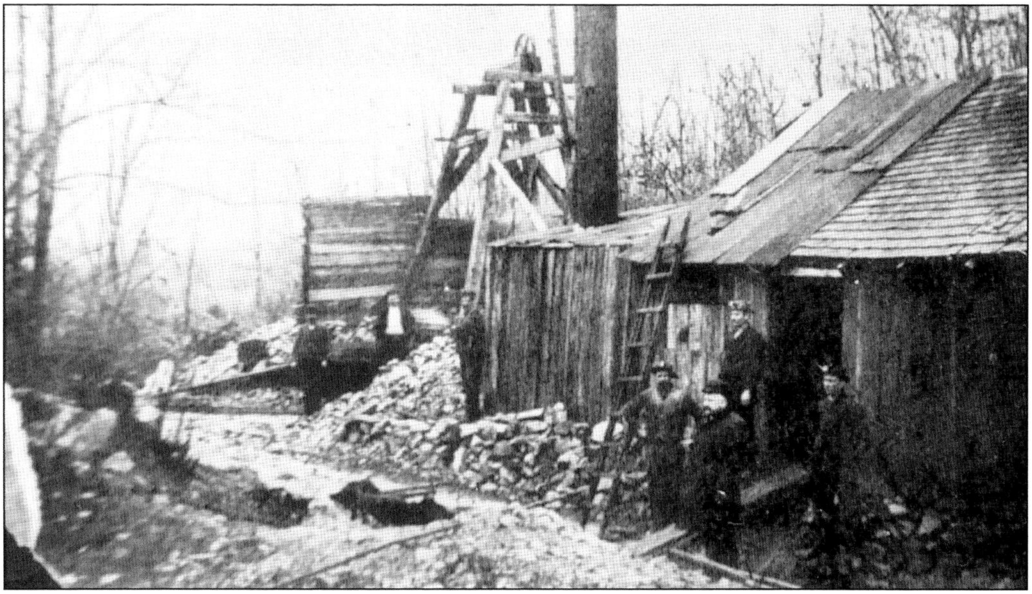

In the early 1800s, the Weldon Mine was in operation. The mine consisted of a series of pits and shafts. The Weldon Mine had a history of opening and closing from 1868 to 1890, when a concentrator was erected. The concentrator removed the phosphorus from the rich ore, but it was a very expensive process and, by 1901, all operations had ceased. In 1902, the mine was sold, but the coal strike caused it to close forever. The Lower Weldon Mine started *c.* 1873, but little success was evident and it was abandoned before 1896.

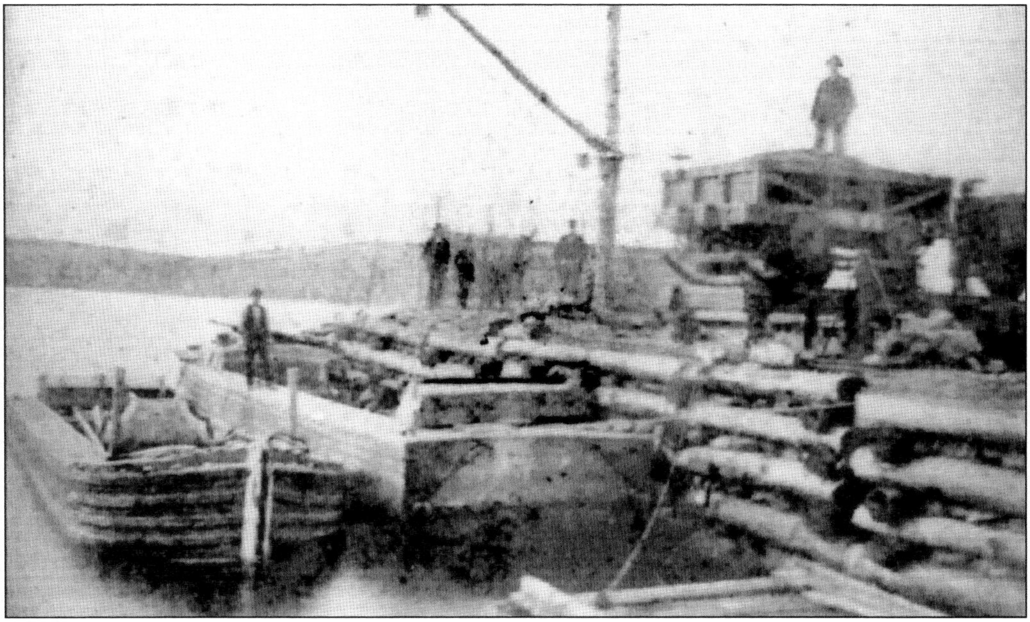

The ore from the Weldon, Ogden (Edison), and Hurdtown mines was originally brought to the Nolan's Point docks via horse and wagon. However, once the Ogden Mine Railroad was operational the ore arrived via train. Once at the dock, as seen in this damaged image, the gondola car that contained the ore was unloaded into waiting Morris Canal boats. The boats transported the ore to refineries and forges.

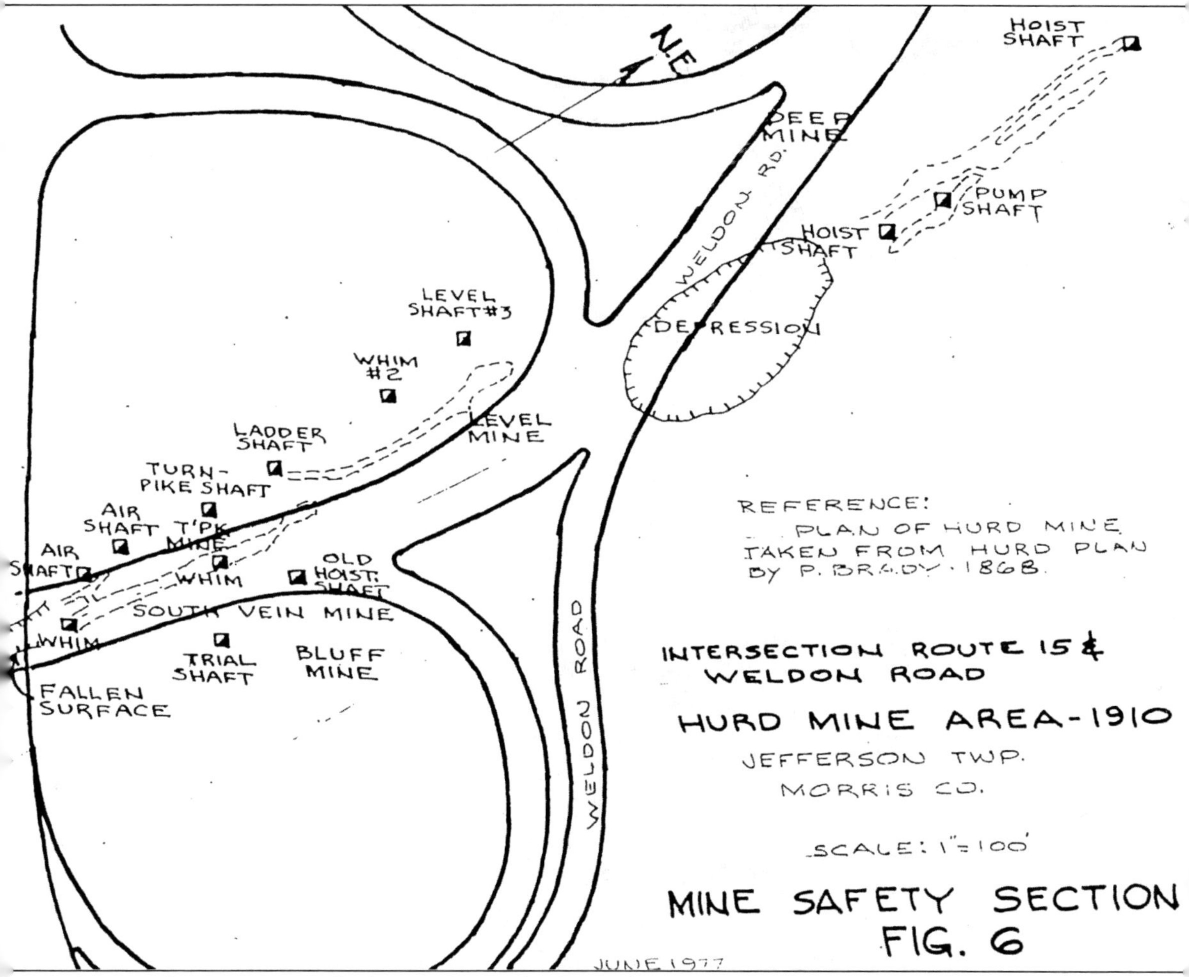

The Hurdtown Mine, which was located where the Route 15 overpass for Espanong and Weldon Roads is currently located, belonged to the Glenden Iron Company from the mid-1850s to 1893, when the Mount Pleasant Mining Company purchased it. By 1895, a depth of approximately 5,500 feet had been reached, but the ore vein was very stringy. Productivity dropped drastically and the mine eventually closed for good.

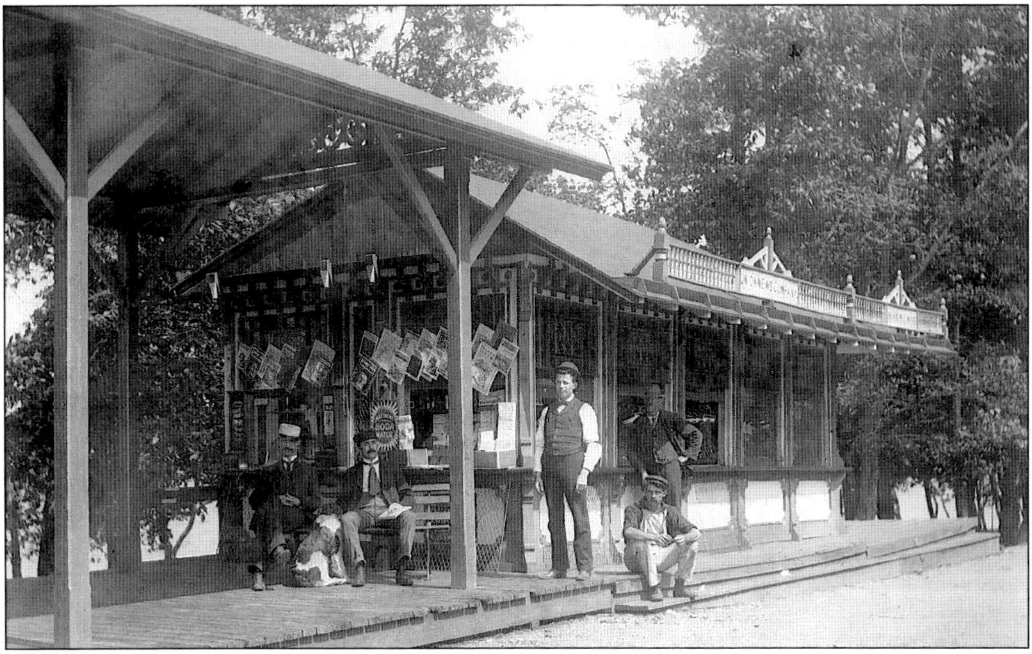

The Union News Company was located near the Central Railroad station on Nolan's Point. The agent, S. Elander was proud of its 20th Century Iceless Sanitary Soda Fountain. Cigars, tobacco, candy, ice cream, postcards, novelties, magazines, and papers were readily available, as seen in this *c.* 1910 photograph.

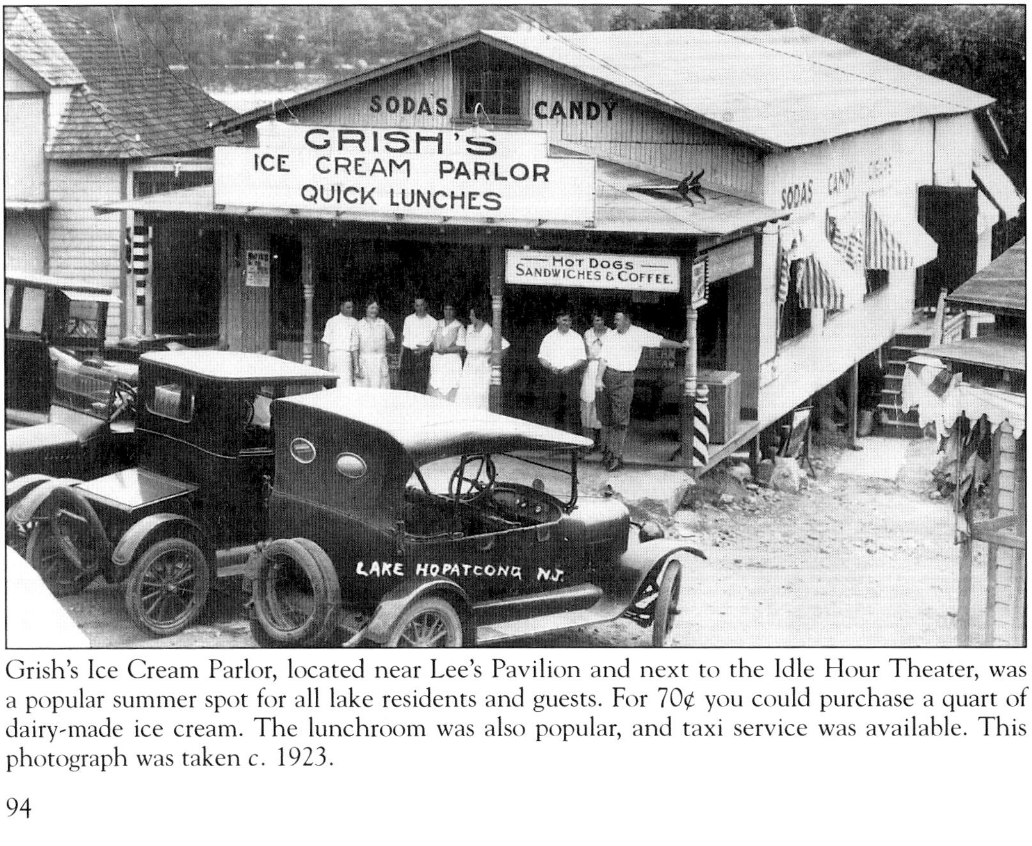

Grish's Ice Cream Parlor, located near Lee's Pavilion and next to the Idle Hour Theater, was a popular summer spot for all lake residents and guests. For 70¢ you could purchase a quart of dairy-made ice cream. The lunchroom was also popular, and taxi service was available. This photograph was taken *c.* 1923.

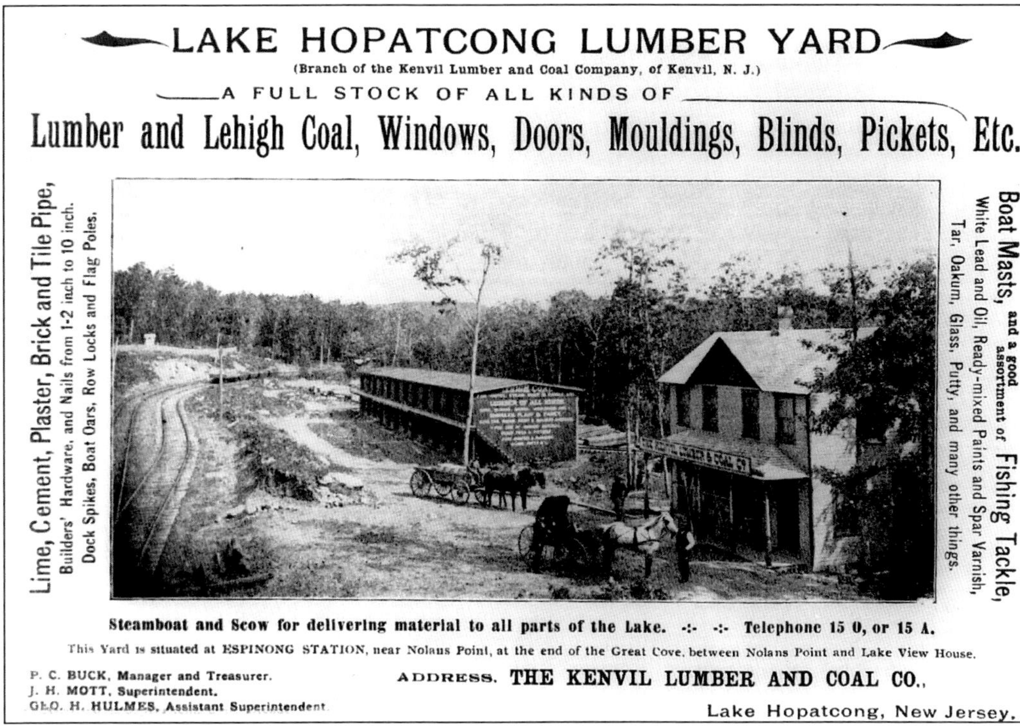

A full line of supplies was available from the Kenvil Lumber and Coal Company, which was located on the main road from Hurdtown to Mount Arlington. Today, Jefferson Lumber is located here and these buildings still exist.

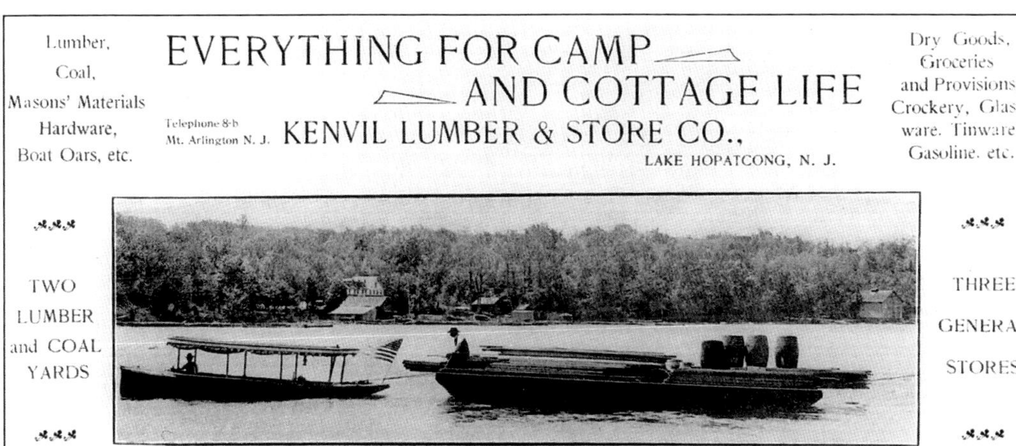

Deliveries around the lake were made via this boat and barge. Unlike today, home deliveries were free of charge in the early 1900s. Although island living was made easier because of this service, it ended with the advent of automobiles.

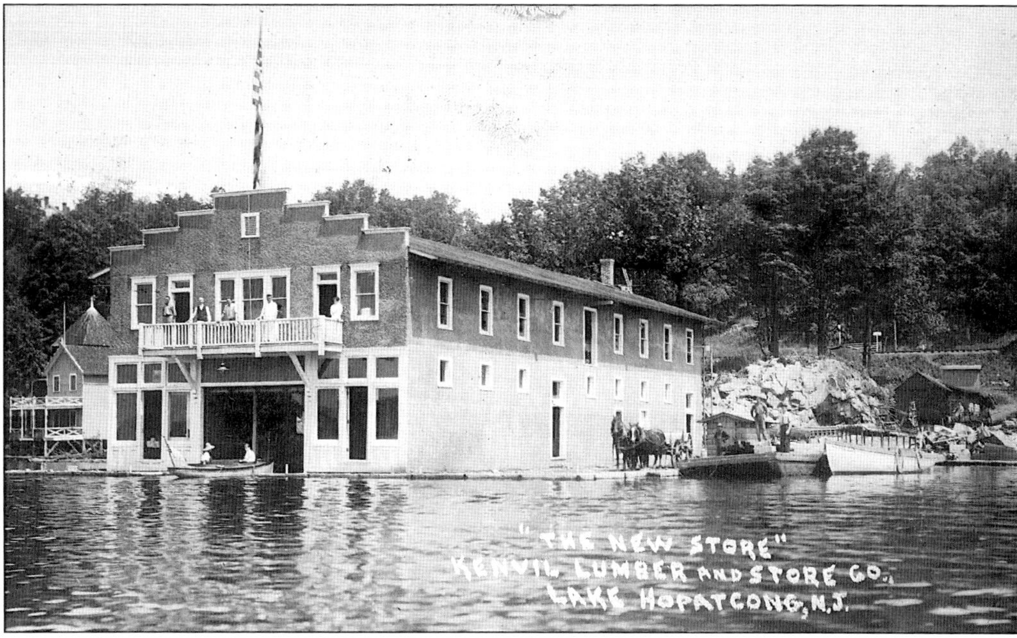

During the winter of 1909, the new Kenvil Store was erected in Great Cove by the Kenvil Lumber and Store Company. The store was constructed on a solid cement pier where launches could enter.

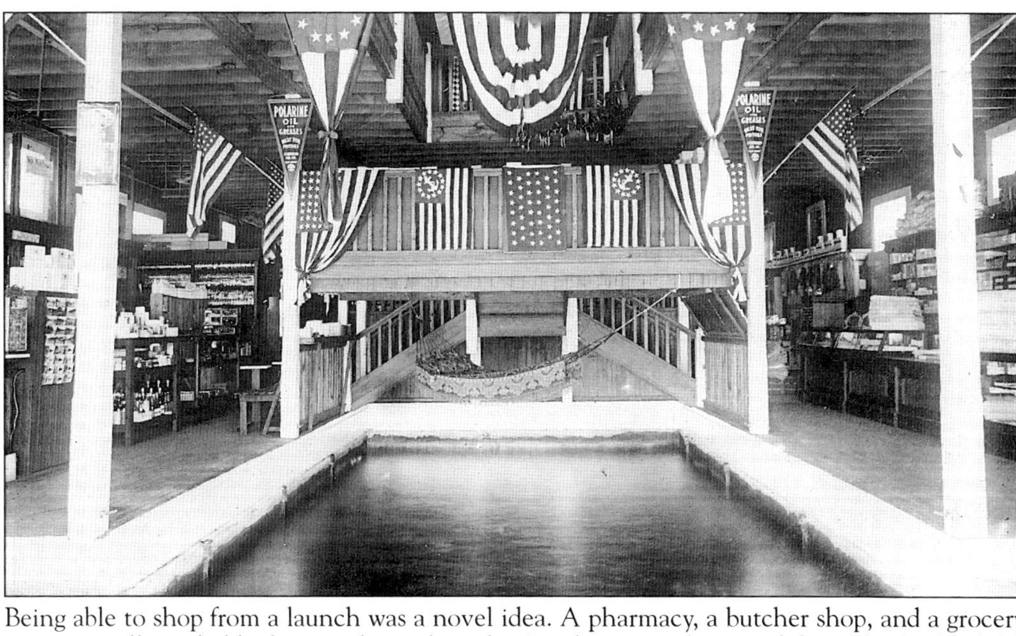

Being able to shop from a launch was a novel idea. A pharmacy, a butcher shop, and a grocery area were all reachable from within a launch. Gasoline was also piped from the back of the Kenvil Store into launches.

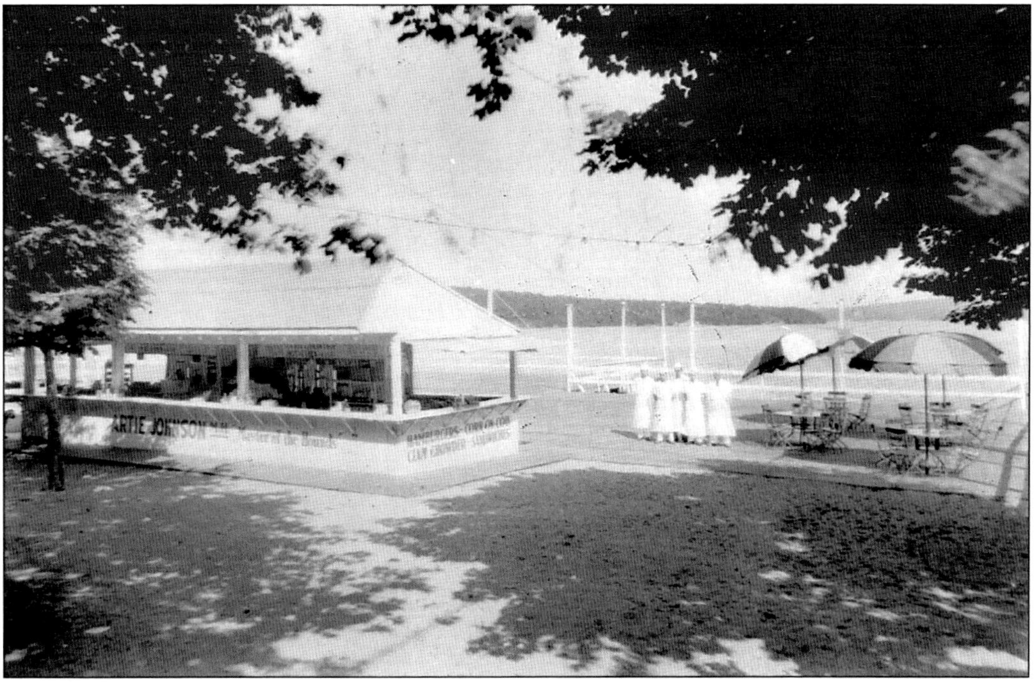

Artie Johnson, better known as "master of the hounds" for making great hot dogs, ran a refreshment stand at the Nolan's Point Amusement Park beginning in the early 1900s. During the 1930s, Johnson built and operated a tavern and dance hall that is currently called Valerie's.

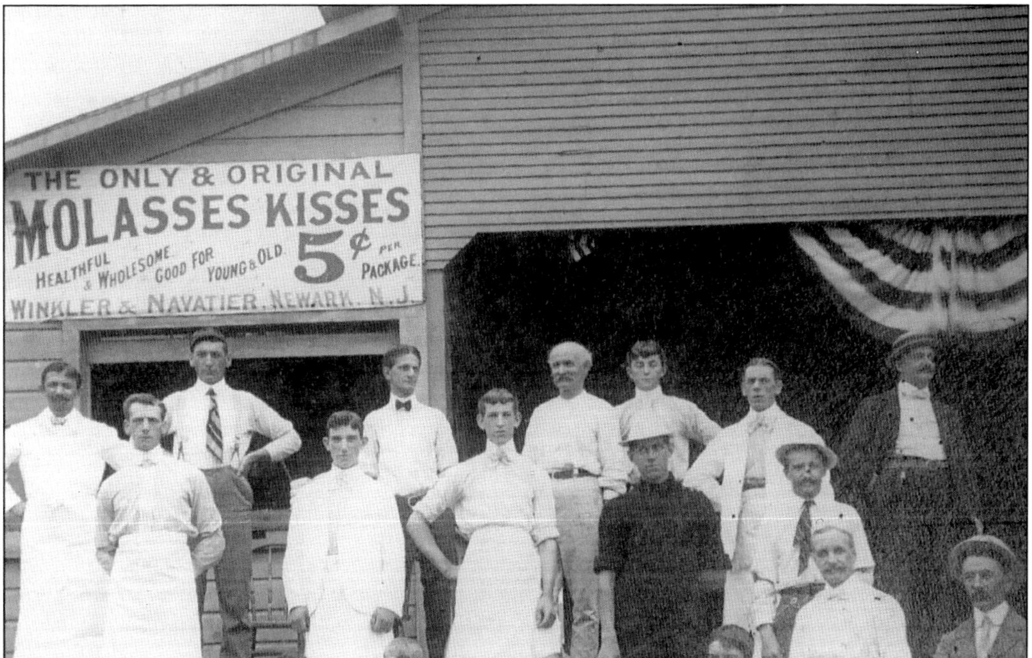

During the summer season of 1906, Winkler & Navatier, would bring Molasses Kisses to Allen's Pavilion. The kisses were made in Newark, and were delivered by train to their Nolan's Point store.

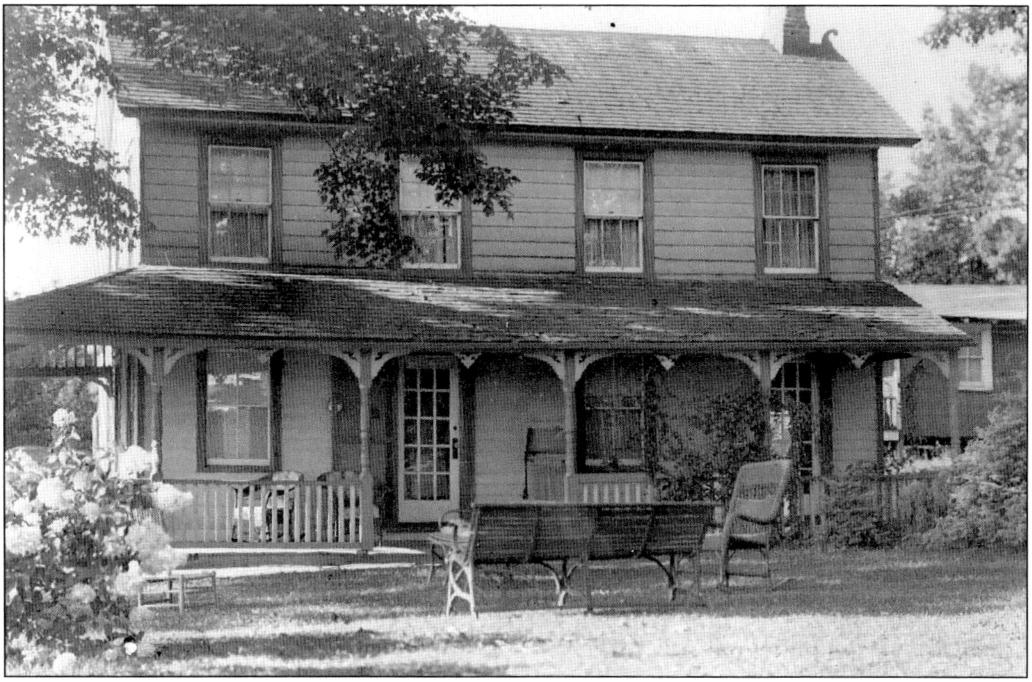

This Nolan's Point home was originally owned by Stephen B. Shaffer. It was built in the mid-1800s, and he lived there until his death in 1899. Shaffer was a firm believer in preserving the knowledge of our past and had gathered a large Native American (Lenape) artifact collection. W.J. Harris lived in this house after Shaffer's death.

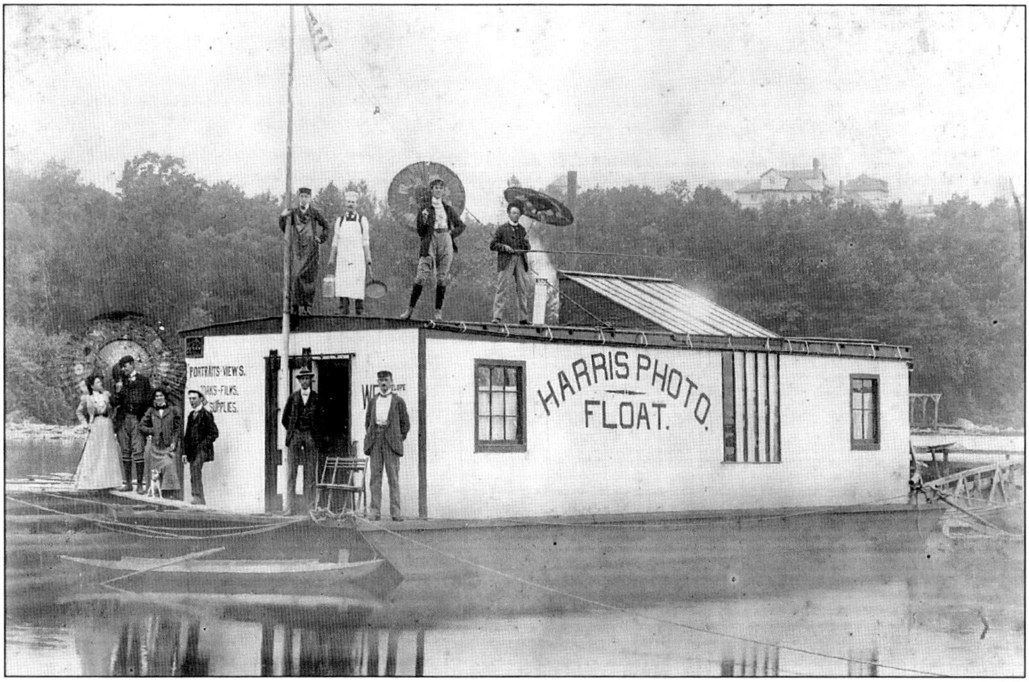

Employees and guests are busy showing off the Harris Photo Float. The skylight in the rear of this float was used to help with the photograph-developing process.

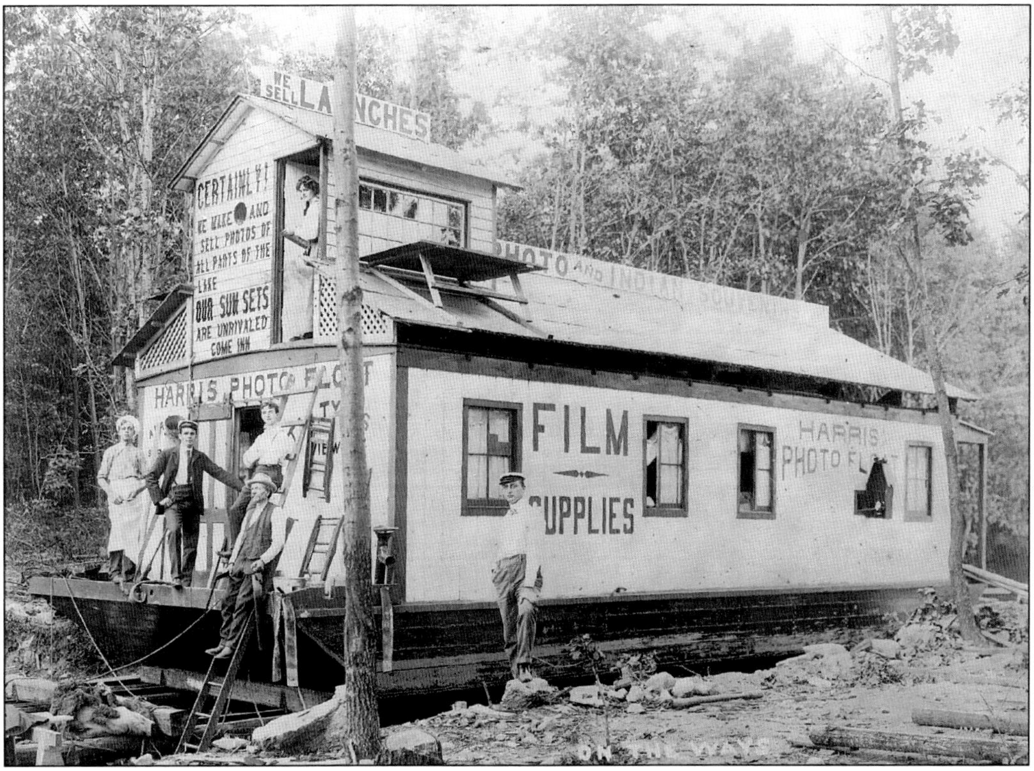

Prior to 1902, Mr. Harris decided to give his float a new look. In order to have more advertising space, Harris added a tower. The locals often commented that it "looked like a church." Unfortunately, in 1903, a knot popped and the float sank. It was moved to the Breslin Dock in Mount Arlington, where it remained.

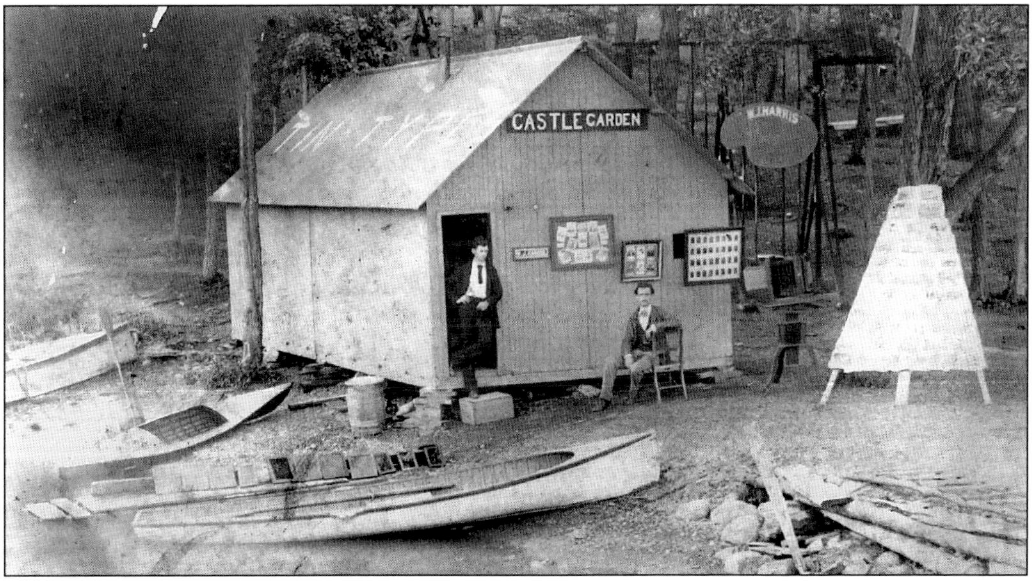

In addition to his permanent studio next to Lee's, Harris had a portable studio in Castle Rock. Tintypes, film, and postcards were also available at the Castle Rock location.

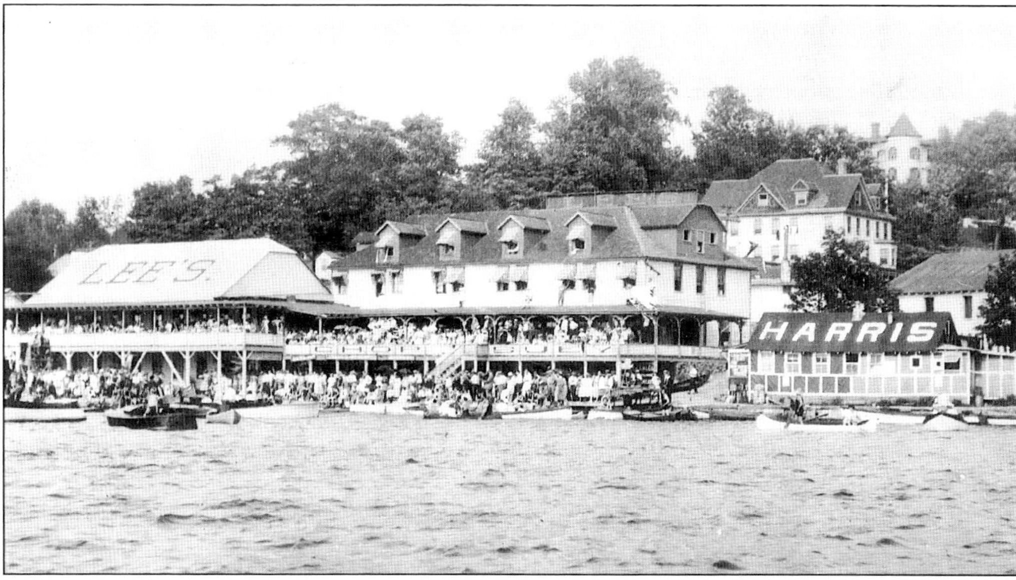

At the studio next to Lee's Pavilion, Harris sold and developed film and also took pictures. Unfortunately, the studio burned in 1924, and Harris did not rebuild.

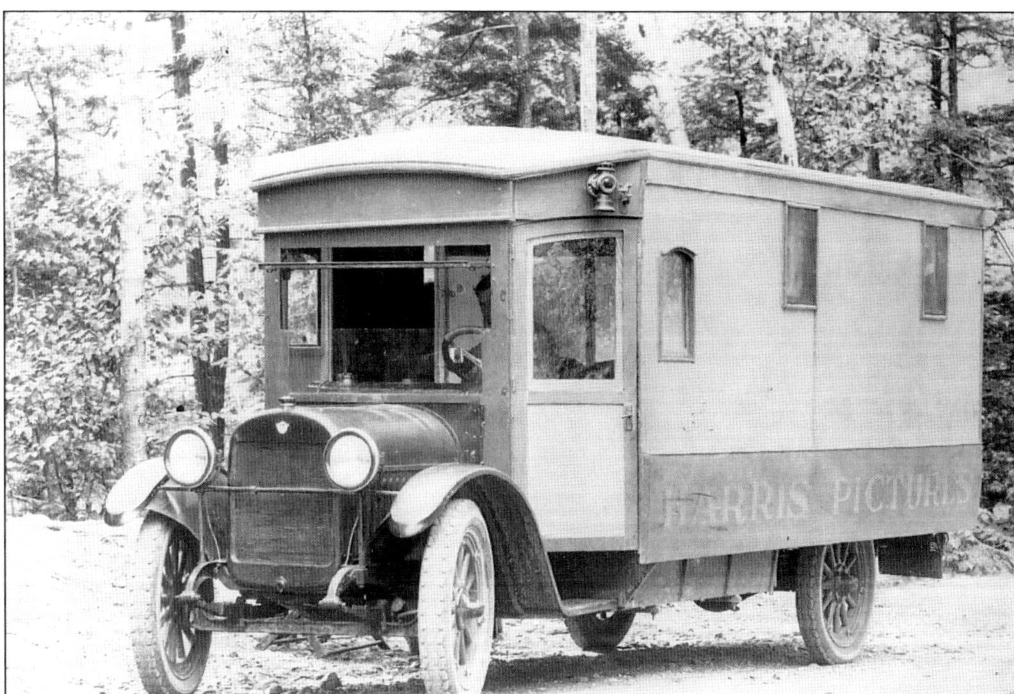

In the winter season, Harris traveled south to St. Augustine, Florida, in his RV. According to his business card, he only allowed five days to reach Florida.

In 1847, the family of Ans B. Decker, who was a renowned fisherman and bait maker, arrived at Lake Hopatcong. By 1852, Decker's father, Maurice, had begun stocking the lake with pickerel. The Decker family lived on Raccoon Island and operated a guide service for freshwater fishing on Lake Hopatcong, Swartzwood Lake, Culver's Lake, Green Pond, and Budd Lake.

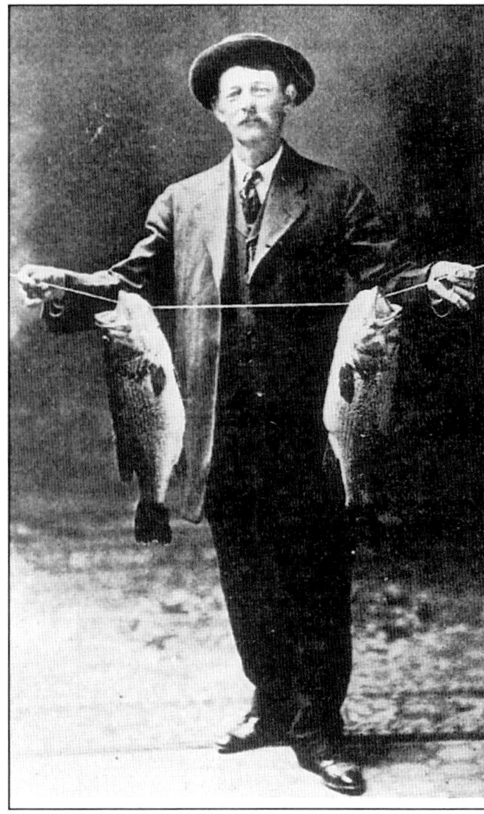

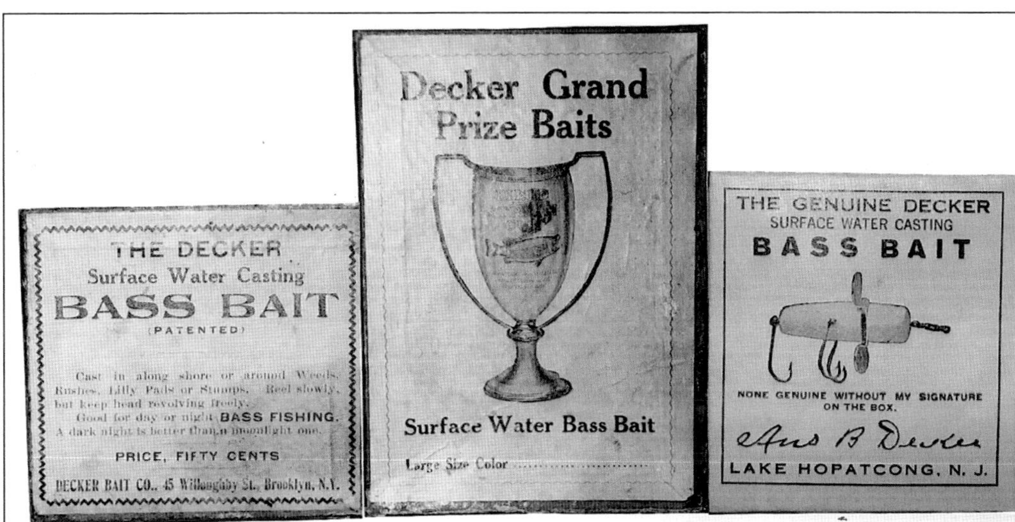

Ans Decker is known as "the father of the wooden bait." His bait and signed boxes are highly collectible. At the age of 14, Ans B. Decker accidentally discovered that bass would jump out of the water after chips of wood. He immediately added three single hooks to the wood and made "fool bait." The center photograph shows a bait box that has a picture of the first grand prize given by *Field & Stream* for the largest big-mouthed bass. The bass was caught by Decker on his surface-water bait.

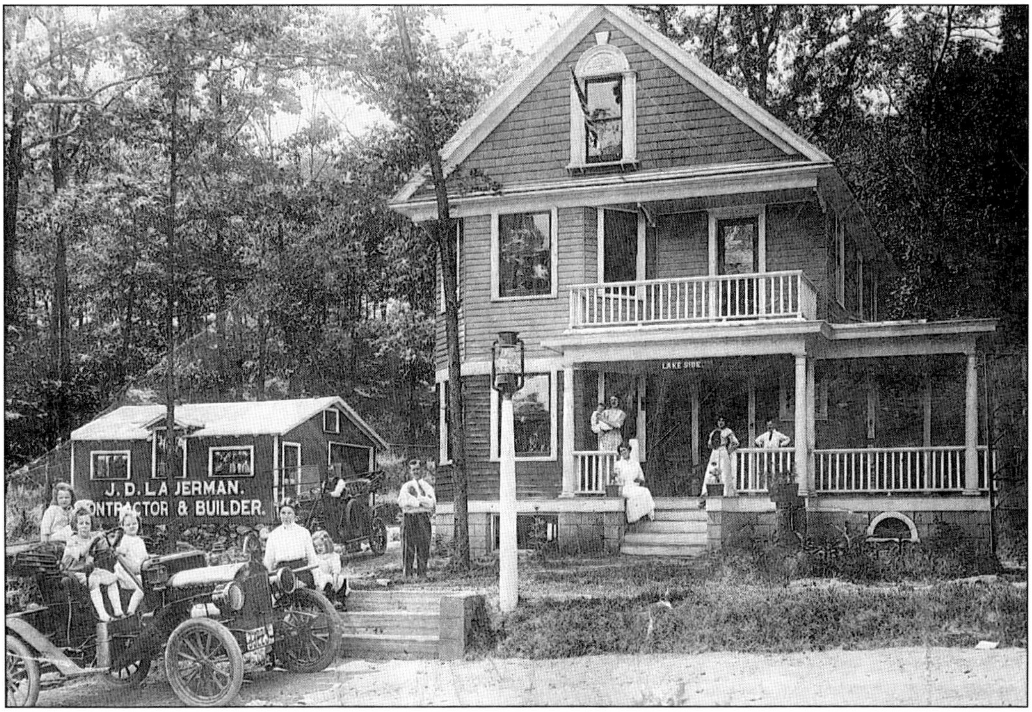

John D. Lauerman, a craftsman, lived on Stonehenge Road along the Central Railroad tracks. He was a builder and contractor who constructed many of the local houses and businesses. No job was too small or too big for Lauerman. Playhouse Park was one of his many undertakings. Lauerman did not believe in contracts, and he felt that a handshake was enough. Lauerman's family still resides in Jefferson Township.

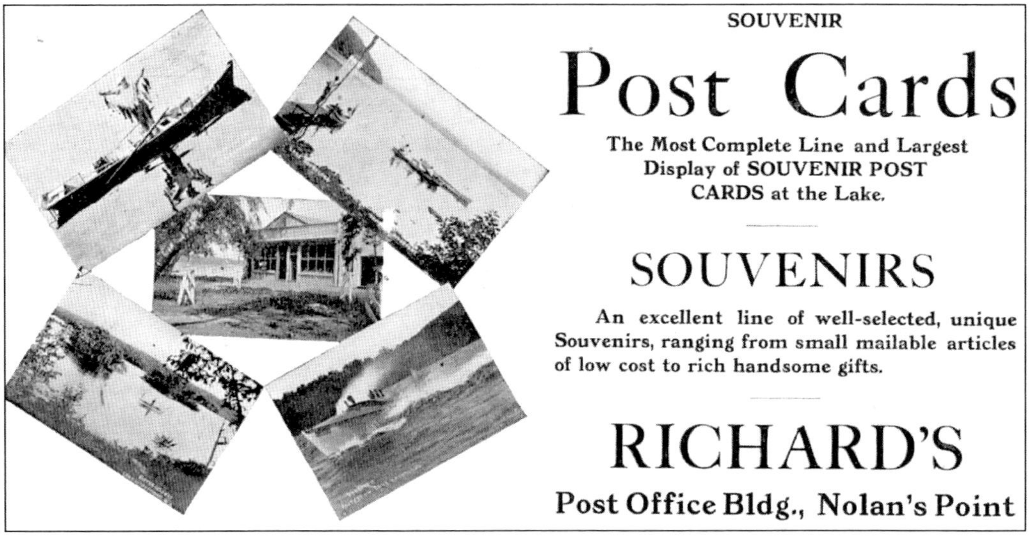

Mr. and Mrs. William Richards had a souvenir store on the other side of the Lake Hopatcong Post Office located on Nolan's Point. They had a complete line of small mailable gifts, mailing cards, candy, and lake souvenirs. If postage was needed, Mr. Richards would sell you stamps and then mail the items.

PHONE HOPATCONG 555 P. O. BOX 64

SPEED BOATS AND MOTOR BOATS FOR HIRE

SIGHTSEEING TRIPS AND MOONLIGHT TRIPS

MOTOR BOAT REPAIR SHOP

ESTIMATES CHEERFULLY GIVEN

GAS AND OIL

CAPT. F. R. CRATER, MGR.

NOLANS POINT LAKE HOPATCONG, N. J.

Frank R. Crater, owner of Crater's Tavern (formerly Allen's No. 3) was an enterprising young man. He was not only a tavern owner but also a postmaster, a boat captain, a repairman, and an outing organizer.

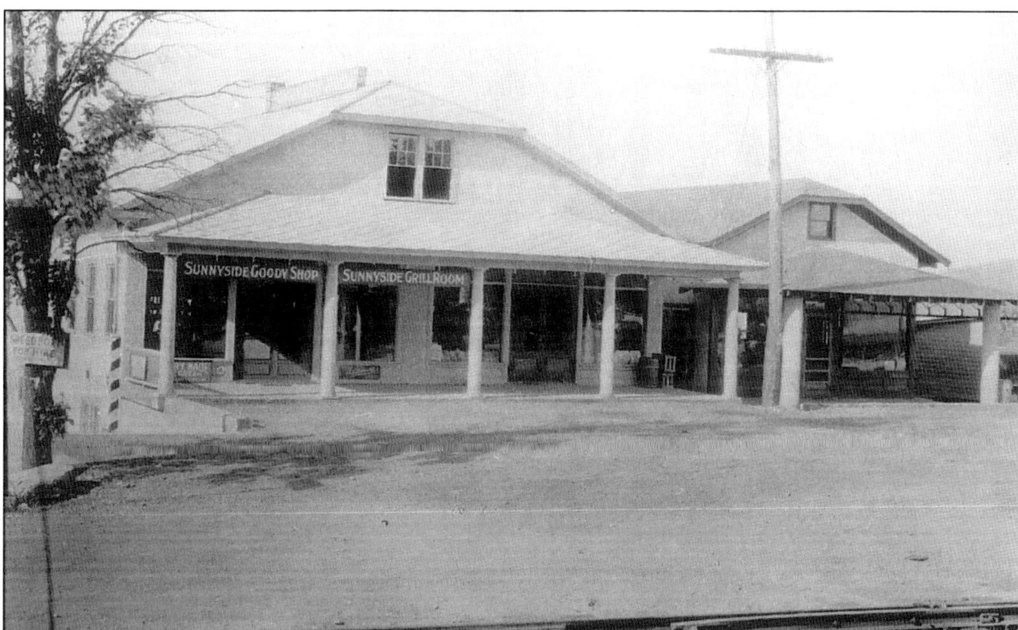

After the Nolan's Point fire of 1924, many new shops were constructed: a goody shop, a grill, and a meat market occupied the ground level floor, and a barbershop and bait store were available on the lower level of the building.

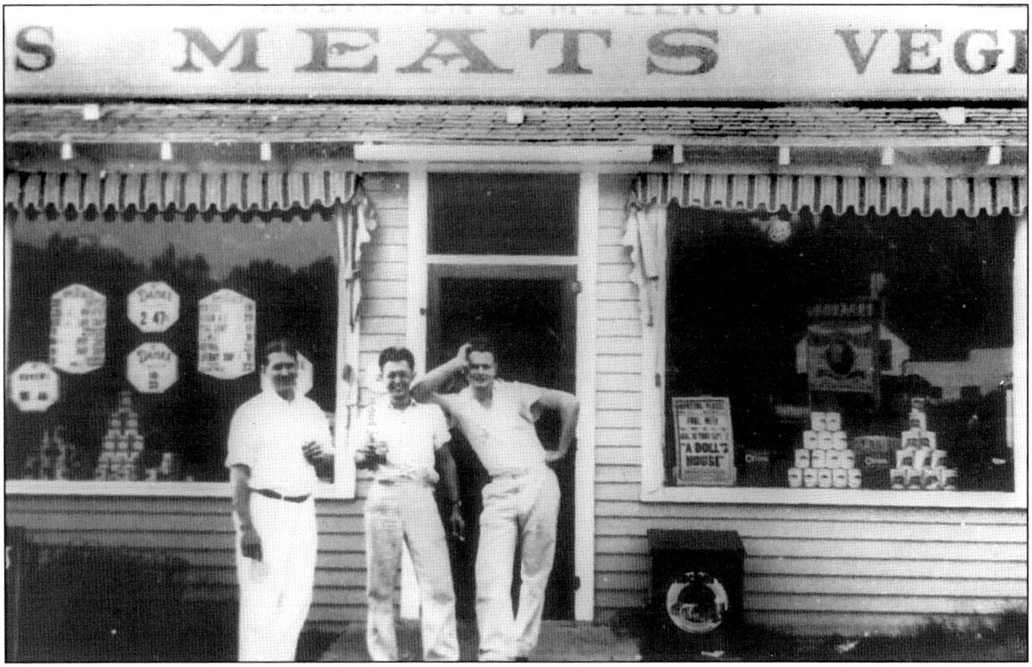

Directly across the street from the Espanong Hotel was a small neighborhood market called the Espanong Store. Joseph Patrisco, proprietor, would make arrangements to deliver orders to any part of the lake. If planned a day ahead, home-killed broilers were available. By the mid-1930s, the Robinsons and Mc Elroys took over the market. This market is currently a deli.

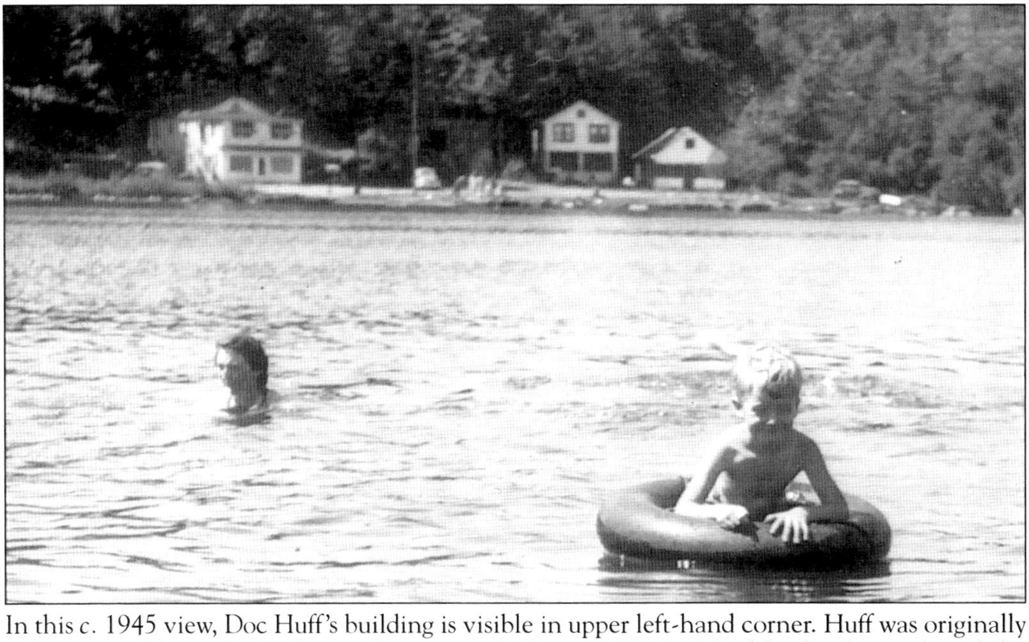

In this *c.* 1945 view, Doc Huff's building is visible in upper left-hand corner. Huff was originally a dentist, and his wife, Leah, ran the tavern. In June 1956, the Mitchko family purchased the tavern and renamed it Tiny's. Additions have been added to the original structure, but it has remained a tavern.

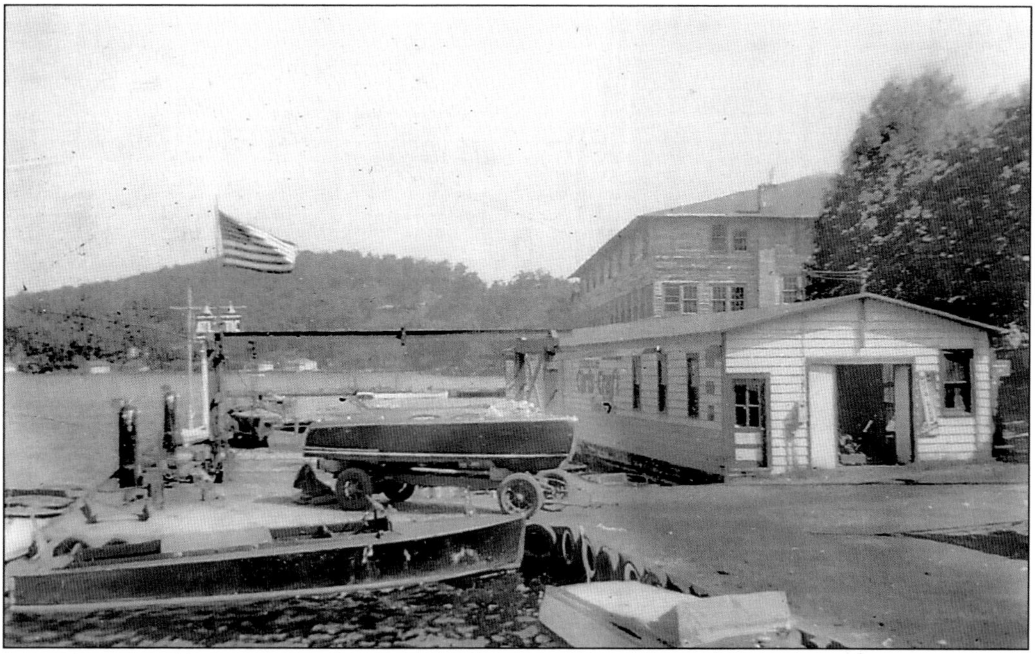

Next door to Allen's No. 3, Henry Green, a former Jersey City resident, owned and operated the Lakeland Marine Base on Nolan's Point. He was an authorized dealer for Century and Gar Wood Boats. A repair shop, parts department, storage, and boat-building area were on site.

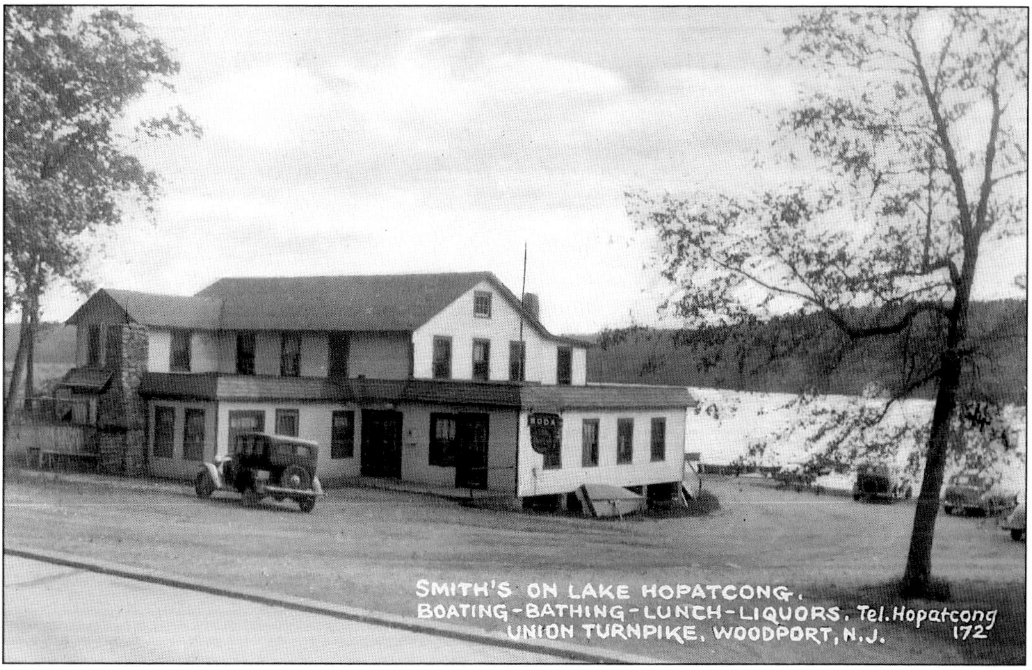

Smith's, better known to the locals as Smitty's, was built by Agustice V. Smith c. 1921 on property that was purchased from the Chamberlain family. Over the years, docks, a showroom, a repair shop, and storage areas have been added. The facility has recently changed hands.

Live . . . this summer on the water!

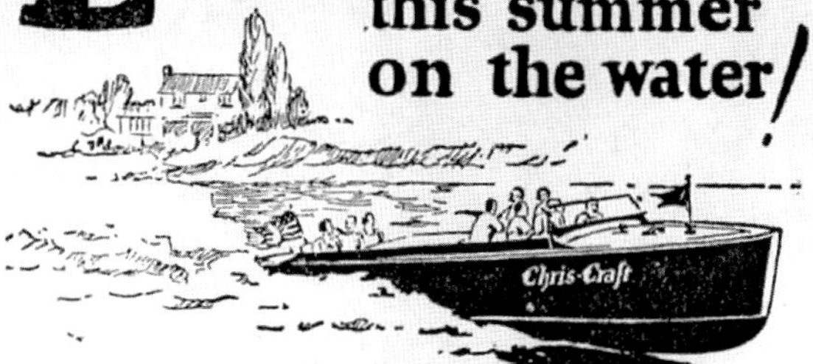

LET a Chris-Craft speed you away from the city's heat and dust . . . break the monotony of business and household routine . . . provide safe, clean, healthful sport for the children.

A Chris-Craft is as useful as your family car . . . and as instantly available. Easy to drive and economical in operation. Seating capacity eight to fourteen.

CHRIS SMITH & SONS BOAT CO.
Algonac, Michigan

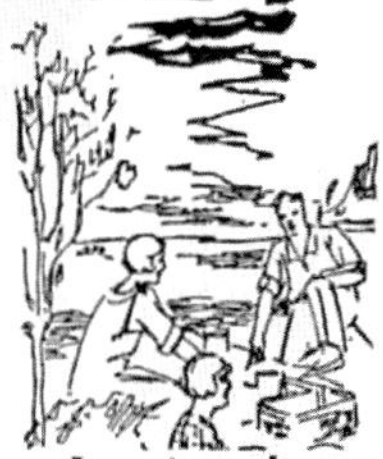

Investigate the new Chris-Craft Deferred Payment Plan.

$2235 to $9750 *22 to 30 Feet—30 to 45 Miles an Hour—82 to 200 Horsepower.*

Chris-Craft $2235 to $9750

WORLD'S LARGEST BUILDERS OF ALL-MAHOGANY MOTOR BOATS

Competition Proves the Evinrude

EVINRUDE VICTORIES

May 20—Nolan's Point, 1st Place, Class C.
May 30—Lake Mohawk, 1st, 2nd, 3rd, Class C Amateur.
May 30—Lake Mohawk, 1st, 2nd, 3rd, 4th, Class C, Free-For-All.
July 4—Brady Park, 1st, 2nd, 3rd, Class C.
July 14 & 15—Nolan's Point, 1st, 2nd, 3rd, 4th, 5th, Class C, Amateur.
July 14 & 15—Nolan's Point, 1st, 2nd, 3rd, 4th., 5th, Class C, Free-For-All.
July 22—Lake Mohawk, 1st, 2nd, 3rd, 4th, Class C.
Aug. 1—Sunnyside, 1st, 2nd, 3rd, Free-For-All.
Aug. 5—Greenwood Lake, 1st, 2nd, 3rd, 4th, 5th, 6th, Class C, Amateur.
Aug. 5—Greenwood Lake, 1st, 2nd, 3rd, 4th, 5th, 6th, Class C, Free-For-All.
Aug. 5—Greenwood Lake, 1st, 3rd, 4th, Unlimited Class.
Aug. 13—New Bedford, 1st 2nd, Class C and Unlimited.
Aug. 18—Green Pond, 1st, 2nd, 3rd, 4th, 5th, Class C.
Aug. 19—Brady Park, 1st, 2nd, 3rd, Free-For-All.
Aug. 26—Lake Moosic, Scranton, 1st, 2nd, 3rd, 4th, Class C, Amateur.
Aug. 26—Lake Moosic, Scranton, 1st, 2nd, 3rd, Unlimited Class.
Aug. 26—Lake Moosic, Scranton, 1st, 2nd, 3rd, 4th, Class C, Free-For-All.
Aug. 26—Philadelphia, 1st, 2nd, Class C, Free-For-All.
Aug. 26—Philadelphia, 1st, 2nd, Unlimited Class.

The above mentioned races, run in this locality, were, with one exception, all won by local boats and EVINRUDE motors. This is but a reflection of EVINRUDE'S unceasing country-wide victories. 95% of these winning boats were BABY WHALES!

EVINRUDE MODELS—6, 12, 16 H. P.—all roller bearing & ballbearing equipped, $150 and up.

BABY WHALES—12 & 14 foot lengths.

FAMILY OUTBOARD BOATS—to carry 6-8-10 people, $100 and up.

ON DISPLAY at our SHOWROOM

MAKE ARRANGEMENTS NOW FOR WINTER STORAGE AND BOAT AND ENGINE REPAIR WORK
TO BE DONE DURING THE WINTER — REASONABLE RATES
OUR MODERN MACHINE & REPAIR SHOP IS OPEN ALL YEAR

Hockenjos & Hockenjos

Great Cove — Lake Hopatcong, N. J.

Phone Hopatcong 24 - 138

By the mid-1920s, Hockenjos & Hockenjos had begun business in Great Cove. Boating was still very popular on Lake Hopatcong, and new models and types were introduced yearly. Local races, using Evinrude motors, were held to demonstrate the superior quality of the product. Chris Crafts became very popular and were available at Hockenjos & Hockenjos.

What was originally part of the Consumer Coal & Ice Company complex near Callaghan's Cove eventually became Jack's Beach, named after Jack Butler. The building was constructed out of icehouse doors.

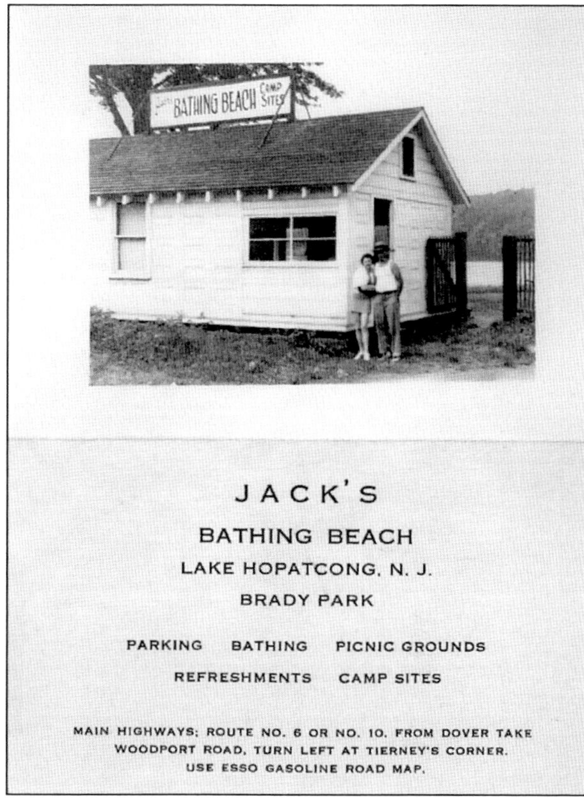

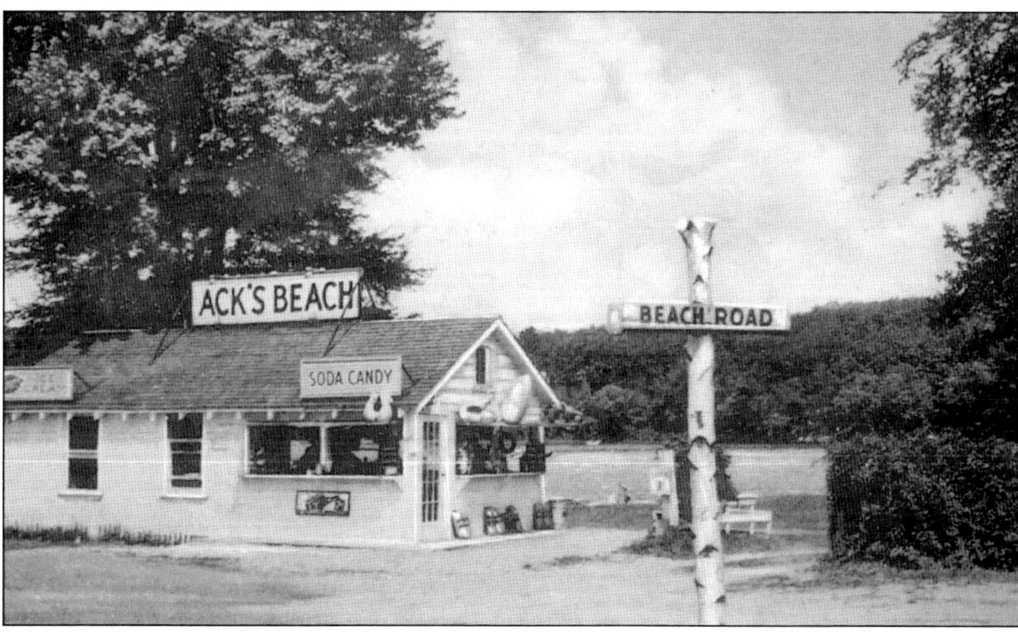

Henry and Ruth Ackerman changed the name of Jack's Beach to Ack's Beach *c.* 1952. Windows were added to the front and sides of the building, and beach toys and refreshments were available.

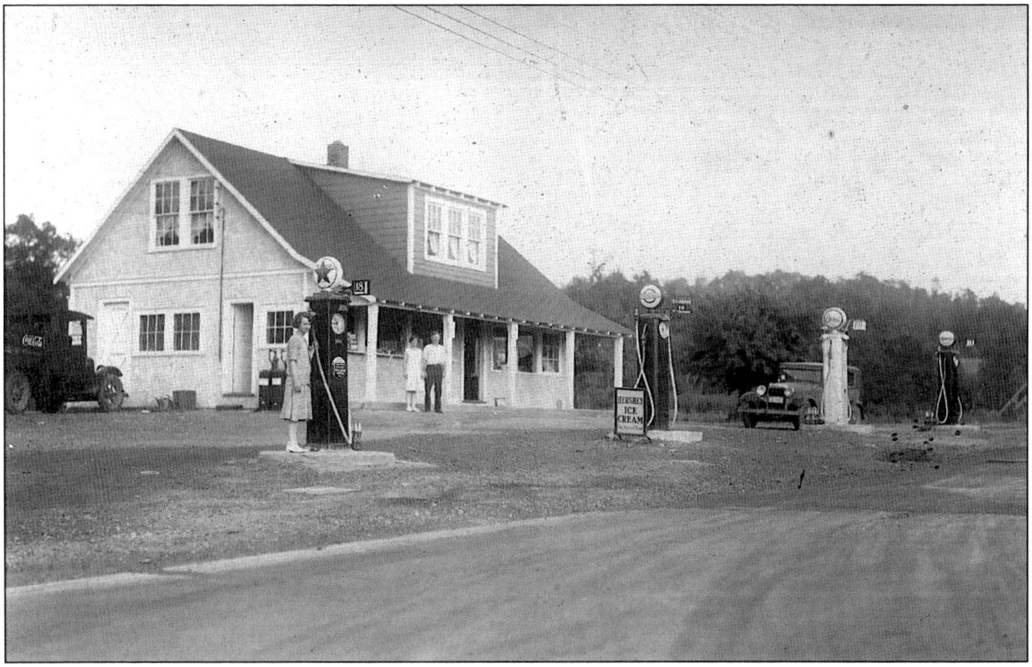

Increased automobile usage and local development created a need for gasoline stations. William and Ellen Briggs opened a gas station and snack bar *c.* 1933 on property currently occupied by McDonald's and the shopping center. Eventually, the couple added a tavern. Prior to the construction of the Jefferson Township Firehouse, fire equipment was stored on this property.

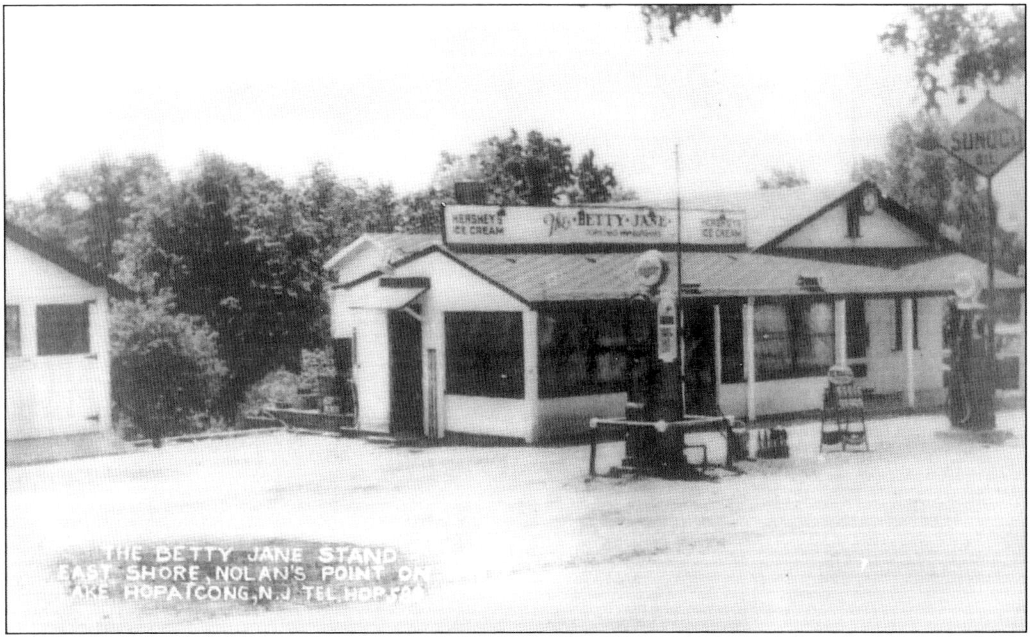

In the early 1930s, George Hulmes sold property on Espanong Road to Robert and Clara Slockbower. The Betty Jane was constructed and named after their two daughters. Originally, it was a gas station and refreshment stand, and it eventually became a tavern. Recently, this building has been renovated and is currently called Anthony's Lounge.

Seven

HELPING HANDS

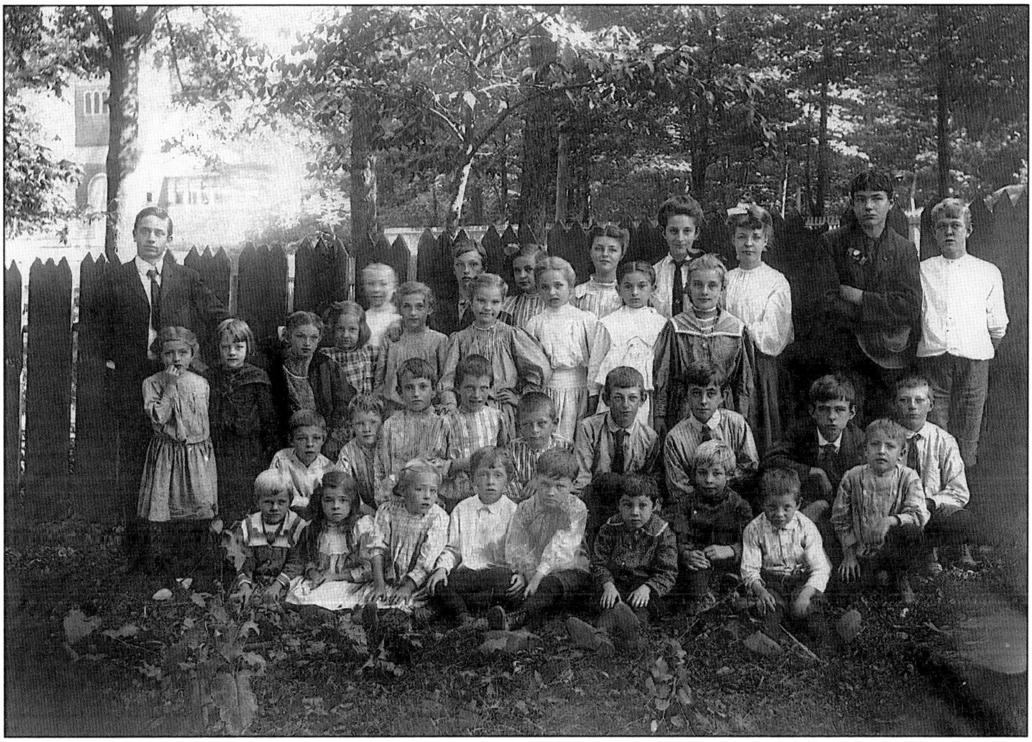

Located diagonally across the street from the Lake Hopatcong United Methodist Church was a one-room schoolhouse for kindergarten through eighth grade. Children of local business owners Myrtle C. Hulmes and Irene Richards attended this school from *c.* 1906 until 1910, when the school closed and they were transferred to the Nolan's Point school.

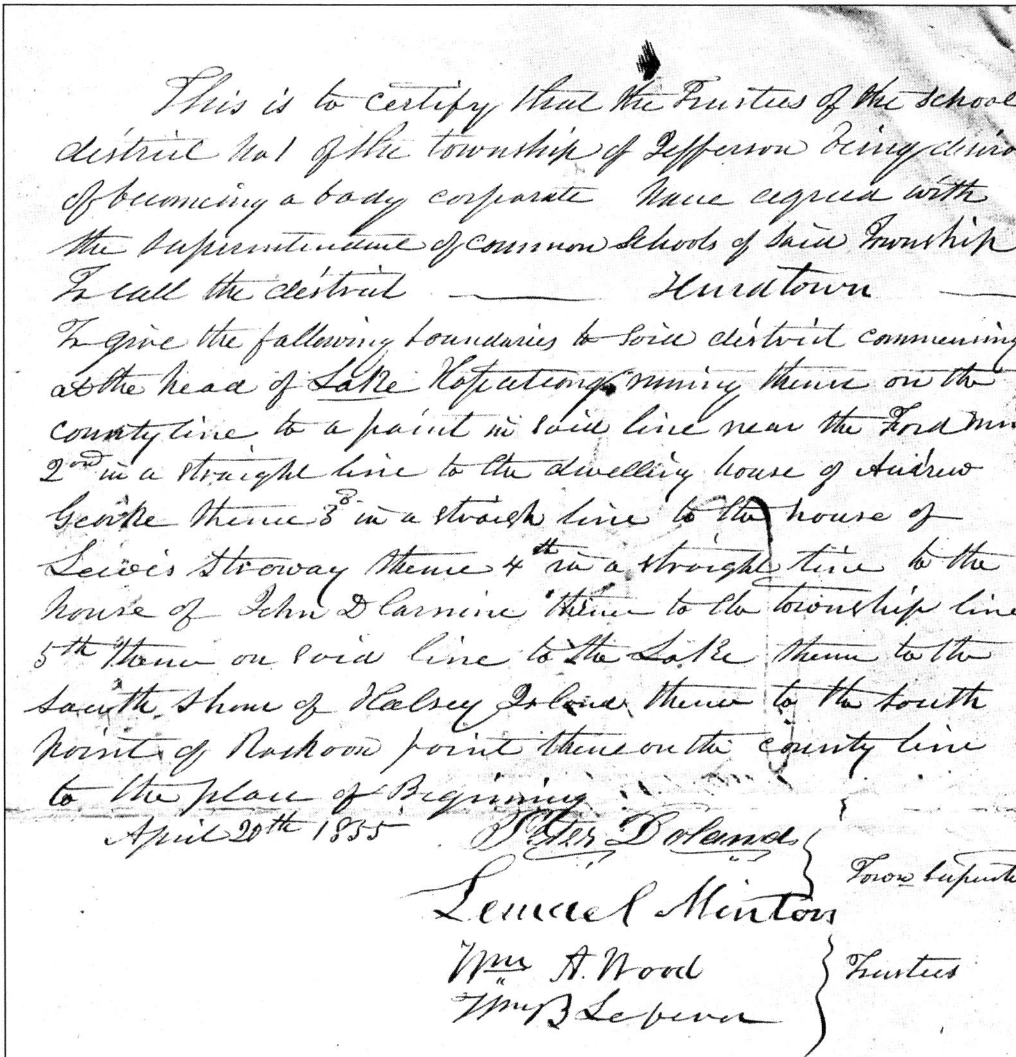

This is to certify that the Trustees of the School district No 1 of the township of Jefferson being desirous of becoming a body corporate have agreed with the Superintendent of Common Schools of said Township To call the district —— Hurdtown —

To give the following boundaries to said district commencing at the head of Lake Hopatcong running thence on the county line to a point in said line near the Ford Min[illegible] 2nd in a straight line to the dwelling house of Andrew George thence 3d in a straight line to the house of Lewis Stroway thence 4th in a straight line to the house of John D Larmine thence to the township line 5th thence on said line to the Lake thence to the South Shore of Halsey Island thence to the South point of Raccoon point thence on the county line to the place of Beginning

April 20th 1855

Peter Doland } Town Supert

Lemuel Minton

Wm A. Wood } Trustees

Wm B Lefever

On April 20, 1855, Jefferson Township Superintendent Doland and trustees Minton, Wood, and LeFever signed the documents that created the Hurdtown School in District No. 1 of Jefferson Township.

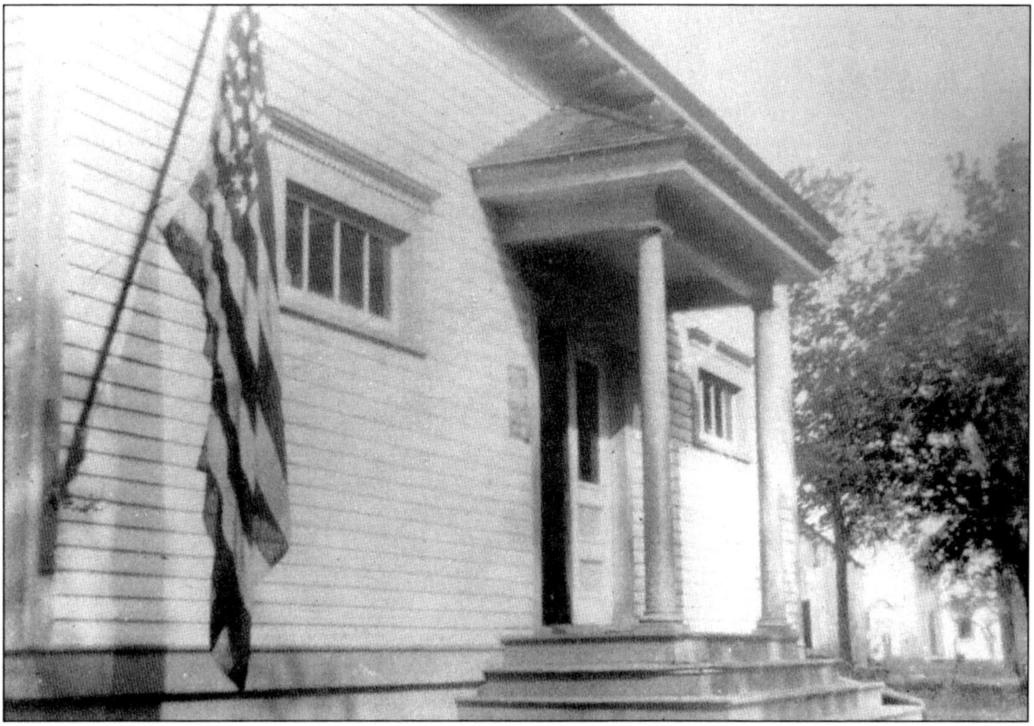

The Hurdtown School was located on the Union Turnpike (Route 181). This school was larger than the Nolan's Point School and also housed children from kindergarten through eighth grade.

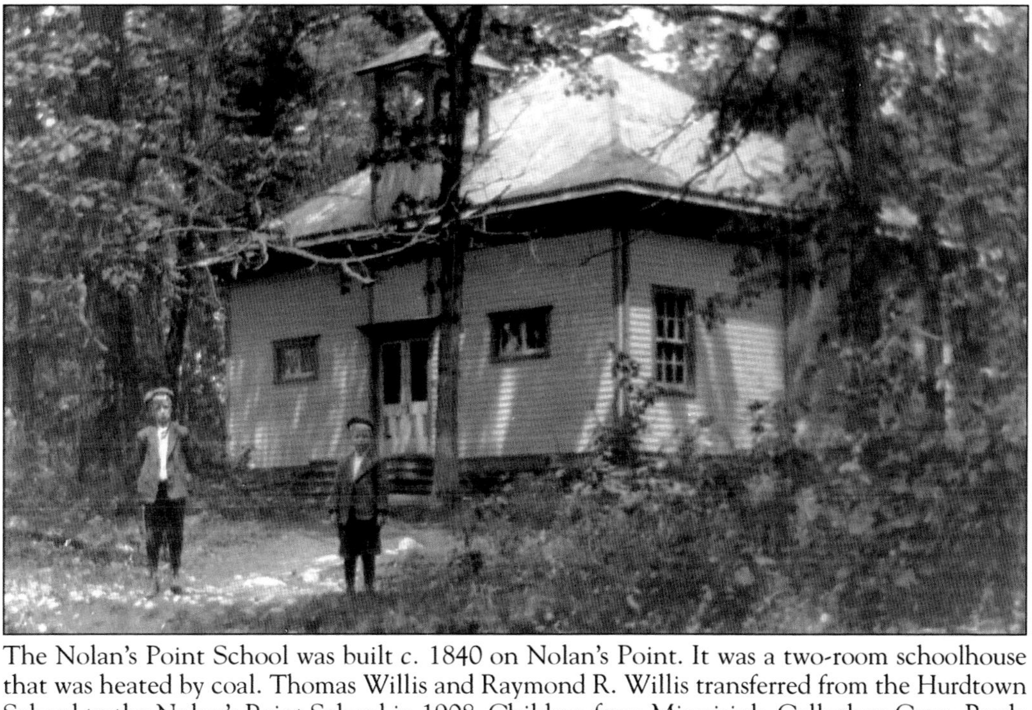

The Nolan's Point School was built *c.* 1840 on Nolan's Point. It was a two-room schoolhouse that was heated by coal. Thomas Willis and Raymond R. Willis transferred from the Hurdtown School to the Nolan's Point School in 1908. Children from Minnisink, Callaghan Cove, Brady Park, and Espanong attended the Nolan's Point School until the consolidated school opened.

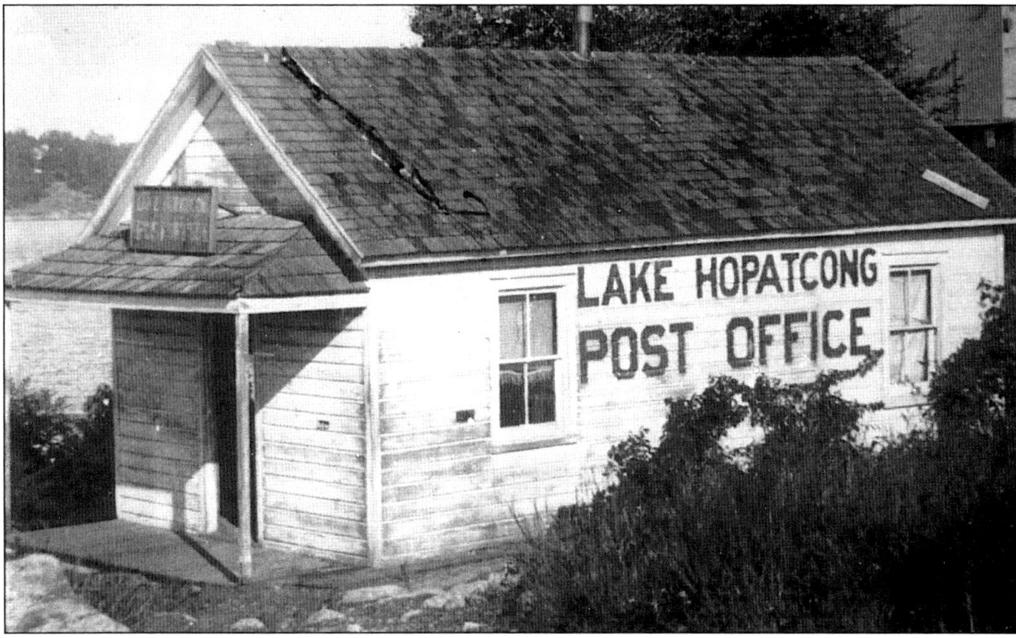

In 1890, the Lake Hopatcong Post Office was located in today's Jefferson House parking lot. Franklin Schaffer built this structure, and Charles Edwards was made postmaster. His sister Annie Edwards was assistant postmaster and, in 1894, became postmaster. Eventually, the post office moved to Allen's Pavilion No. 1. Every time Allen's burned, the post office was rebuilt.

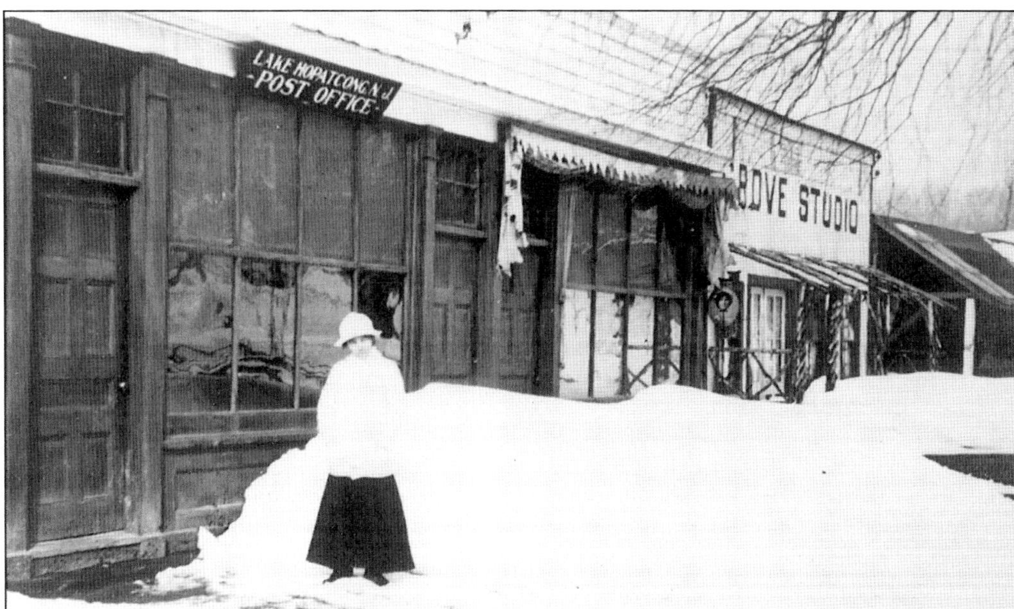

The post office was located next to Allen's Pavilion and shared a building with a souvenir store. William Richards was postmaster and his wife, Etta, had the souvenir store. You could buy postcards from Etta and step across the store to buy stamps from her husband. In the winter, the post office had a crew of two: a postmaster and one helper. Two more helpers were added in the summer.

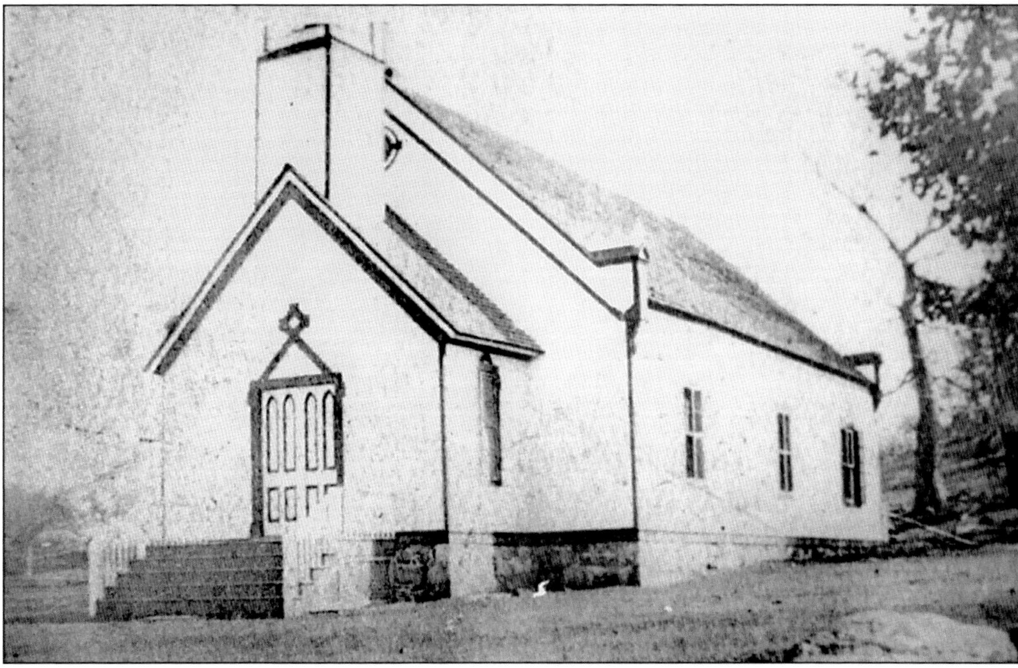

Hurdtown's Methodist Episcopal Church, located between Route 15 North and South, was built *c.* 1870. The Hurd family had close ties with this church. For a time, Hurdtown's Methodist Episcopal Church was joint circuit with the Lake Hopatcong Church. The minister would travel by horse, canoe, or ice skates between locations each Sunday.

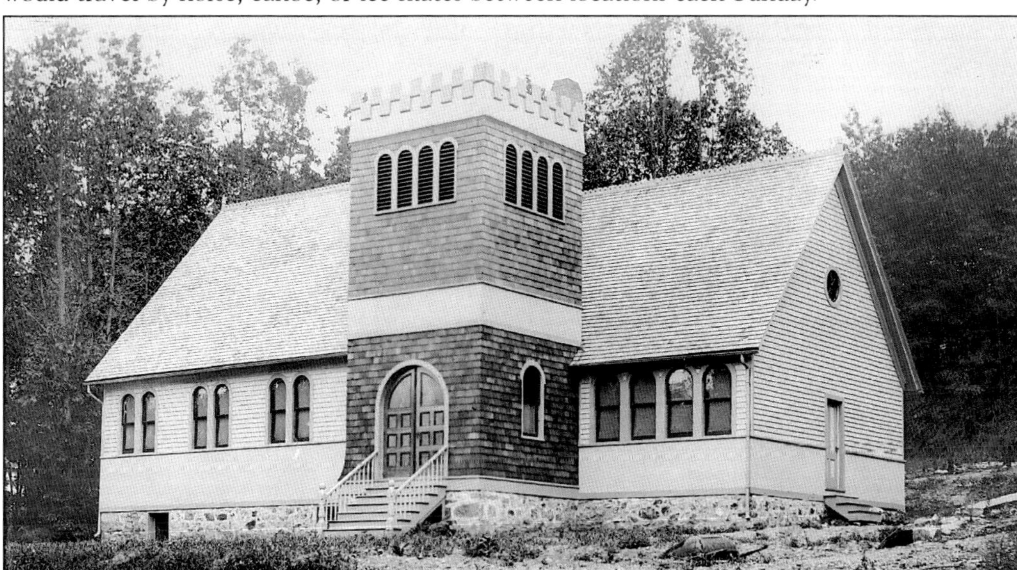

The Lake Hopatcong Methodist Episcopal Church, located on Howard Boulevard, was built in 1873. In the fall of 1889, it was destroyed by fire. Rebuilding commenced, and the Honorable Sen. L.A. Thompson of Somerville came to the rescue. He offered to finance the rebuilding of the church on the same site. The building was dedicated in 1901. Six years later, the women of the church made a payment of $500 to Senator Thompson, who had surprised them by making the $500 a donation.

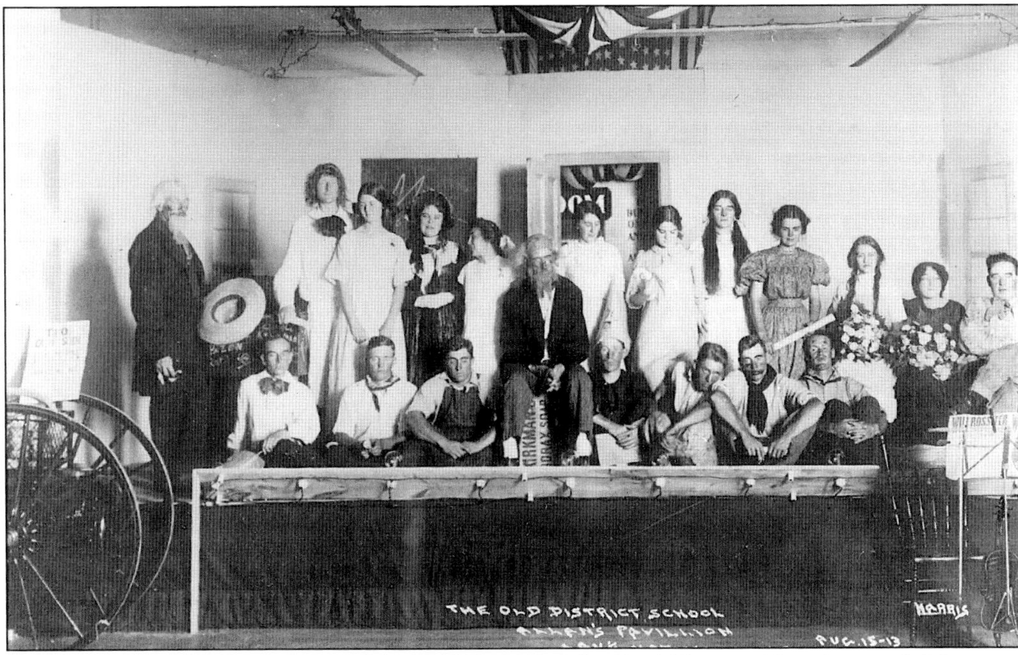

Seen here is the newer version of the Old District School. A *Farce in Two Acts with Music* was presented by the Christian Endeavor Society of Lake Hopatcong Methodist Episcopal Church on August 15, 1913, at Allen's Pavilion on Nolan's Point.

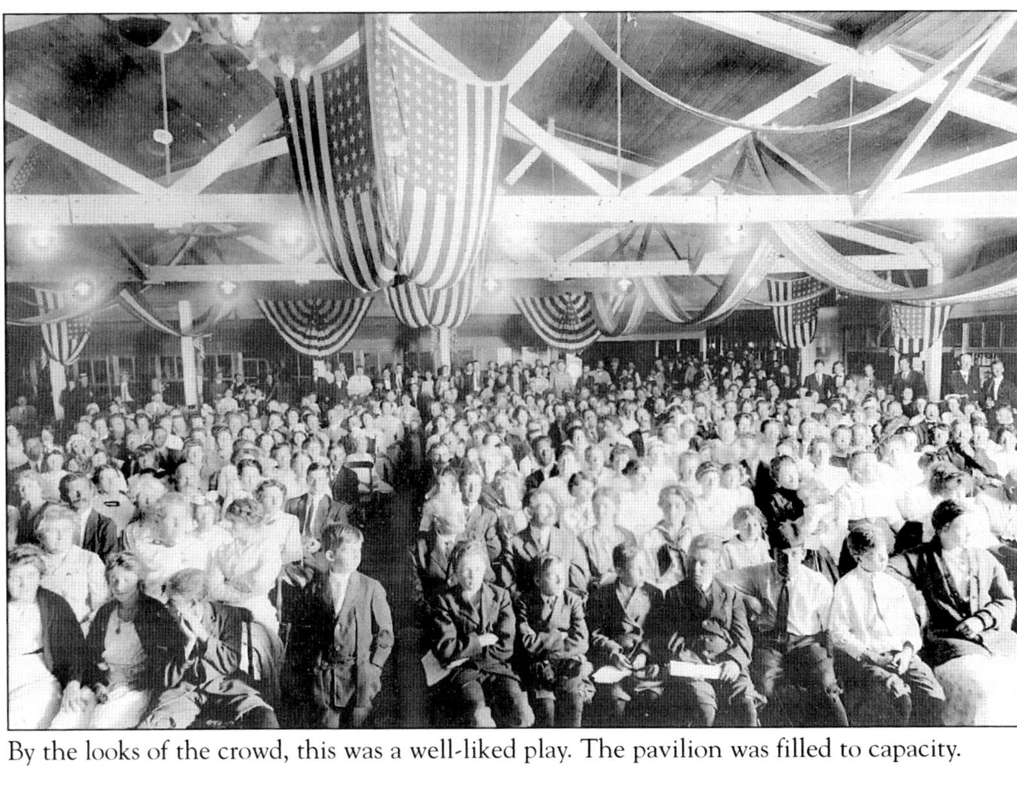

By the looks of the crowd, this was a well-liked play. The pavilion was filled to capacity.

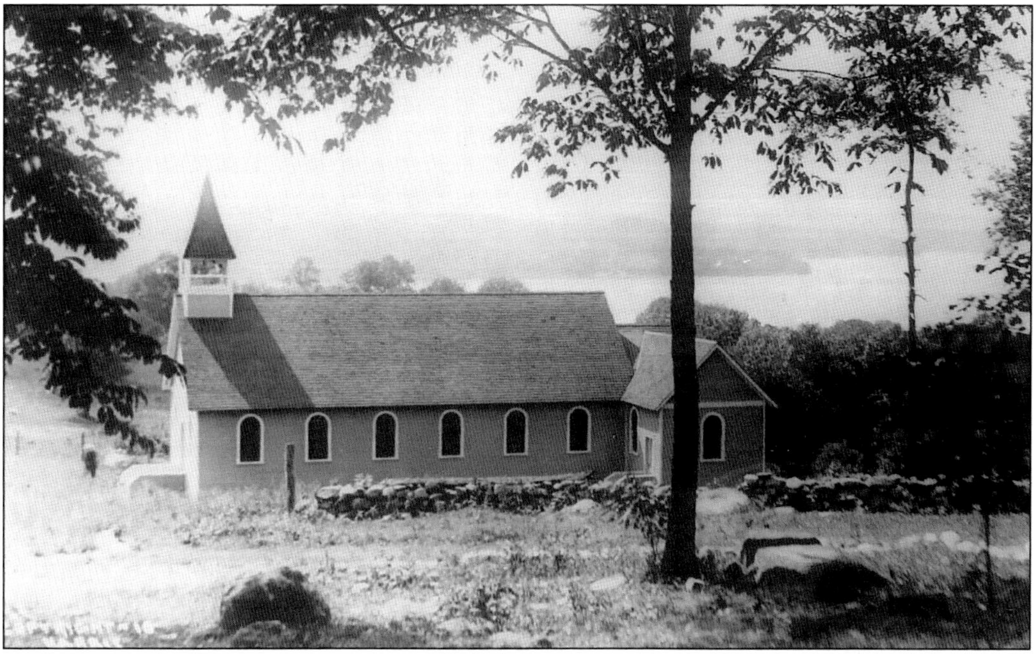

The Star of the Sea Roman Catholic Church was located on the heights of Nolan's Point. The Brady family donated this land for religious purposes. As seen in this *c.* 1910 photograph, the church served the Nolan's Point area.

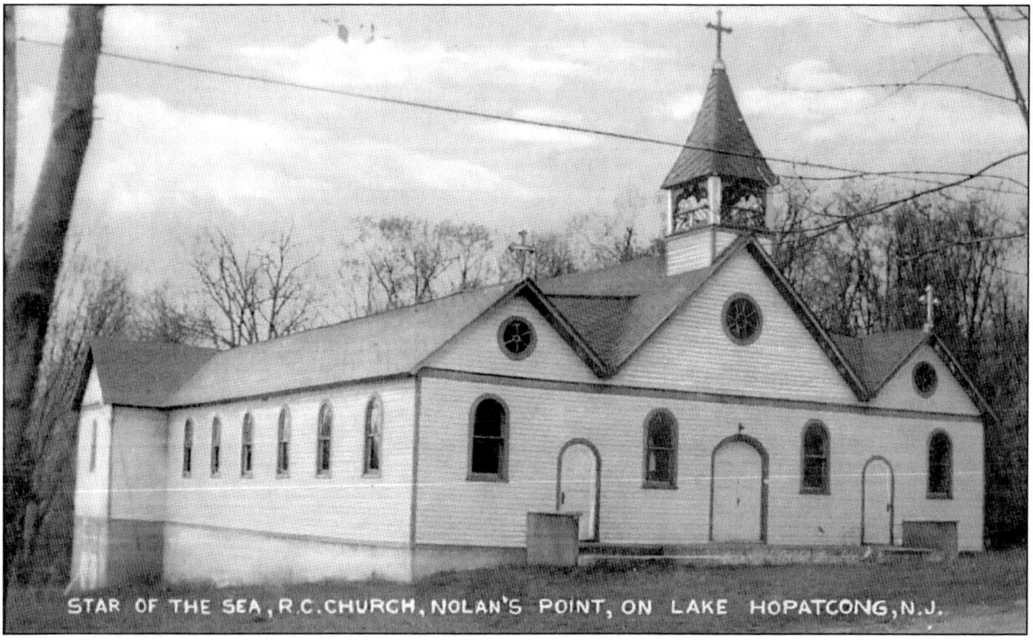

As the summer community grew, it became necessary to enlarge the church. By putting on shows, the vaudeville performers helped to earn the money to build the additions. The church burned in 1965, and a new one was built on what is now Espanong Road.

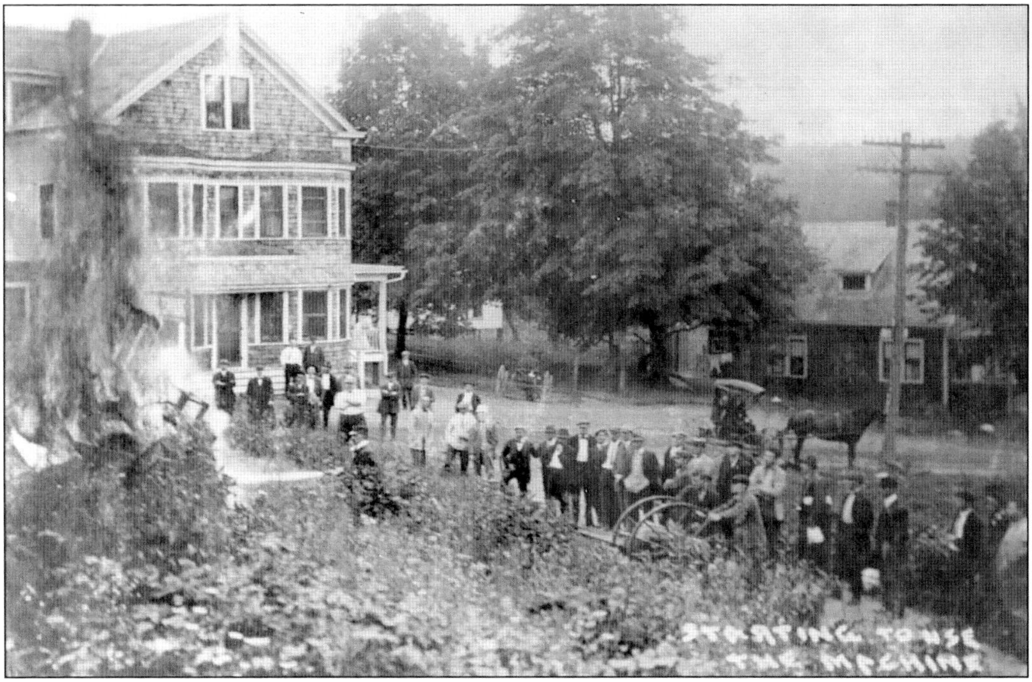

One of the earliest Jefferson Township fire organizations was known as the Espanong Fire Brigade. In order to become accustomed to the latest firefighting equipment, volunteers set a practice fire in front of the Espanong Hotel, as shown in this c. 1913 image .

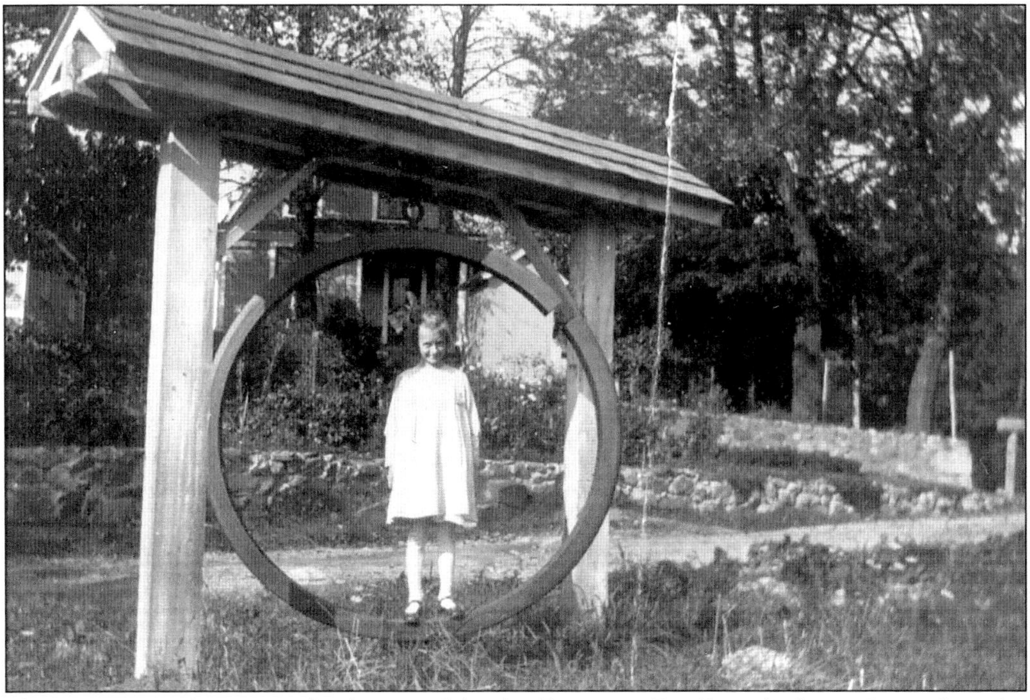

This gong, one of two, was the fire signal for the Espanong Fire Brigade. It was located on the corner of Espanong Road and Stonehenge Road.

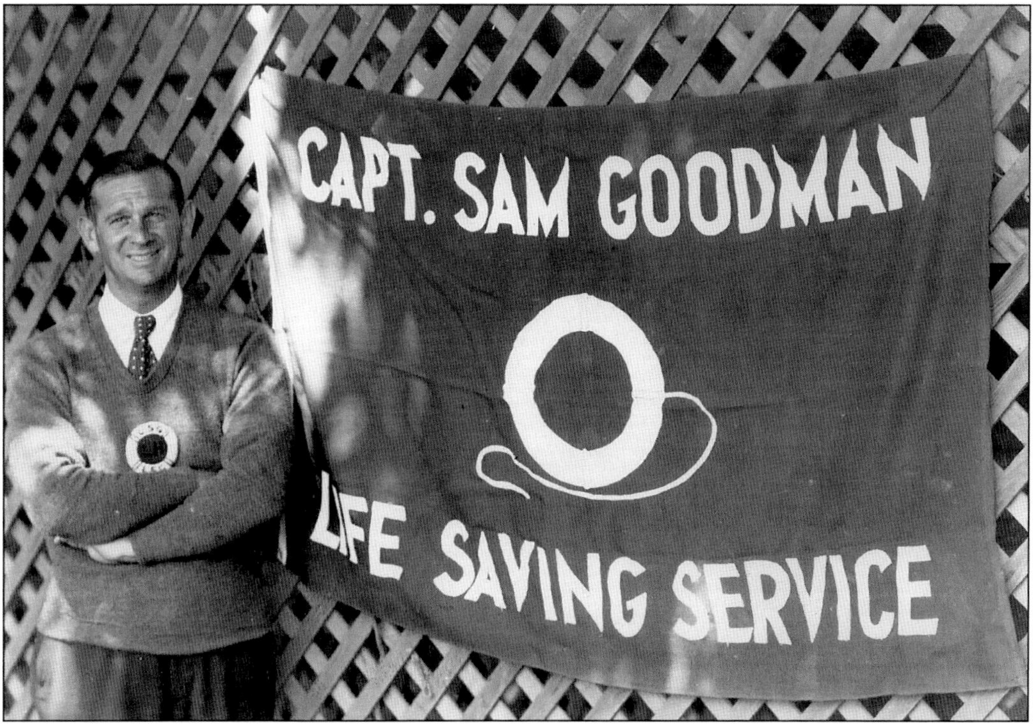

For many years, Capt. Sam Goodman had a self-appointed lifesaving service for Lake Hopatcong that he operated from Nolan's Point. He also taught lifesaving to local youths.

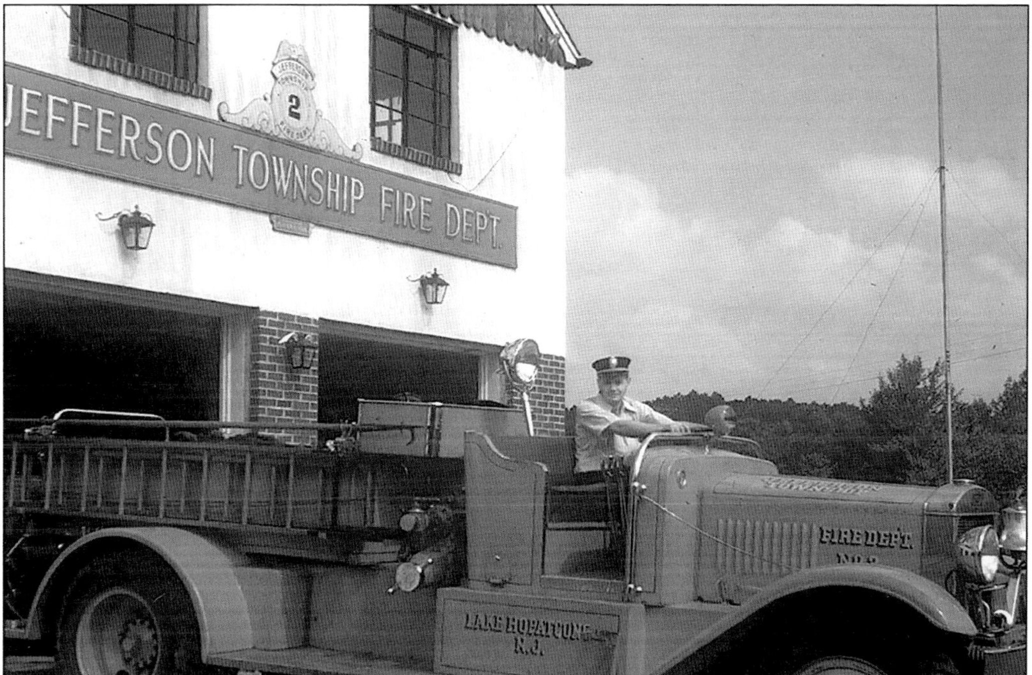

On April 2, 1942, the Lake Hopatcong Fire Association was established. On May 6, 1942, the name was changed to the Jefferson Township Fire Company No. 2.

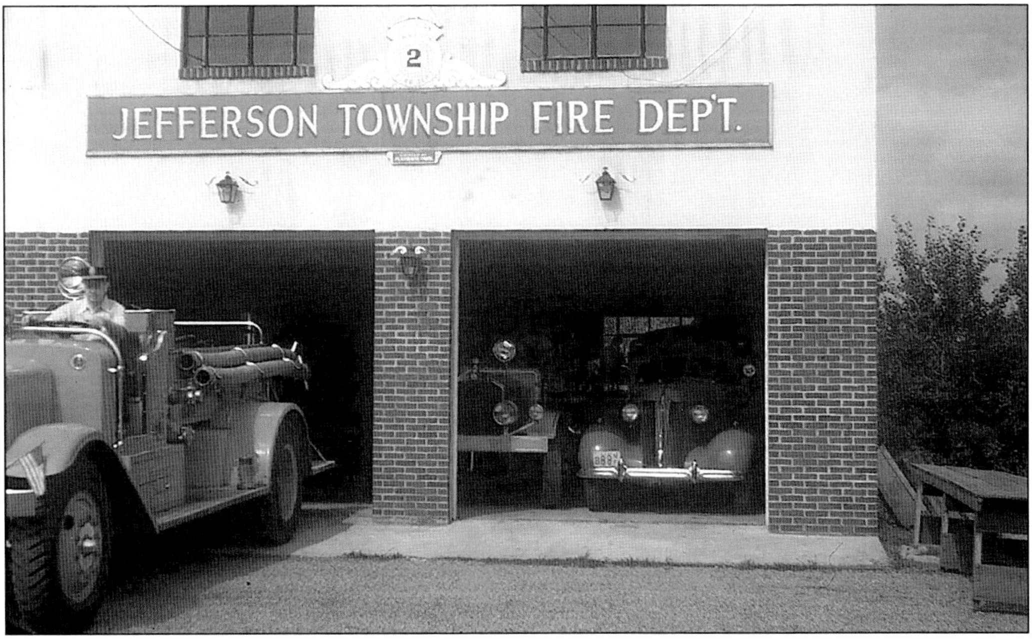

By 1945, the Jefferson Township Fire Company No. 2 established a rescue squad. The second bay of the firehouse was used to accommodate an ambulance. In 1972, the rescue squad separated from Fire Company No. 2 and obtained its own building on Route 15 South.

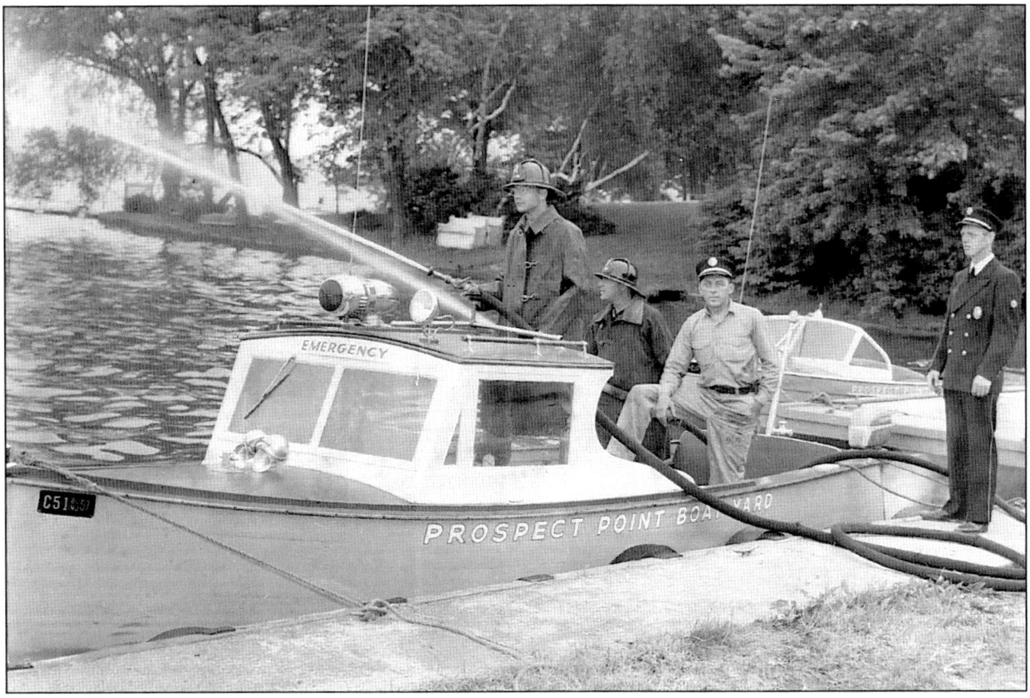

Since inhabited islands and many shorefront homes existed in Jefferson Township, the need for a fireboat became evident. This *c.* 1950 photograph shows one of the first fireboats built and maintained by Samuel Sutphen of Prospect Point Boat Yard. Today, a fireboat continues to be a vital part of Jefferson Township's fire apparatus.

Eight

New Beginnings

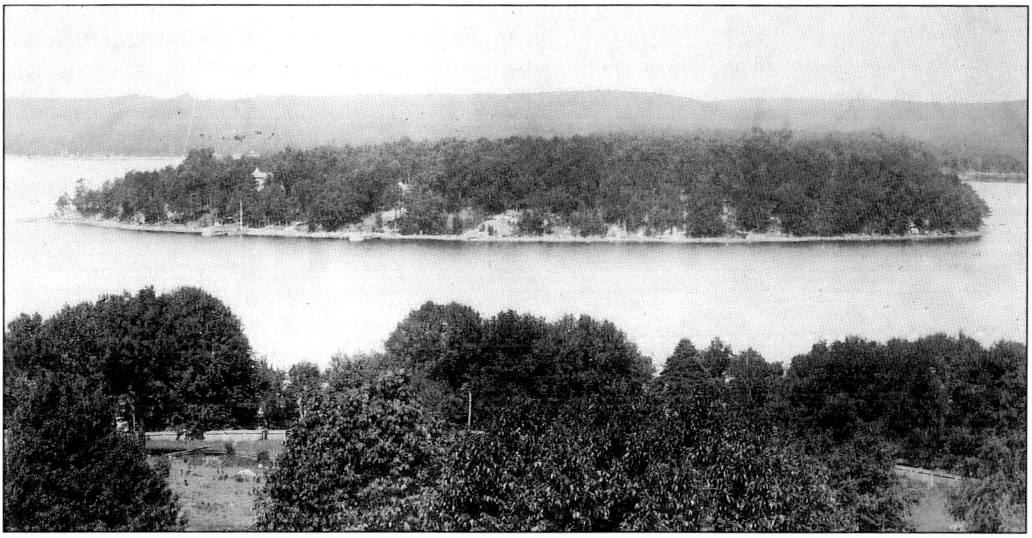

Halsey Island, located across from Nolan's Point, consists of approximately 30 acres of land. By c. 1811, this large island was owned by the Hurd family, who also owned the Hurdtown Mines. Unlike Raccoon Island, Halsey Island had a very slow start. By 1898, only two cottages existed on the island.

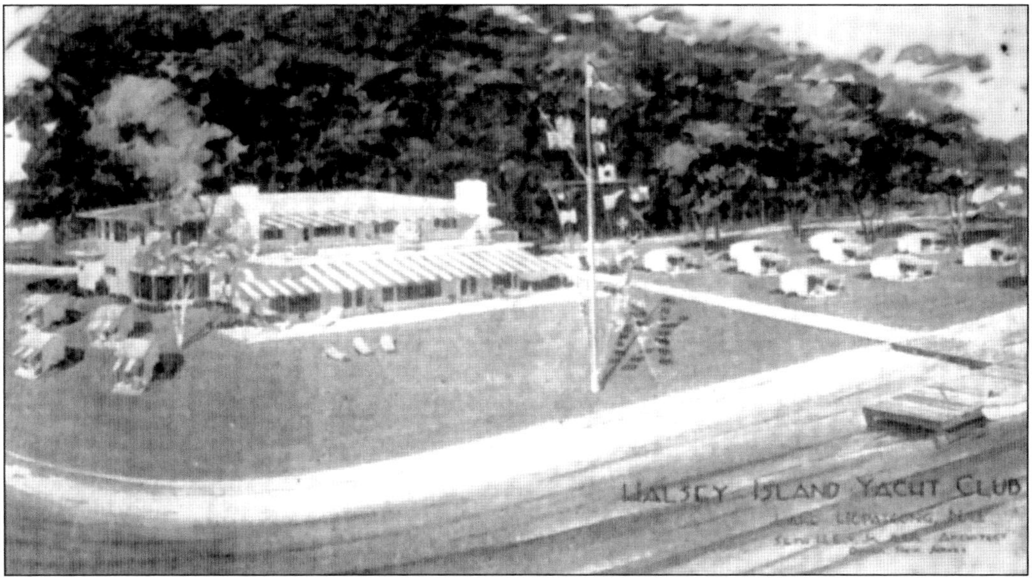

It was not until 1948 that the Hurd family sold the majority of Halsey Island to the Halsey Island Company. Harry Lynn dreamed of developing a residential community that would have a large, modern yacht club. The yacht club cost approximately $150,000 and was designed by Seth Ely Jr. of Dover. This plan never came to fruition, and today there are still only 19 summer homes on the island.

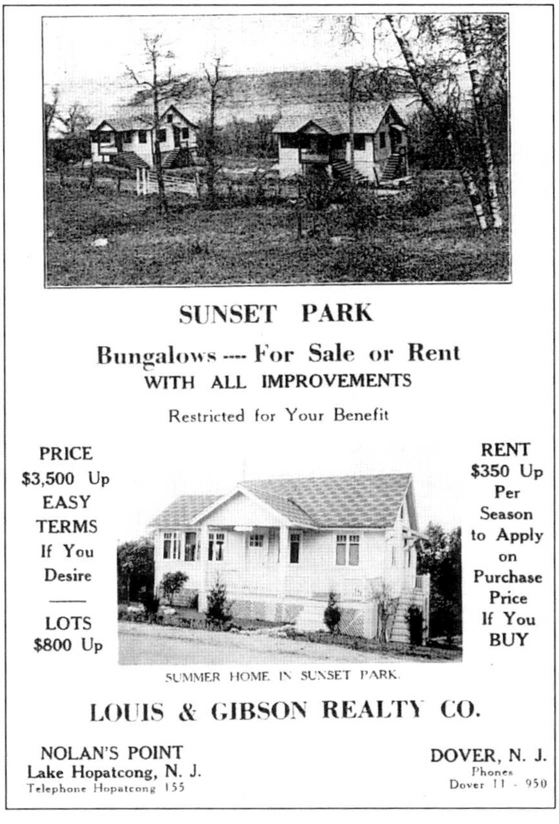

Seen here *c.* 1926 is Sunset Park, which was going to be a dream summer development of Abe Louis on Nolan's Point Road. Spectacular views of the lake and Halsey Island were to be a major rental and selling point. However, about three bungalows were built. These bungalows have been converted to year-round homes and are still being occupied.

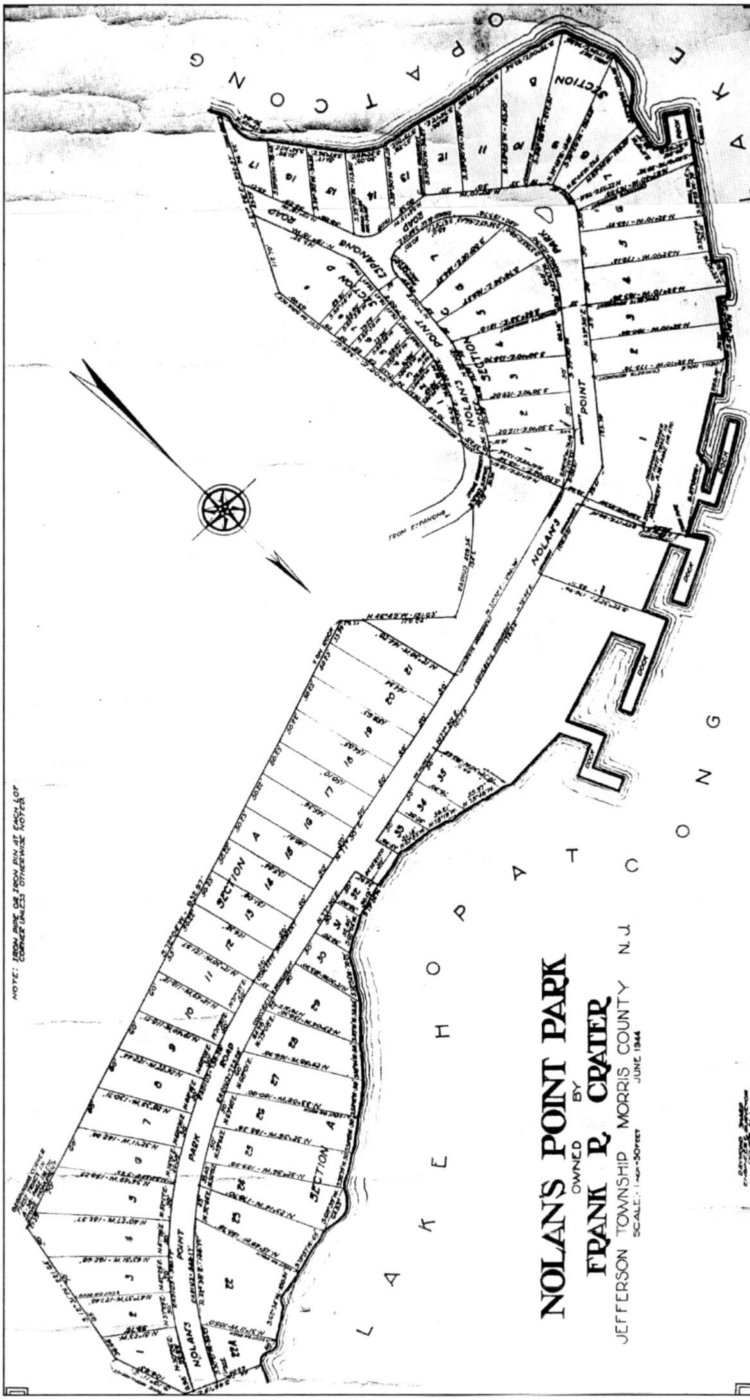

By June 1944, Frank R. Crater—owner of Allen's Pavilion No. 3 and the property where the Nolan's Point Amusement Park and picnic area was located—subdivided this area into Nolan's Point Park for a future housing development. The property extended from Nolan's Point to Castle Rock. Anyone who purchased property was entitled to use the bathing beach located on the shores of Lake Hopatcong.

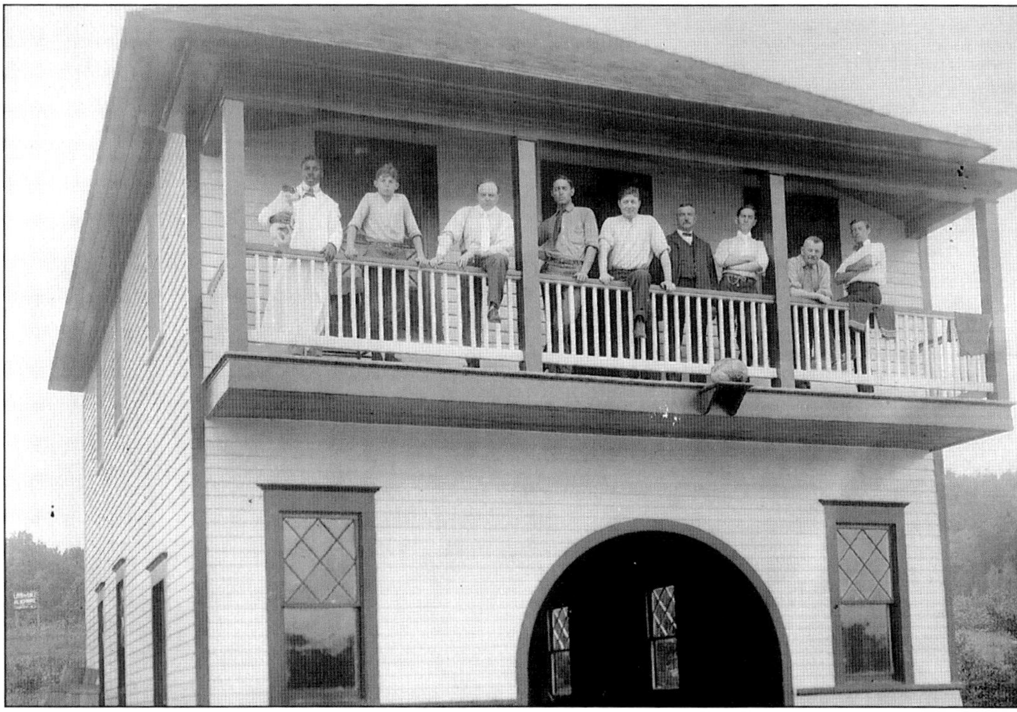

In July 1905, George W. Badeoff of Newark drew up the plans for the Shadow Lawn Boathouse in Prospect Point. Mr. Wilcox, a carpenter, agreed to build the boathouse for the sum of $1,900. By the early 1920s, it was renamed the Prospect Point Boathouse. Bathing, fishing, rowing, and a Russian tearoom were available at this location.

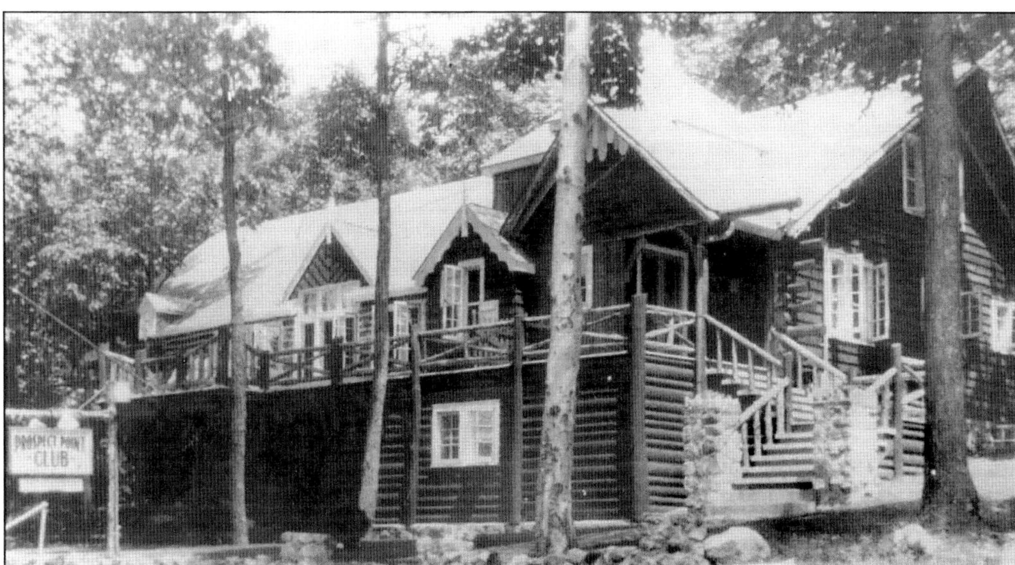

As the Prospect Point community grew, its residents wanted to have a community club. Eventually, the Prospect Point Club, located on Schwarz Boulevard, was built. Dinners, dances, and other community activities were held there. Unfortunately, the club burned and was never rebuilt.

By 1889, Burtis and Oscar Megie of New York advertised lots for sale on Raccoon Island. These lots were usually 100 feet wide and 200 to 600 feet deep. Most lots sold from $500 to $1,000 and only cash was accepted. As early as May 1890, many lots were sold and seven or eight cottages had been erected. A very nice arrangement was made with the hotel that opened on June 1, 1890; lot and cottage owners could eat at the hotel.

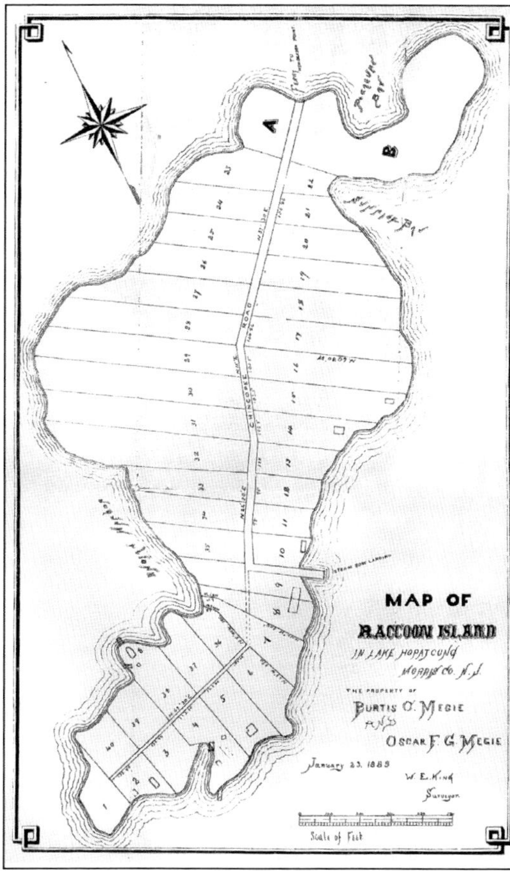

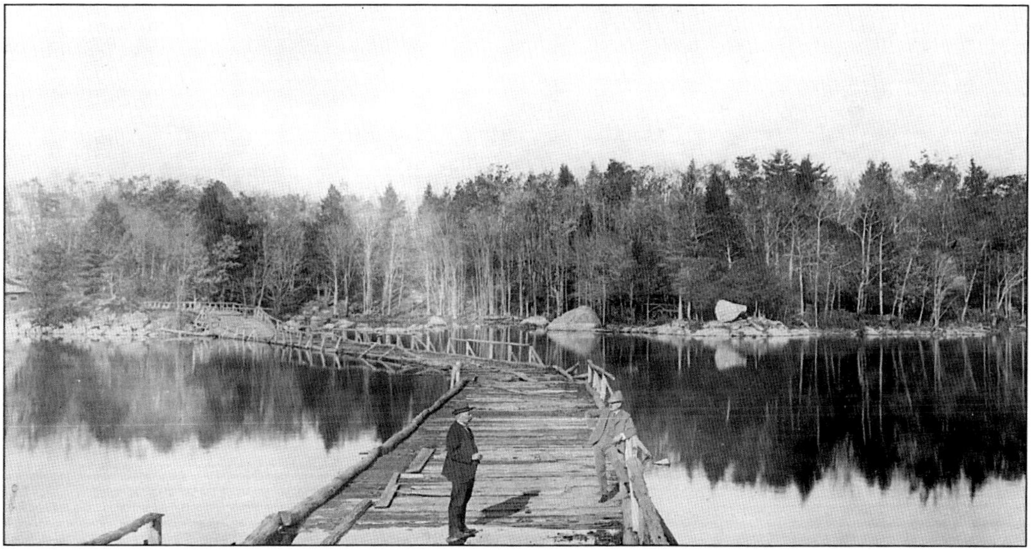

The Chincopee Bridge, which connected Raccoon Island to the mainland, was built of wood planks c. 1890. However, the ice had destroyed it by 1899. The Raccoon Island residents fought for a replacement bridge, which was approved in 1928 but never came to fruition because of the Great Depression.

OPENING OF CHINCOPEE BRIDGES.

The Cottagers and Guests at the Hotels and Boarding Houses on Lake Hopatcong are cordially invited to attend the

OPENING

of the Chincopee Bridges connecting Raccoon Island with Henderson Point, on

Saturday Afternoon at 5.30 o'clock.

Those coming in Launches, Sail or Row Boats, will please rendezvous in Henderson Bay, just west of the Bridge. A dock will be provided for landing.

John S. Gibson, Esq., of Dover, Editor of the "Iron Era," will make a short address.

A Special Boat will stop at all Stations on the Lake, to convey those wishing to attend the Opening, to and from the Bridges, at Excursion Rates.

O. F. G. MEGIE.

Raccoon Island, July 15, 1891.

N. B.--Music will be furnished by the Netcong Silver Cornet Band.

This invitation was circulated around Lake Hopatcong. Residents and visitors were welcome.

Something Seldom Seen at Lake Hopatcong

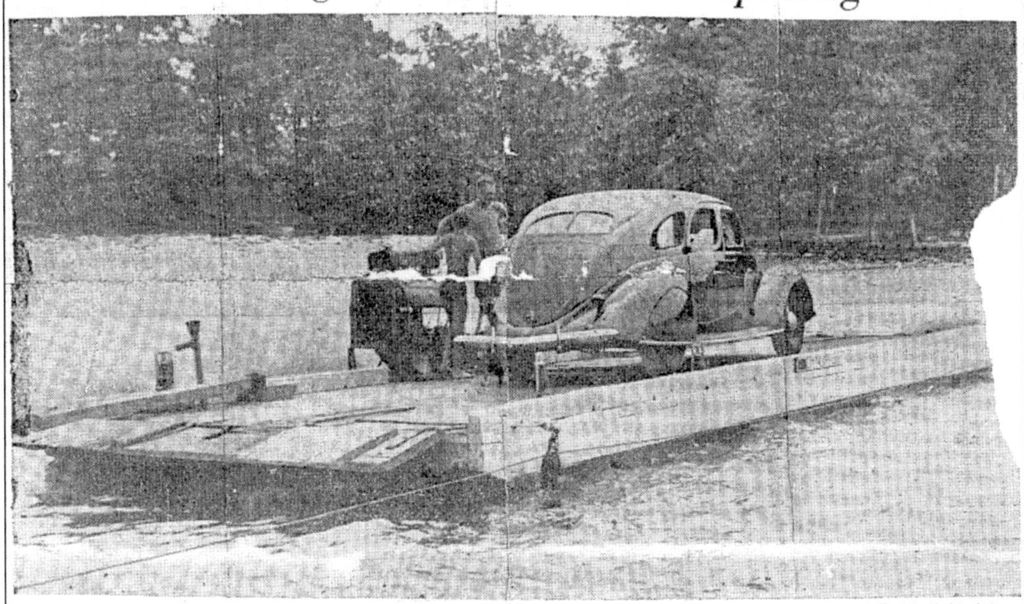

Arthur S. Hecht photo

Of the thousands who spend their Summer vacations every year at Lake Hopatcong, N. J., relatively few have seen this primitive auto ferry running from the mainland to Raccoon Island.

Since the Raccoon Island Bridge was never replaced, an alternate transportation source was approved. The Raccoon Island Ferry went into operation in 1932.

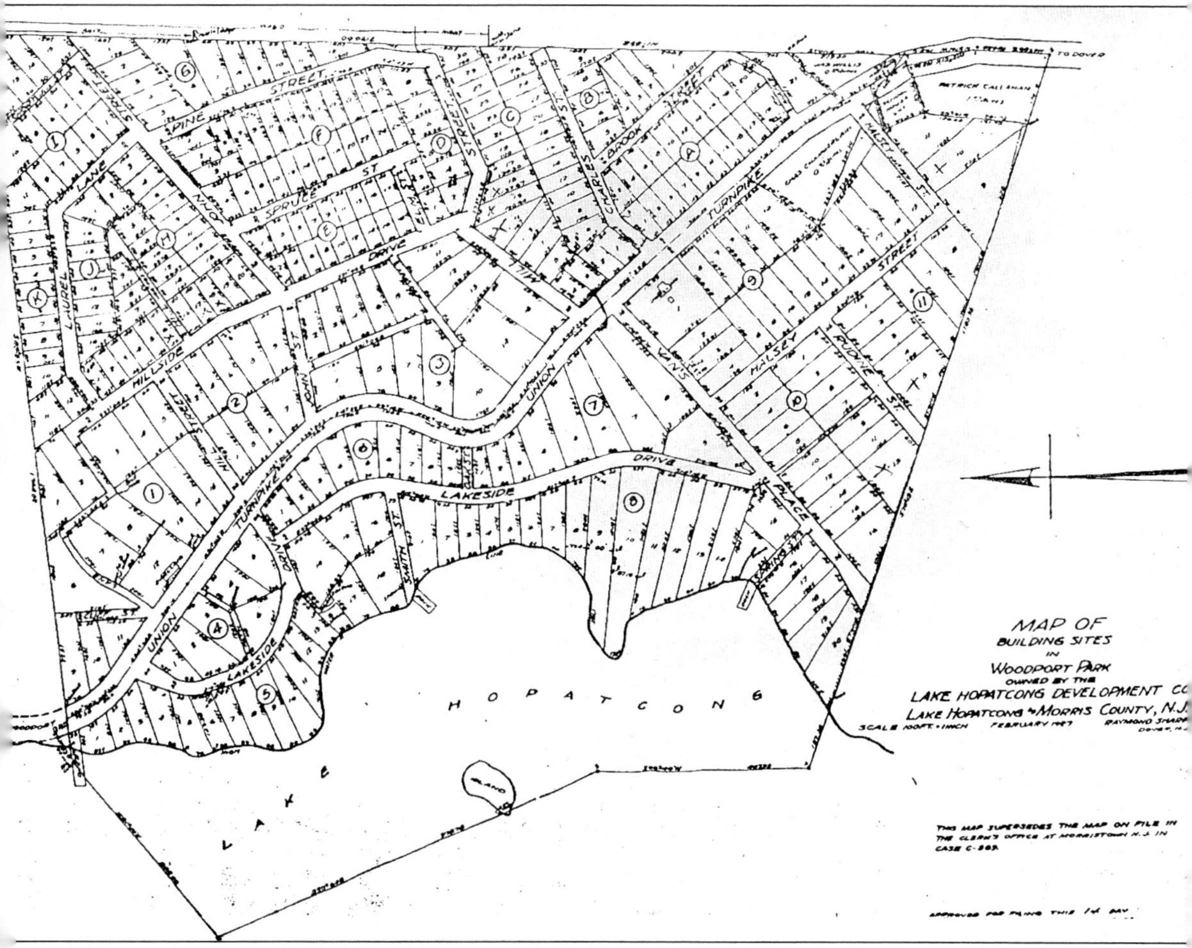

In February 1927, Raymond Sharp, a surveyor from Dover, updated the plot map for the Woodport Park in Woodport. The Woodport Park was owned by the Lake Hopatcong Development Company. The development was situated on both sides of the Union Turnpike (later Route 15) and extended along the shores of Lake Hopatcong. Like most developments during the time, the lot sizes were small. Many summer homes were built, and they would eventually be converted to year-round residences.

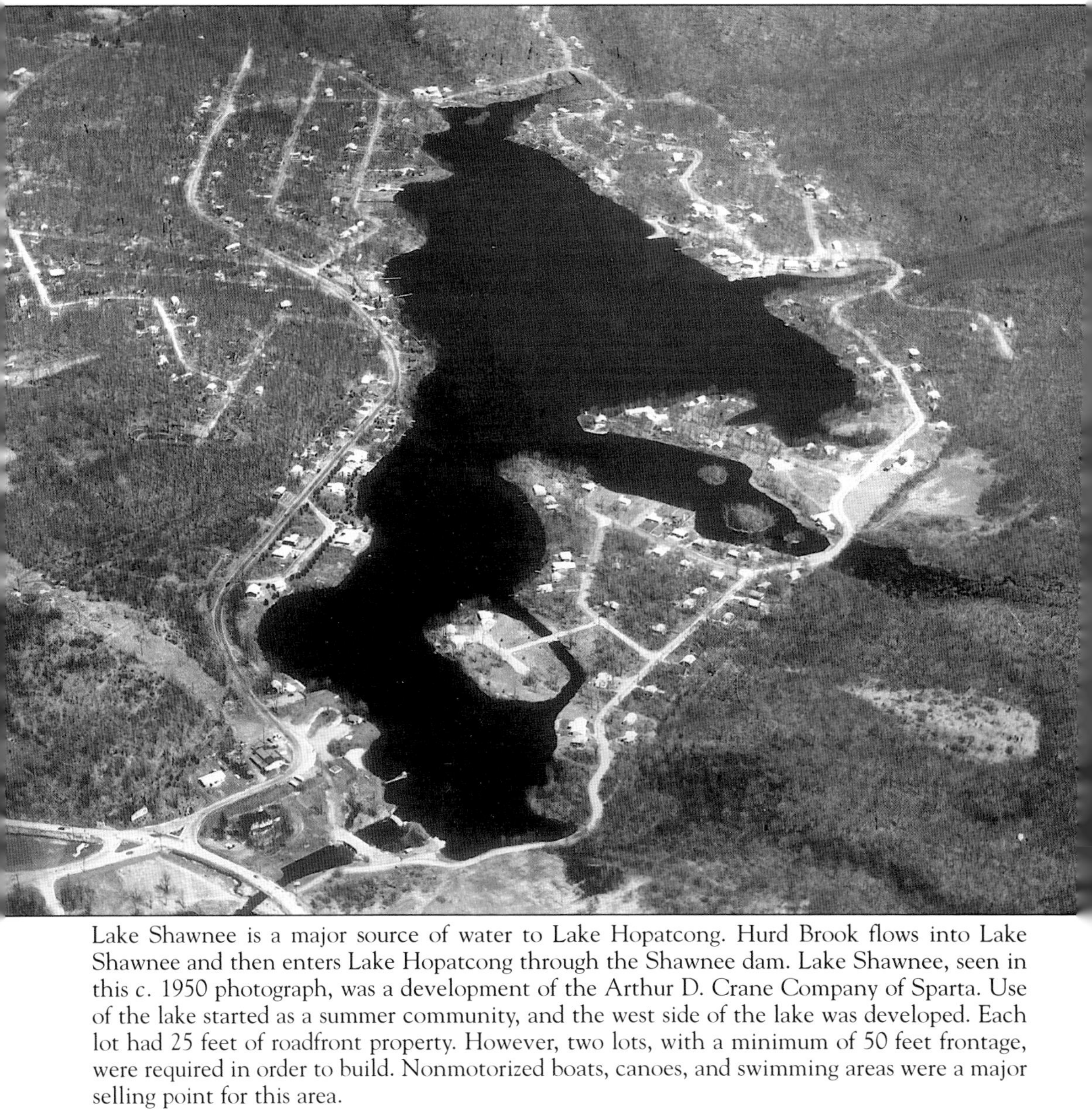

Lake Shawnee is a major source of water to Lake Hopatcong. Hurd Brook flows into Lake Shawnee and then enters Lake Hopatcong through the Shawnee dam. Lake Shawnee, seen in this *c.* 1950 photograph, was a development of the Arthur D. Crane Company of Sparta. Use of the lake started as a summer community, and the west side of the lake was developed. Each lot had 25 feet of roadfront property. However, two lots, with a minimum of 50 feet frontage, were required in order to build. Nonmotorized boats, canoes, and swimming areas were a major selling point for this area.

Just as Lake Shawnee is a major water source to Lake Hopatcong, so is Lake Winona. As the water runs down the mountains, it flows into Lake Winona and then enters Lake Hopatcong through Bright's Cove. The Arthur D. Crane Company developed Lake Winona at around the same time as Lake Shawnee and Lake Forest. Of the three areas, Lake Winona is the smallest and was probably developed first.

Property owners at

LAKE WINONA

Enjoy all of these:

★ **EASY ACCESSIBILITY** — Less than an hour's drive from Jersey's Metropolitan area.

★ **YEAR 'ROUND VACATION PLEASURE** — for the entire family. How the children enjoy the summer and winter fun!

★ **BEAUTIFUL MOUNTAIN SETTING** — Cool restful nights for sleep.

★ **PRIVATE SANDY BEACH** — Plenty of room for soaking up the sunshine.

★ **ALL MODERN CONVENIENCES** — Year-'round water mains, electricity and telephone.

★ **DIRECT ACCESS BY BOAT** — to the largest fresh water boating and fishing area in New Jersey — over 50 miles of picturesque shoreline.

★ **FULL OWNERSHIP OF LAND** — No leases —Title by Warranty deed.

★ **COTTAGE SITES FOR EVERY TASTE** — Lakefront, hillside or mountain sites with panoramic views.

★ **LOW PRICES — GOOD TERMS** — No other lake community can offer so much for so little.

★ **COMPLETE BUILDING SERVICE** — Plans, specifications and every assistance given in building. We will build your cottage or help you or your contractor build it for you.

DON'T WAIT UNTIL THE BEST LOCATIONS ARE GONE

COME OUT TODAY!

The Arthur D. Crane Company

Office on the Property

Mail Address — Route 6A, Sparta, N. J.

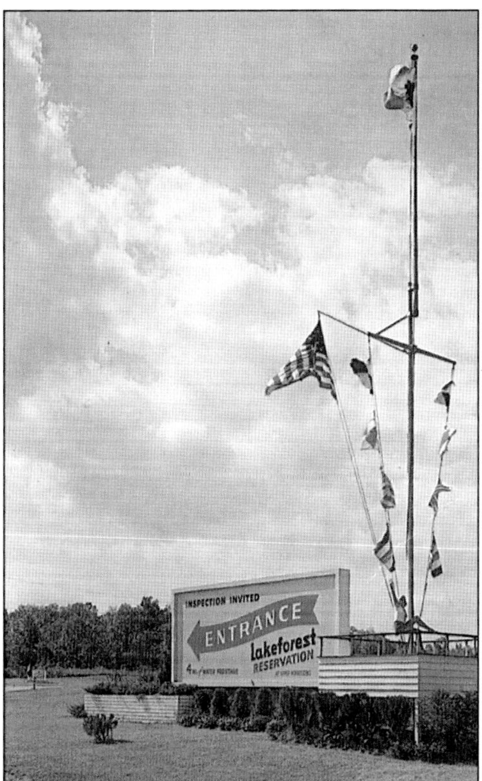

The entrance to Lake Forest is just off of Route 15. A large billboard and flagpole with nautical flags mark the entrance, seen here *c.* 1955. After passing the billboard, guests registered and passed a gatehouse. There was also a gatehouse on Ripplewood Drive, near today's Espanong Road. As time passed, the gatehouses were eliminated.

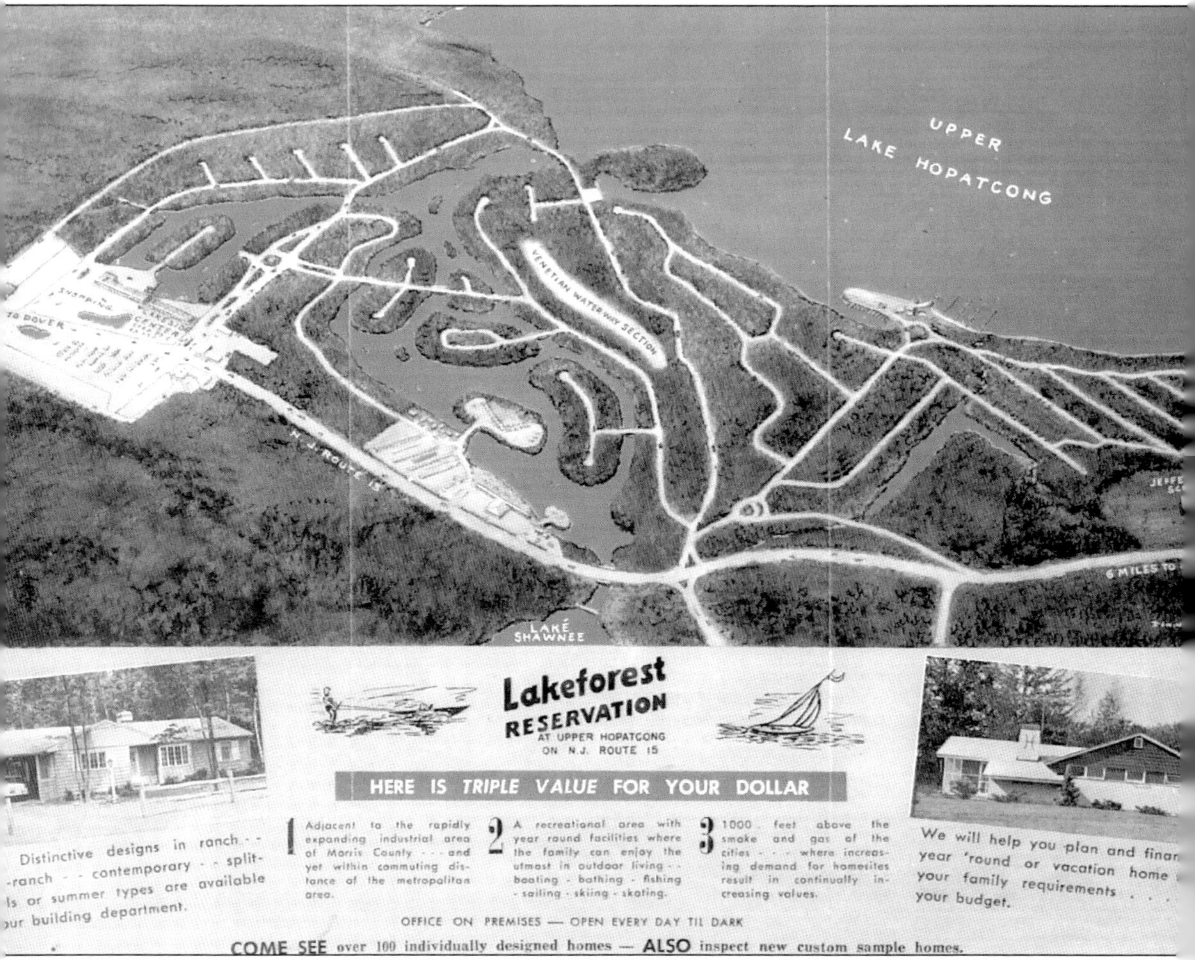

By the 1950s, the Arthur D. Crane Company formulated its ideas to start the Lake Forest Reservation at Upper Lake Hopatcong. Unlike Lake Shawnee, this development was a planned year-round community. The community was designed to set a new high in harmonious living in a friendly, congenial, invigorating atmosphere.